CIO Perspectives

Dean Lane

In conjunction with:
Office of the CIO
Consortium of Information Systems Executives
San Francisco State University

KENDALL/HUNT PUBLISHING COMPANY
4050 Westmark Drive   Dubuque, Iowa 52002

CONTENTS

SECTION FOUR
Learning and Growth   193

SECTION FIVE
Historical Perspective   237

DEDICATION

To my wife, Debbie,
to my children, Brian and Heather
and my parents, Kathryn and Paul Benson

FOREWORD

John Thompson, CEO Symantec

Today, information is much more than a resource. It is nothing less than the currency of our age, and as such is invaluable. It is worth more than a company's infrastructure, databases, applications and networks—combined. Given the significant investments in IT and the importance of it to the company, it's important that CIOs get it right.

This places considerable responsibility upon the CIO and their organization to deliver solutions that enable the company to increase revenue, improve customer satisfaction and reduce costs. CIO Perspectives provides a 'primer' for current and future CIOs on best practices, giving guidance on how to effectively leverage IT resources and ensure that IT investments provide the maximum benefit to the organization.

As I have spoken with CIOs all over the country I've noticed a shift. No longer are people talking about how they have to cut costs and do more with less. Instead, our conversations almost always get back to how they can improve business processes and help their companies grow. Operating globally with customers on one continent, suppliers on another, and competitors on yet another demands businesses be able to adapt to local processes while keeping in mind the overall strategic picture. In addition, globalizing business operations makes enterprises more reliant on information technology to manage interdependent supply chains and networks of suppliers, partners and customers from all over the world. It's a big job and the business challenges are complex—spanning multiple organizations—and cannot be solved or managed by just one group.

This reliance, in turn, places a greater priority on the CIO to keep the infrastructure safe, secure, up, and running.

Today CEOs look to the CIO and their team to contribute to business growth and efficiency. CIOs today need to be both a technology leader and a business leader. They are relied upon to think strategically and creatively about how to leverage IT to add value to the overall enterprise. CIOs must turn IT into a source of innovation and value creation, not just a service or a cost-center. Experienced CIOs use their know-how and technology to solve business problems and to help reduce enterprise-wide costs and operating budgets. And because of this, they are recognized as indispensable corporate leaders who can harness the power of technology by aligning IT to the changing needs of the business.

Driving business growth requires that the CIO work closely with the rest of the senior management team. CIOs need a seat at the executive table to help other leaders understand what IT can do to support the overall strategy. Today it is critical to have IT integrated into the core of the business.

When I was first asked to write the foreword for CIO Perspectives, I was interested and somewhat intrigued. The fact that all proceeds of this book go to the CIO Scholarship Fund definitely caught my attention. You see, every penny of revenue from this book goes to fund under-privileged students who are pursuing a career in Information Technology. Even more eye-catching than that was the thirty Silicon Valley CIOs and IT professionals that collaborated to bring this important work to completion.

CIO Perspectives addresses many of the challenges CIOs face today, provides practical tips to help CIOs manage these challenges, and offers insights into what will be required of IT leaders in the future. I believe it is a valuable tool for IT and business leaders alike, helping them understand how to harness IT to improve the business.

PREFACE

CIO Perspectives is a compendium of original contributions from some of the top CIOs in Silicon Valley. It is hard to argue with experience! Each CIO is sharing his or her experience on some facet of IT management issues and/or challenges.

Organization

The contributions are classified according to their impact on the four perspectives of the balanced scorecard (BSC): financial, customer, internal process, and learning and growth. In the final analysis, it is important to understand how the contribution will affect the performance measurement of an IT organization.

The first section, however, digresses from IT organization to define who are the IT people and what they do in an organization. It covers establishing identity and marketing—two themes that have been lacking in the CIO repertoire.

The following four sections follow the BSC perspectives. The CIOs volunteered to contribute according to their interest. The chapters are presented in their own words.

Audience

CIO Perspectives is being written primarily for business and information technology (IT) practitioners. In the late 1990s, business books attracted a large and diverse group of readers. Business and investment books took a dive after the 2000 stock market crash, but seem to be reviving at present. This book is being targeted at the following diverse audience:

- IT specialists and consultants. Organizations with top- and middle-level IT managers have many employees who deal with strategic, tactical, and operational IT issues.
- Business managers at all levels, from CXOs to middle managers.
- Companies who adopt the *CIO Perspective* as their mantra.
- MBA students. Faculty can use this book either as a text or as supplemental readings for a graduate MIS course.

If you do not belong to any of these categories but still enjoyed reading the book, we would appreciate receiving your feedback.

Office of the CIO Series

This manuscript is being published under the emblem of the Office of the CIO, and in the future we expect to add additional publications under the same logo. Please look out for our logo.

Every book is a journey; in this case, however, the series published by the Office of the CIO is more like positive steps in the search for the Holy Grail. Each contribution to the series will hopefully bring additional enlightenment to managing technology.

We want to thank all our contributors for sharing with us their thoughts and experiences and for working so diligently to put them down in words.

Finally, this publication and others to follow are meant to diffuse the rumor that CIO stands for *Career Is Over.* Contrary to popular belief, CIOs are all alive and kicking, and they are concerned about the future of corporate management in the twenty-first century.

Sam Gill and Dean Lane, March 2007

ACKNOWLEDGMENTS

This book is the result of the experience, knowledge, and wisdom of colleagues who contributed their time and hard work during their precious few hours away from their jobs. The diverse topics that we develop in each chapter are not just interesting, as certain theories might be; they are the judgment and conclusions of real-world experiences and implementation successes and failures. Thirty people helped make this book a reality. Most of them have more than twenty years of experience in the information technology field. They did this selflessly and for zero pay, as all funds generated by this book will go to the CIO Scholarship Fund, which provides scholarships to underprivileged students pursuing a career in information technology.

I am especially grateful to Dr. Sam Gill and Ms. Jennifer Diamond, who have worked closely with me on this book. Without them, this book would never have been a reality.

Other outstanding people need to be recognized and thanked as well:

- Tony Guerrero, for assisting me with the vision and technical content.
- Marti Menacho, for her vigilant review of chapters written, chapters revised, chapters rewritten, chapters reviewed, chapters re-reviewed—well, you get the idea.
- Martin Wegenstein, for his dedication, counsel and advice to numerous contributing authors.

These individuals, plus all of this book's contributors, bring wisdom and experience to bear on issues facing companies—especially their employees in information technology. I would like to thank them for sharing their thoughts, methods, and tricks of the trade.

SECTION 1
Finance and Performance

1.1

Mergers and Acquisitions

Mark Egan

Introduction

I had just reached my six-month milestone in the newly created CIO position and was beginning to feel comfortable with my role. We had worked very hard to develop our information technology (IT) strategy and had started to deliver on some of our longer-term projects. The new IT management team was in place, and the staff was beginning to work together as a team.

I was reading the paper before my first meeting of the day, and was very surprised to see that our company had just announced a major acquisition that promised to reshape our industry! Then my phone rang, and my boss, the company CEO, asked me to come right over to his office to discuss the acquisition. On the way over to his office, one of my newly hired directors stopped me and asked if she would have the same role in the combined organization. I promised to get back to her later that afternoon. My boss was unusually busy that morning and asked me to develop an integration plan by next week, as he was committed to considerable cost savings in the combined organization, especially in the IT group. I left his office in a daze and decided to call my wife and cancel the two-week vacation that we had planned for next month.

The question I pondered was, "What do I do next?" My position had just expanded considerably, and we were going to play a critical role in the success of the combined company. I was going to have to take charge and assume a leading role through the massive change that will be required to successfully complete a major acquisition.

Overview

Chapter Organization

This chapter is about managing change during a merger and acquisition (M&A) activity, as it is a major undertaking to successfully complete an IT integration effort. I first provide an overview of the many challenges facing CIOs today, including integration work during M&A. I then introduce a model for managing change that can be applied to any significant change within your organization, including M&A. Guiding principles for successful integration are also covered in this section. They offer a quick summary of best practices for IT integration. M&A survival guide is covered in the next section. It reviews the three major phases of integration: measure/evaluate, improve/integrate, and manage/run. The survival guide is organized by people, process, and technology, as these are the key components of your integration program. Merger of equals is a unique M&A situation, and this topic is covered next. I review the issues that you will be faced within these situations, as well as strategies for addressing them. The final section summarizes key practices for successful M&A integration efforts. I have been responsible for the IT integration in more than thirty-five M&A transactions. I wish you the very best in completing your work in record time!

CIO Perfect Storm

CIOs today are faced with considerable pressures to perform our jobs. Security threats, such as viruses and worms, are making it difficult to ensure the reliability of our systems on a 24/7 basis. Regulations such as Sarbanes-Oxley (SOX) are placing restrictions on how we run our IT operations. Finally, M&A is increasing for some industries, and we need to rapidly complete the IT integration work in order for the business to realize the full benefits of the transaction. These are three examples of pressures that have created a situation that I refer to as a "CIO Perfect Storm," depicted in Figure 1.1.

As IT professionals we are focused on enabling our businesses to offer new products and services, and these challenges have raised the bar in terms of what it takes to deliver. Going forward, we can use a major business change, such as M&A, as an opportunity for the IT organization to influence significant positive change within the organization.

Merger and Acquisition Trends

The world is getting smaller for some industries today, and CIOs need to be prepared to assume a leading role in M&A. The financial services industry, for example, has undergone significant changes over the past few years. Use of the Internet has devastated the retail brokerage industry, with online trading putting many brokers out of work, since trading can now be done for less than $10. Technology has also gone through considerable changes. The communications industry is starting to resemble the original AT&T before it

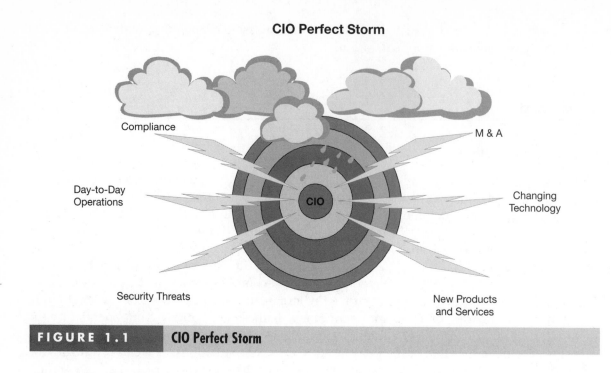

CIO Perfect Storm

Compliance

M & A

Day-to-Day Operations

CIO

Changing Technology

Security Threats

New Products and Services

| FIGURE 1.1 | CIO Perfect Storm |

was broken apart in 1984. Finally, the enterprise software industry is now dominated by just two vendors, Oracle and SAP, as the result of a spree of M&A activity. Behind the scenes, CIOs have been working overtime to ensure the integration work to support these changes is completed as quickly as possible.

CIO Role in M&A

CIOs need to carefully balance the need to quickly complete the integration work while minimizing any disruption to the business operations. Technology is pervasive—from basic communications such as e-mail, to enabling your customers to enter their orders and check on the status of delivery—and every system must work in a seamless fashion when two companies are combined. Business operations are also intertwined with their supporting systems, and employees and customers become very familiar with these systems. They find it very difficult to change. We must become *change agents* within the company to accomplish the seamless integration of such complex processes. Of course, we live under the ever-present constraint that we cannot impact the day-to-day business operations.

It is important to have an overall framework to ensure consistent, repetitive, and predictable M&A integration, and I will introduce one that you can use in this section. I refer to this framework as the Rapid Response Integration Model, shown in Figure 1.2. Staff both inside and outside the IT organization can use it to understand the work required to complete M&A integration.

This model provides an overall framework, with two disclaimers. First, it is important to note that no two M&As are the same. This model is not a cookie-cutter prescriptive

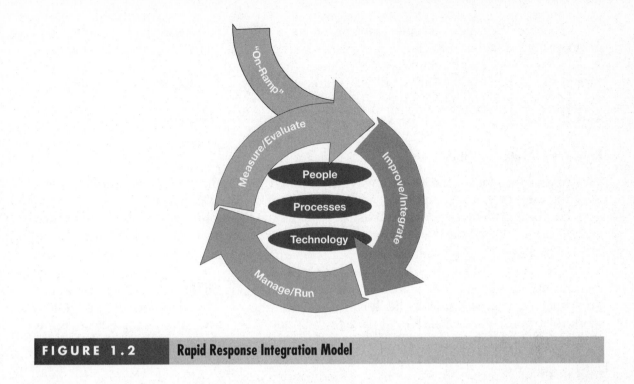

FIGURE 1.2 | **Rapid Response Integration Model**

approach, as each M&A will have unique challenges that you will need to address in order to be successful. Second, the entire company needs to operate within a consistent framework, along with the IT organization. With these two assumptions in mind, the model can be used to communicate the many activities going on simultaneously during IT integration.

The model starts with an *on ramp* that monitors the environment to anticipate major changes, such as regulations, security threats, and M&A. The more you look out for potential changes to your environment and proactively prepare, the easier it will be to manage the ensuing change. The on ramp leads to the three components of the Rapid Response Integration Model: the phases and the elements that these phases affect. The three major phases of the model include measure/evaluate, improve/integrate, and manage/run. The elements are people, processes, and technology.

Measure/Evaluate Phase

During the measure/evaluate phase of M&A, you will have the ability to evaluate the company or business you plan to acquire and thus develop your detailed integration plans. The first portion of this phase is often referred to as the *due-diligence period,* when you conduct a detailed evaluation of the company that you plan to acquire. I would encourage you to become actively involved, if you can, during this time frame, as many assumptions are made regarding time necessary to complete the integration work, cost savings, and business impacts. It is essential that you are included in the decision making. This is followed by a public announcement; several approval steps, depending on whether the acquired company is public or private; and finally, the actual closing of the deal, when the acquired company ceases to exist.

I consider this the most important phase, as considerable work can be completed to develop your detailed implementation plans and determine your IT strategy for the combined company. It is important to note, especially in the case of a public company, that you cannot direct the IT organization of the acquired company during this time frame, although you can participate in joint planning. The major outcome from this phase is a detailed integration plan that you can immediately begin executing once the deal has been closed.

Improve/Integrate Phase

This phase includes all the execution work required to complete the integration. It starts with the day the transaction closes, commonly referred to as *Day 1*, and all the remaining activities to complete the work. This is the bulk of the heavy lifting for the IT integration and reflects how well the planning work was done in the previous phase of the project.

I recommend that you plan to complete this phase in no more than ninety days, with the understanding that size and complexity of the acquired company will have a bearing on your ability to achieve this goal. Enormous pressure will be placed on the IT organization during this time frame, as the business is counting on IT to complete the integration work in a rapid, seamless fashion. I have found ninety days to be a reasonable time frame, and recommend that you develop strategies that can be completed within this time, even if you have to develop less than elegant solutions, as the business will find it very difficult to operate on multiple systems for longer periods of time.

Manage/Run Phase

This is the final phase of the M&A integration and most, if not all, of the work should be completed at this point. If your ninety-day integration plan was completed successfully, you should be in a position to reevaluate the IT organization and governance program to ensure it is working for the combined business and make any necessary adjustments. Some very long lead-time work, such as integrating product-licensing systems, may extend into this phase, but the majority of the work should be completed.

People, Processes, and Technology

People, processes, and technology are the three major elements that you need to address in each phase of integration. People are by far the most important and challenging element of M&A work. Employees do not like change, and the IT organization becomes a major change agent within the organization to convert to common systems for the combined business. Employees are also going through major personal changes during this time frame, with fear of losing their job, working for a new manager, and having to learn new business systems and processes.

Processes are the second area, and these include the business processes to run the combined organization, in addition to the internal IT processes such as change control to manage your organization. Considerable effort must be placed on understanding the processes of the acquired company and mapping these to the processes of the combined company. I will discuss this in more detail in a later section and offer suggestions on how to accelerate this effort.

Finally, technology must be addressed, and decisions must be made on which business applications should be used for the combined company and which standards will be followed, as it is unlikely the two organizations are using the same ones. This is an area that the IT organization needs to move very quickly to make these decisions and communicate them to the business, as you do not have a lot of time to debate—you must move into integration mode.

Guiding Principles for Successful M&A

The following are recommended guidelines for rapid, successful IT integration, based on my experience with more than thirty-five M&A transactions:

1. *People are number one.* It is important to first address people issues, such as whether someone has a job in the combined organization and who the manager will be, before you can expect to make a lot of progress.

2. *Speed is king.* You need to move very quickly during M&A integration, as the business is counting on being able to operate in a combined fashion, and IT is essential to this effort. You should plan to complete your integration activities in ninety days or less, with the understanding that larger, more complex M&A may require more time.

3. *There must be IT governance.* You need to set up IT governance board, with executives that represent all business functions, for oversight and rapid decision making, as you need to quickly resolve issues so you can focus on completing the integration work.

4. *Design for scale and reliability.* It is important to have a flexible IT architecture that can easily support the combined organization in a highly reliable manner.

5. *Use common project management methodology.* You need to follow a consistent project management methodology for the combined organization as quickly as possible to ensure successful integration planning and execution.

6. *Communicate effectively.* Clear communication on the IT integration strategy is essential, so everyone can understand the changes that are planned and they can execute accordingly.

7. *Align IT with other business functions.* It is important that the IT organization is closely aligned with business priorities, and critical business decisions such as what products that will be bundled together are made quickly, so the IT group can develop plans to support these decisions.

M&A Survival Guide

This section drills down into the three major phases of IT integration and provides best practices that can be used for each area. Table 1.1 provides an overview of the major activities in each of these phases.

The M&A integration summary provides a quick overview of what you should be focused on during each of the three phases. It separates these activities into people, process, and technology categories. It is important to note that each M&A integration effort is unique, and some of these activities may fall into another phase. For example, in the case

TABLE 1.1	M & A IT Integration Summary			
	Measure/Evaluate	**Improve/Integrate**		**Manage/Run**
		Day 1	90 Day Plan	
People	Finalize IT organization model	Announce new IT organization	Evaluate new IT team	Re-evaluate new IT leadership
	Joint planing of IT management	Assume control over key IT operations	Regular staff communications	Ongoing IT planning meetings
	Establish reward & retention plan	Communicate reward and retention program	Monitor program progress & reward staff	Reward high performing staff
	Meet business leaders at new company	Status on integration activities to new business leaders	Establish rapport with new business leaders	Ongoing meetings with business leaders
Process	Finalize governance model for IT	Implement IT governance model	Monthly governance meetings	Re-evaluate IT governance model
	Establish communications & change management program	Establish 24 × 7 command center	Publish IT integration dashboard	Publish IT metrics for combined organization
	Finalize project management methodology	Operate under project management methodology	Project management methodology training	Integrate project management into IT training program
	Identify small number of critical IT processes	Begin implementing critical IT processes	Integrate key IT processes	Continuous process improvement program
Technology	Finalize scalable IT architecture	Implement critical IT functions	Publish combined IT Roadmap	Deliver programs according to 6 quarter IT roadmap
	Inventory applications & integration strategy	Complete cutover to key business systems	Complete business application cutover	Complete long term integration (e.g. licensing)
	Identify risks of acquired businesses (e.g. security)	Implement risk mitigation plan	Implement long term risk solutions	Ongoing risk management program
	Finalize technology decisions & standards	Communicate technology standards	Migrate to new IT technology	Ongoing technology review & standard setting process

of a simple acquisition of a smaller company, you can accelerate many of the integration activities into the measure/evaluate phase and quickly decide on appropriate roles in the combined organization. By contrast, in the case of a much larger company that is comparable in size to your company, you may not be able to announce any organization changes until the deal has been approved and you are operating as a combined company. Keeping this in mind, I will now review each of the three major phases in more detail.

Measure/Evaluate Phase Overview

This is the most important phase of the M&A integration effort, as you have the ability to plan out your work, without the pressure of operating the IT organization for the combined company. I strongly recommend that the CIO and his leadership team become heavily involved during this phase, as it is essential that you have a well-thought-out plan that you can execute once the transaction has been completed and you are operating as a single organization. You may have regulatory constraints during this time frame, such as announcing leaders for the new organization, so you need to be very diligent on focusing on those areas in which you are not restrained.

Measure/Evaluate Phase—People

As mentioned previously, the most important issue to address involves critical personnel, as the IT organization will not be able to operate effectively until you have answered the following three questions for the entire staff:

1. Do I have a job in the combined company?
2. If I have a job, who will be my manager in the combined company?
3. What is my new role and scope of responsibility?

The IT employees will be totally focused on these three questions and will not be able to concentrate on their work until they are resolved. For this reason, I recommend that you step back and concentrate in this area, first starting with the IT organization model. When integrating a smaller company that might not have a formal IT organization, this will be very simple, as you need to decide whether you can find a role for these employees in the organization. Larger IT organizations may require more time, and you can also use this as an opportunity to reevaluate your existing IT organization model and staff and make adjustments. These adjustments may include the addition of a new leader to head up a function that previously did not exist, such as the establishment of an independent quality assurance (QA) function, as a result of a larger development organization. You may also want to reevaluate your existing leaders who may not be performing at an optimal level and use this opportunity to move someone else into their role.

One final point is that it is important to identify meaningful roles for key members of the acquired company, as this will send a clear message to the staff that you value their contribution and want them to be part of the future organization. This may not be possible for a number of reasons, and it is equally important to let them know their status and assist them in finding a new role outside of the IT organization. It is essential to include the staff from the acquired company in your planning activities and begin to operate as an integrated organization as quickly as possible. It will take time for your combined organization to bond as a team. The sooner you get this process going, the faster you will complete this effort and focus on providing IT services to the combined company.

You should also establish a reward and retention program for IT staff that either motivates staff to work very long hours for a period of time or provides an incentive for staff to stay with the company until key portions of the integration work have been completed. This program would include retention bonuses for staff that will be terminated after a finite period of transition time.

You also need to meet with key business leaders of the new company to establish relationships and plan the integration work. In most cases, these individuals will experience considerable change during the IT integration, and it is important to establish a good rapport, as you will need their help to manage their organizations through the change that will occur during this period.

Measure/Evaluate Phase—Processes

Your IT governance program needs to be established. You can use your existing model as a starting point and make adjustments as required. I recommend that you quickly begin holding integration planning meetings and have an executive governance board that oversees your plans and makes any decisions that are required. Your executive governance board should include executives from all the business areas, chaired by a senior level executive, ideally the CEO or COO of the company. IT needs to take a leading role here, as all the organizations within the company are going through the same process. Unless a formal program is in place, you will not be able to confirm that your plans are aligned with the business and obtain rapid decisions from business leaders.

You need to quickly get a few processes in place to ensure your program is running smoothly and everyone understands your plans going forward. Communication is essential during times of massive change. I recommend that you have someone assigned to this area for all IT integration work. Communication studies have proven that you need to tell someone several times before it finally sinks in and they understand what you are saying. Combine this with all the chaos going on with employees worried about their jobs, and business changes necessary to operate as a combined company, and it is challenging for everyone inside and outside the IT organization to comprehend your plans and support them.

I had the luxury of a full-time communication person who managed the communication program for our integration work, and she developed a comprehensive plan for all three phases of the program. Communications included everything from broad employee communications on what to expect from the IT organization in areas such as their e-mail system, to very targeted communications to individual groups on changes to their specific business application. If you don't have a trained communications professional to dedicate to this effort, I would recommend that you contract other staff to assist in this area.

Project management methodology is key, because you need to quickly communicate in a common language during your integration effort. I recommend that you adopt your existing methodology and train the acquired IT organization. This enables you to develop project plans that are consistent and provides a common understanding of what someone means when they are talking about certain activities such as integration testing. You can think of IT integration as one very large project for which you need a plan that means the same for all parties involved in the process. Time should be set aside to train the acquired IT organization on your project management methodology, terminology that is being used, and any tools that are available. A common dashboard of IT activities should be developed quickly and used to communicate the status of the program, as shown in Table 1.2.

The dashboard should identify the key tracks of the program, such as the integration of your financial systems. It should include current status, issues that need to be resolved, and overall rating of *red, yellow,* or *green* status. This can be an effective tool to raise awareness of critical issues that need management attention while you have time to avoid impacts to the overall integration schedule.

Business processes inside and outside the IT organization must be reevaluated during an integration project. Whenever possible, I recommend that the acquired company follow your business process, as this is the quickest way to complete your integration work. This is not to say that the acquired company may not have well-thought-out processes that you may choose to adopt; however, I would always err toward using your business processes unless you identify a compelling reason to do otherwise.

The major effort is to understand the acquired company's business processes and train its employees on the changes required to follow your business processes using your exist-

TABLE 1.2		IT Integration Status Dashboard			
Track	**Subtrack**	**Major Day 1 Activities**	**Measure of Success**	**Status/Issues**	**Overall Status**
G & A	Finance	Revenue reporting	High-level daily revenue reports reflect both companies	Preliminary plan drafted, but not approved	Red until Finance plan locked and approved
		Expense Controls	All expenses managed using onsistent controls		
		Ledger integration	Ability to close books		
	HR	Single source of employee information	Managers can use one system to manage all employees on HR-related matters	Plan drafted and working priority of application interfaces	Yellow
		Integration with other applications	Other business functions' applications reflect changes in employee population		
Sales, Marketing & Services	Sales	Automated discount authorization process	Order management is able to verify discounts approved by Sales	Business process to be completed in 30 days	Yellow
		Customer Account reports	Sales account managers have single report reflecting customers from each company	Draft report under review	
	Marketing	Web site look-and-feel rebranding and containing appropriate corss-linkages	Customer able to locate product information from both companies on web site	Plan for Day 1 drafted	Green
		Joint marketing campaigns	Leads resulting from joint campaign can be routed to the correct lead management system	Plan for Day 1 drafted	
	Services	Phone/Call Center support for customer handling	A misdirected customer call can be handed off to the correct call center smoothly	Plans to be finalized in next 30 days	Yellow

ing systems. This is not an activity that the IT organization can do alone. You need to facilitate this effort with the business leaders from the major functional areas such as finance and sales, as they will need to manage through this change to ensure their staff is trained, in order to be successful. The acquired company's leaders may not have experience in doing process reengineering work, so you will need to identify this gap quickly and hire staff to assist in this area. You cannot complete your IT work until the future business processes have been locked down.

From an IT internal process perspective, I also recommend that you follow your existing processes and just train the acquired staff on your processes, as you do not have the time to reevaluate this area. There may be exceptions here as well, although I would consider them rare. You need to pay close attention to this area, as smaller companies often have very informal processes in areas such as change control, and you need to quickly get them trained to follow more mature processes. If you have a much larger company, then I recommend that you focus on a few critical processes, as this will enable you to concentrate on areas of greatest risk. Areas that I recommend include handling and prioritizing of IT work requests, change control, and systems monitoring. Once you have these under control, you can expand into other areas, as it will take some time to operate as an integrated organization.

You should also review your plans for Sarbanes-Oxley (SOX) compliance for the combined company. If you follow your existing business and IT processes, you should be in a good position to demonstrate how you will run the combined company. It is a good idea to get your auditor involved in this process early to ensure that your assumptions are valid and you have adequate time to test your controls for the combined company.

Measure/Evaluate Phase—Technology

The first step in this process is to develop a detailed inventory of the applications and technology employed at the acquired company. This will enable you to compare and contrast its technology with your existing IT portfolio of applications and make decisions. I recommend that you initially focus on any application that your customers will interact with, and on systems that support the order processing and shipment functions. The primary objective is to determine if you can run the combined company on your existing business systems, as this is the most straightforward process to complete your integration work. You want to identify any changes that may be required. Unless you have a compelling business reason, I would strongly recommend that you adopt a model to quickly assimilate the newly acquired company on your existing business applications. Debates on technology are nonproductive, they can be emotional, and they waste valuable time that you don't have during M&A integration.

Standards are sometimes quite challenging for an IT organization. The most difficult are those that directly impact the end users, such as laptops, PDAs, cell phones, and e-mail. If you always wanted to get wireless e-mail rolled out but did not find the time, and your newly acquired company has this capability, you may want to consider a broader rollout for the combined company, as your new users are going to be quite upset when you take this capability away. This was the most frequent question raised during one of the integrations that I was responsible for. I decided to adopt a broader program for the company, not because this was the highest priority, but because I did not want the IT integration to be a bad experience for the newly acquired company.

This is an area where you want to leverage your IT governance function, as you should have leaders from both organizations involved in the evaluation process and supporting your decisions. You should strive to finalize all technology standards for the combined business and broadly communicate them during this phase so you can turn your focus to implementation as quickly as possible.

It is likely that you will be asked to identify cost savings. Outside of reducing staff, most of these will come from the technology area. I recommend that you quickly evaluate retiring systems, combining your licensing agreements, and reducing communications expenses as possible means to achieve savings. Pay close attention to all contracts from your acquired company, as they often have automatic renewal clauses. You may need to quickly cancel these contracts to avoid another year of fees. Communications costs are a large component of the IT budget, and redesigning your network to include the acquired company can often be a source of cost savings. Also, smaller IT organizations do not always have the expertise or time to evaluate communications expenses, so you may want to examine this area.

From an architecture perspective you need to determine if you can run the combined company with your existing systems with acceptable performance and reliability. If any of your business applications or infrastructure is already stressed, you could use this as an opportunity to enhance this area. For example, can you existing e-mail system handle the additional employees, or do you need to rearchitect your infrastructure to increase the number of servers or upgrade the hardware? Can your online order processing system handle an additional 20 percent volume, or do you need to upgrade this system? These are areas that you need to quickly assess and for which you will need to develop mitigation plans, as you will be operating as a combined company shortly.

You also want to identify any risks, such as information security, with the acquired company. In the case of a smaller company, they may have had a very small I.T. organization and were not able to implement basic security products such as anti-virus or anti-spam protection. I recommend that you quickly do a thorough assessment of their security technology to identify any gaps and put a plan in place for remediation, as they will soon be part of your combined organization and you are responsible for any security incidents that occur.

Your governance board will need to approve your migration plan. Thus, you need to develop a *future state* architecture for the combined company that you can broadly communicate to gain acceptance and support. I recommend that your presentation be highly graphical in nature and brief, as you will be communicating with staff at all levels and understanding of IT, and they all need to develop a common understanding of your plans. Of course, as with every other procedure, this presentation needs to be completed as quickly as possible, so it can be presented whenever it is needed.

Measure/Evaluate Phase—Summary

At the completion of this phase you should have your organization model addressed and the new IT leaders should be meeting on a regular basis and starting to work together as a team. All the IT employees should know if they have a job and who their new manager will be, unless you have a business or regulatory reason for not disclosing this information.

Your single integrated plan should be completed, and you should have completed multiple tests of your Day 1 cutover activities. The entire IT team should be trained on a consistent project management methodology and using similar terminology, as you cannot afford to have differences in this critical area. Broad communications should be occurring on the status of the IT integration work, and regular meetings should be scheduled with the IT staff.

Finally, your architecture should be scaled to support the combined business, and you should publish the IT roadmap for the next year. Critical decisions that affect the end users, such as e-mail, PDAs, and laptop standards, should be approved by the IT governance board and communicated to employees. Major business risks, such as information security, should have been addressed with mitigation plans.

Improve/Integrate Phase—Overview

This phase is all about execution, as your success will depend in large part on the quality of work that was done in the measure/evaluate phase. Enormous pressure will be placed on the IT organization to enable the company to communicate effectively and to operate in a seamless fashion with your customers. This is a great opportunity for the IT organization to have a very visible and positive impact on the combined company.

This phase consists of two major activities: Day 1 and your ninety-day integration plan. Day 1 consists of all the activities that you plan to complete on the first day that you operate as a combined business. Your ninety-day integration plan is all the remaining activities that must occur in order to integrate the two businesses. I strongly recommend that you plan to complete your integration work in ninety days or less, as extending this beyond that time frame can be very costly and will affect the overall success of the transaction. Larger or more complex M&A may require more time, although I would encourage you to always strive for completing the IT integration work as quickly as possible.

Improve/Integrate Phase—People

If for some reason you could not announce the organization earlier, I recommend that you quickly hold a meeting with the entire IT team to communicate the new organization and answer team members' questions. It is essential that all staff members know if they have a job, who they will be working for, and what their role and scope of responsibilities will be in the combined organization. Regular sessions should be held with the IT staff, at all levels, to provide an update on integration activities and to answer questions. It will take several quarters for staff to fully integrate, so it is important for the new IT leaders to be very visible during this time to ensure that team members are working toward common goals.

Prior to Day 1, you cannot usually direct the staff in the acquired company. However, on Day 1, you need to immediately take control of key operational functions such as the operations, network, and security functions. You are now responsible for these functions, and any issues that occur are now on *your watch.* It is very possible that you will not have been fully briefed on outstanding issues; it is important to get the details of these issues so you can understand any risks and develop mitigation plans.

This is a great opportunity to evaluate your new IT staff in action, as you will be under considerable time pressures, and they will have to deliver. Staff that is not performing as required should be counseled during this time frame to ensure that they understand their new roles and performance expectations. Make sure that everyone understands your reward and recognition program; this can be a great incentive to staff who will be working very long hours during this first ninety-day period. Non-monetary recognition is also important, and using IT communications meeting to highlight accomplishments can be a great motivator to the staff.

You should also be meeting with key business leaders on a frequent basis to ensure that their issues are being addressed in a timely manner. This is a great time to establish a positive rapport with business leaders, such as finance and sales, and to demonstrate the IT organization's ability to enable them to run their businesses. It is a good idea to contact them on Day 1 to ensure that everything is going smoothly from an IT perspective, as you can often address simple issues very quickly and make a very positive impression.

Improve/Integrate Phase—Process

From a process perspective, you should establish a 24/7 command center to manage all the Day 1 cutover activities. The command center would be staffed around the clock and would include the employees who developed detailed integration plans, who understand the dependencies and key assumptions in the plan, and who know who to contact with issues or questions. Depending on the amount of work that needs to be completed, you may want to have the command center operational a few days before Day 1, continuing until it is no longer needed. The command center should be providing regular updates, coordinating all IT activities, and serving as an escalation point for any issues that occur.

Your IT governance should be in place by now. I recommend that you have formal updates at least monthly to ensure that key business leaders are kept informed on integration progress, troubling issues are resolved, and critical decisions are made. Your integration dashboard should be published weekly during the next ninety days to provide everyone with an update on progress and to highlight any issues that need to be addressed. The IT team should be trained on your project management methodology. It should become routine that the team contributes to the integration dashboard. Follow-up training on your project management methodology should continue for the next ninety days to ensure that all the staff are trained and are following this methodology when doing their day-to-day jobs.

Critical IT processes, such as change control, should be integrated for the combined company. I recommend that the acquired company adopt your business processes, as you do not have time to reevaluate this area initially; you need to focus on speed. During your first ninety days, you should have plans to address critical IT processes, including those required for regulatory reporting such as SOX, as you will need this in place for a period of time so your compliance program can be verified during your testing process.

Improve/Integrate Phase—Technology

It is essential to enable communication between employees and your customers. Getting all employees on a common HR and e-mail system is key to communications. I recommend that you plan to have this work completed on Day 1 whenever possible, although some of this work may extend beyond this date. Your Web site should be integrated from a customer perspective, even if that means that you have links between two separate Web sites, as you want to appear as a single company to your customers. Financial control is also important, and I recommend that you integrate your key financial systems such as the general ledger and your planning and budgeting systems. Managers must be able to understand the budgets for the combined company.

Depending on the size and complexity of your integration, your order processing and shipping systems may or may not be able to be integrated on Day 1, although you should plan to complete this work by the end of your ninety-day plan. Your remaining business systems should also be integrated within your ninety-day plan. It is very difficult for your company to operate on multiple systems for long, and this is a reasonable time frame to complete this work. It may require creative solutions to accomplish this task; however, it will become increasingly difficult to support systems beyond this time frame, as you may no longer have the staff that originally developed them.

Your IT roadmap for the combined company should have been published by Day 1, and you now need to monitor progress on delivery. The business will not stop, and you will need to continue to deliver new features and functionality beyond the ninety-day plan. Your roadmap should extend for one to two years, so management can understand what they can expect from these capabilities. Technology standards should be communicated, if you were not able to do so earlier, and any upgrades or conversions should be included on your roadmap. Standards that affect end users, such as those regarding PDAs, should be implemented as soon as possible, because they can be *wins* for the IT organization, and you want to quickly eliminate any issues that could be disruptive to end users.

Key risks, such as information security, should have Day 1 mitigation plans that you immediately execute while you provide long-term solutions. Ninety days should be the goal to implement longer-term solutions, as you want to be creative and avoid postponing your ultimate solution. These key risks need to be reviewed by your governance board, as you may be acquiring a much smaller company that has a much more relaxed risk profile, and this may mean disruptions to services while you implement your plans.

Improve/Integrate Phase—Summary

As I mentioned previously, this phase is all about execution, and you need to complete a considerable amount of work on Day 1 and during your ninety-day plan. Your organization should begin working as a team using consistent processes and methodologies such as project management. You need a very detailed plan for your first ninety days; you should be providing regular updates to the business on integration progress. This is a great opportunity to demonstrate the capabilities of your combined IT organization.

Manage/Run Phase

The manage/run phase is all about getting back to business as usual after the initial ninety days. It is a good time to step back and reevaluate the new IT leaders and determine if they have the skills to run their expanded groups. You may want to make minor adjustments to the organization model or assign new leaders at this stage, as you are now expected to deliver the IT roadmap in the coming year, and you need to have the right team in place. High-performing staff should be rewarded at this point to recognize their efforts to ensure the success of the IT integration work.

If you plan to do additional M&A in the future, you may want to identify key staff that is responsible for this function on an ongoing basis. One of my managers led this effort for me; he did an outstanding job of leading all M&A activities as one of his job responsibilities. He identified key staff within the organization that also had this project responsibility, and we had an M&A Dream Team that consistently completed integration work in ninety days or less.

Your governance program should be evaluated to ensure that it is meeting the needs of the new business leaders. This is a good time to make required adjustments. You should also establish ongoing meetings with key business leaders to ensure that you are aligned with their business goals and are delivering appropriate IT solutions. M&A integration is a great opportunity for you to spend a lot of time with key business leaders. You will want to continue this communication on a formal and informal basis.

Your ongoing IT training program should address any remaining gaps in understanding your project management methodology, as all employees should have a basic understanding by now. Metrics should be published regularly and used to drive behavior within the IT organization. Your broad communications program should continue, as employees should be settling in their roles, and need a forum to raise any recommendations on improving the organization. Considerable progress should have been made on IT processes and you should now be in a continuous improvement program to identify areas for further improvement.

From a technology perspective, you should be focused on delivering your IT roadmap and making adjustments on a quarterly basis. All business applications should be integrated at this point, and you need to be bold and retire legacy applications from the acquired company, as you will want your staff focused on delivering new capabilities. Longer-term solutions for any risks that were identified during the earlier phases should now be on your IT roadmap. An ongoing process should be in place to evaluate new technology and update standards on a regular basis.

Special Considerations—Merger of Equals

Quite a bit has been written about *mergers of equals.* Not many of these mergers have been very successful in delivering the results in terms of increased sales, improved customer satisfaction, or improved profitability. I have led major IT activities for three mergers-of-equals transactions and have to agree they are very difficult integration efforts. In this section, I will explore these issues in more detail and offer some suggestions on how to address them.

As I mentioned earlier, M&A is all about managing change. Trying to merge two companies of similar size is like experiencing all of the personal life-changing activities (death, marriage, children, move, and new job) at the same time. You have two companies, with different cultures and values, and they are struggling to define a new culture and values for the combined company. From an IT perspective, you are caught in the middle of this struggle, as employees from each company are very familiar with their business processes and systems, and you do not have a dominant system or set of standards to follow. This requires a very strong IT governance program to assist in the numerous decisions that are very simple when you acquire a smaller company and just migrate to your business systems.

The people who remain present the most difficult issue that you will have to deal with and answering the three key questions: do I have a job, who is my manager, and what are my role and scope of responsibility. I recommend that the two IT leaders work together on an organization model for the combined organization, as one of their first priorities. You may need to complete this work while you are both candidates for the CIO job, and this can be a very delicate process. My recommendation is that you quickly develop a draft organization model, without any leaders identified, that can be discussed with the senior management from the two IT organizations. Several iterations will be required to finalize the model and the fun begins when you start discussing who will lead the new functions. If you can balance the new organization with staff from both companies, this will improve acceptance from the staff that you are following a fair process, and this should continue for the next levels within the organization. The CIO who is chosen to run the combined organization will have to make these tough decisions, will be held accountable for delivering results, and will probably lean toward staff that he or she knows well and who have delivered in the past. The CIO who is not chosen should act in a professional manner to ensure the success of the integration, and avoid becoming political and disruptive during the process.

Once the IT leadership team has been decided, the process needs to be continued throughout the organization by the new leaders until all employees in the organization are accounted for. Employees who feel that they are not getting the best positions during the process might be resentful; the best you can do is to follow a fair and consistent process of evaluating each staff and identifying the most qualified staff for the positions. It is very likely that you will need to reduce your head count during this exercise. I recommend that you freeze hiring as much as possible while you are going through this process, as this can help to minimize the number of positions that you need to eliminate.

Internal politics can get out of hand, so I recommend that you have a consistent and visible process to keep employees informed on the timing of decisions and current status. One effective procedure is to publish a schedule on key organization decisions, such as the date for finalizing the organization model, and provide regular updates to the staff until the entire organization has been announced.

You might find yourself in situations whereby the staff from the two organizations are not working together as a team and are very resistant to any changes from their existing processes. This can get to the stage where you have to have a group session to impress upon them the need to work toward the common goals of the department or find anther role. It is very likely that you will have staff that are very resistant to change, and you are better off not having them in the organization. As the CIO, you may also find yourself with a new boss from another company, who may be very biased toward that company's systems, processes, or staff; and you need to be prepared to deal with this situation and issues that are entirely out of your control. There are no *best practices* for dealing with these types of politics. Ideally, you can focus on doing what is best for the combined company, but you need to be prepared for this situation.

From a process perspective you need to develop a strong IT governance program to raise issues and obtain quick decisions. Ideally, you can get the leaders of the combined company together on a regular basis to review your integration plans and have them make critical decisions. Much more analysis will be required to discuss your proposed plans for aspects such as the e-mail system for the combined company, as each of the former companies will have their preferences and you need to be completely unbiased in your analysis. Strong governance, ideally from the CEO, is required so that decisions made by the IT governance board are final and will not be re-evaluated. This is essential so that the new company can move beyond any staff resistance and cooperate in implementing those decisions. The same governance is required within the IT organization, as it is unlikely that you will have used the same technology and some staff members will be very resistant to any changes.

Clear, consistent communications is essential during a merger of equals. Everyone needs to understand the process that was followed to make these decisions, define future IT strategy, and develop implementation plans. I recommend that the CIO devote a couple hours each week to hold communications sessions with the IT staff, and also that the CIO hold all-hands meetings each month for the first ninety days. This demonstrates the importance of these activities and gives you an opportunity to reinforce your plans. These sessions can be used to confirm the IT strategy, communicate key priorities, and solicit feedback from the team on how the integration has been going. I have also found informal sessions, such as lunches with the CIO, as a good opportunity for staff to ask questions or raise issues in a non-threatening environment.

Getting your integrated IT roadmap can be more difficult, as you have some very tough decisions on which systems to use and your business owners may not have decided on their business strategy for the combined company. Ideally, you can address key financial systems on Day 1; however, your order process and shipment processing will probably require more time, and numerous decisions need to be made. Locking down their future business processes, such as processing customers orders from your web site, is one of the first steps in the process, and your initial focus should be in this area. If you do not have staff that are experienced in this area, you may want to hire a third party who specializes in business process reengineering. Note that this may be a difficult position for the CIO, as the business leaders may need to make some very uncomfortable decisions, such as closing down a redundant call center or discontinuing an overlapping product. However, you cannot make progress in these areas until such decisions have been made. Once the business leaders such as finance and sales have completed this process work, you are in a much better position to determine which systems best support your future business.

In summary, you want to follow all the best practices I described earlier in this chapter; however, they are going to be much harder during a merger of equals. Human nature is to resist change, and you will need to serve as a *change agent* in order to complete the IT integration. You will have to spend considerable time communicating your plans in order to be successful. Your goal as a CIO is to remain focused on integrating these businesses in a rapid fashion, as this is how your company can realize the full benefits of the transaction.

Conclusion

You will continue to be faced with CIO perfect storms during your career, involving such issues as security threats, regulations, and M&A, while you are trying to focus on your day job of enabling your business to offer new products and services. You need to anticipate these challenges and their implications on your environment so that you can formulate plans to address them. You need to take a holistic approach to managing this change and consider the people, processes, and technology areas to ensure you are successful.

IT governance is essential during these changes. It can assist you in accelerating your decision making and gaining support of your plans. Communications is quite important, and I encourage you to over-communicate, as this will ensure a common understanding of your plans and assist employees in managing the changes to their environment. Speed of integration is quite important, and you should strive to complete the IT activities in ninety day or less, as this is essential for the business to realize the full benefits of the transaction.

Finally, this is a great opportunity for a CIO to demonstrate value to the organization and assume a leading role during M&A. I would encourage you to become a *storming CIO* and move out of a back-office role to take charge during these times. Your company is counting on you to deliver, and this chapter will arm you with some of the tools necessary to make that a reality.

Zero-Base Budgeting

Shawn Wilde and Sam Gill

ZBB History

Zero-base budgeting (ZBB) as a method for budgeting is less than forty years old. Yet from its inception in 1969, it has had a profound impact on how people view budgeting. Peter A. Pyhrr, in an article published in 1970, introduced the term *zero-base budgeting* and provided the following explanation: "The budget process is described at Texas Instrument, which instead of adjusting the existing budget for the upcoming year, starts from a zero base viewing all its activities and priorities afresh and creates a new set of allocations for the upcoming budget year."[1]

Pyhrr, in a subsequent article published in 1973, commented on its rapid adoption: "Zero-base budgeting is an emerging process, which has been adopted by a variety of industrial organizations in many sectors of the economy, as well as state and local governments. As it is generally practiced today, zero-base budgeting was developed at Texas Instruments, Inc. during 1969. The process was first adopted in government by Governor Jimmy Carter of Georgia for the preparation of the fiscal 1973 budget, and the process is still being used today in Georgia."[2]

Today, many public and private organizations utilize zero-base budgeting or a slightly modified version, service-level budgeting, which matches spending levels with the services to be performed, for their annual budget process.

Overview

In a recent book *CIO Wisdom*, Chapter 13 provided an excellent overview of budgeting in general and specifically how to develop project or investment budgets. In this chapter, we will focus on the sustaining expense portion of a budget. The most important thing to remember about expense management is that you need to be aware of how well you are performing to budget every month. The reason for this is quite simple; as the executive in charge of a major cost center, your expenses are always discretionary, and if the business needs expense relief, you have to be one of the first to volunteer to reduce expenses. This can happen at any time for any reason, so be prepared by knowing your expense budget and actuals in detail every month. Of course, the upside of the story is that the process helps you understand where growth impacts your expense cost structure and, therefore, what a change in the growth model for the business will do to drive costs. The best way to make this happen is to have a solid process that you and your management team can use to plan and execute a budget.

Why Zero-Base Budgeting?

ZBB is a process for developing a budget and a simple way to think about what a budget says.

As a process, ZBB is a ground-up approach to developing a budget. There are no carry-forwards from the previous year, no sacred cows in the budget, no automatic must-haves or must-dos. Everything in a ZBB must be justified on its own merits. The most common strategy for developing a traditional budget is to take last year's budget and add a percentage for inflation or to take the *trailing twelve months* (TTM) and add a percentage to that for inflation. This may be the simplest way for the CEO and CFO to look at the IT budget for the coming year, but it also implies that all of the assumptions, inefficiencies, and waste in the previous period get carried forward as well. A ZBB process has minimal references to the previous period. Therefore, no expense is automatically sanctioned by the process. Each and every expenditure must stand on its own merits. The benefit to the CIO is that it enforces a discipline within the organization that can produce significant benefit when executed systematically and fairly. Leaving certain expenses out of the process or leaving entire groups out of the process creates its own problems, however. What the ZBB process says about a budget is that for the identified funding, IT can provide an associated level of service to the company, the served employees and customers. If the level of service is appropriate and works for the company, then the budget is a good one and should get approved. If for any reason the service levels are too high or too low, then the budget has a poor chance of being approved, the CIO has just created a career-limiting event.

The process used to develop a ZBB can be whatever works for the organization. For example, some companies use ZBB with required proposals such as existing level (EL), minimum level (ML), and existing level plus new requirements (EL+1). In this process, there can be many proposals. For example, you could estimate the expenses at a minimum level (ML) of 25 percent less than the existing level (EL) and EL+1 at 25 percent above the existing level. Other approaches simply compare the proposed ZBB to the current period, with an explanation of how and why changes occurred. Any systematic approach can work, but the real value is getting to what is being said about delivered services at any budget level.

A ZBB process may not be appropriate for every department, or even every year. It may be more realistic to have different departments follow the ZBB process on different years. What is important is that over time, every department within IT uses the process.

Executive Relationships

In all organizations there exists an earned level of trust among its leaders. For the CIO: this means that your credibility in managing budgets and projects is a key part of your relationship with both the top leadership and your peers. As a member of the executive team, your job is to deliver the business-required level of service at the cost you budgeted/estimated. The job of the executive team is to approve your budget and, consequently, the service levels you are able to provide at the funding level approved. The challenge for you is to clearly demonstrate how service levels and budget are related, and that the process you used to establish the service levels was transparent, consultative, and honest.

Fundamentals

ZBB does not change the fundamentals of budget planning and execution. All budgets need the basic building blocks: a budget philosophy that is consistent with the business, a return-on-investment (ROI) standard and process for investment decisions, a detailed history of past actuals, and sufficient understanding of the current business reality for the company.

- *Budget philosophy.* What is the overall rationale behind the budget: Control? Change? Growth? If your business is not growing, then an increase in the IT budget is not consistent with a control-costs philosophy. On the other hand, if IT is to be used as a vehicle for change, then the IT budget is a strategic budget and therefore will be built up based on the strategic needs of the business. If you are in growth mode, then the drivers of cost need to be highlighted and mapped to the growth forecast in the business.

- *ROI standard.* Every business has some criteria for approving an investment. For some, it will be strictly ROI based and there will be an internal process to develop and calculate the ROI. For others projects may have intangible strategic components or even regulatory requirements that supersede ROI and generate approved projects to that criterion.

- *Past actuals.* History is the only way you can understand your current obligations, and from that you can discover your future obligations which will end up in your budget. One or two years' data are usually sufficient. More than that will just add complexity with little additional value.

- *Corporate factors.* The way your company works, your culture, your values and goals, geographical coverage, size, and business type all of these influences show up in the IT expense budget as specific items required to run IT so as to meet the expectations of management and employees. For example, in some companies the ratio of help desk staff to employees may be 1 to 50; in other organizations it may be as high as 1 to 250. Also, IT may or may not own desktops, laptops, and cell phones. There may also be unspoken assumptions about system uptime or MTTR requirements. Each of these practices has a significant influence on the IT expense budget and must be factored into the budget process. As the CIO you also need to be aware of your industry group and the approximate cost profiles in that group. As often as is practical or whenever data are available, you should measure yourself against your industry group. Alignment is great, beating the numbers is better. But having numbers completely out of the range is a sure sign of trouble.

Developing an Operating Budget

The first step in building an operating budget with ZBB principles is to identify and quantify the fundamentals that apply. Which are the budget philosophy, past actuals and the corporate factors.

Budget Philosophy

- This should be one of three choices: control, change, or conservation. Even if there is an assumed increase allowance for inflation, the overall IT budget will always fit into one of the three choices.
- Once the overall rationale has been identified, the CIO's job is to determine how each function within IT is to be planned. Networking may be growing while application support is staying the same and help desk is shrinking. Each function, role, and responsibility needs the CIO's guidance in where they start and how they plan.

Past Actuals

- In the process of finding real numbers to input to the budget, many of the prior year's assumptions and estimates may have been correct or may have been 100 percent wrong. For example, if you are changing your back-up tape media from one format to another, the start-up cost of seeding the process with new media could be quite high, while continuing to use the same media would consume at a constant rate. Using actuals is the best practice, but only if you know what is in those actuals.
- Past actuals are also where you find expenses that were not in any budget but that happened anyway. Done properly, these costs can provide a realistic calculation of contingency funds needed in the budget.
- Avoid large buckets in your actuals and in your planning. Data circuits should be planned, contracted, and budgeted facility by facility and site by site. Creating too

large a bucket for costs hides inaccuracies and creates black holes of expenses that cannot be tracked. Most companies have reasonable natural account lists for running normal G&A expenditures, but their support for IT is usually weak and incomplete. Since these account lists cannot usually be charged for the use of IT, there are a few ways to approximate the individual account categories of interest to IT:

- Maintain a purchase order register centrally for all IT purchases. Done right, you can always use this list to determine where your spending is going.

- Use the natural account codes as best you can, and if necessary, create departments to hold site-specific or expense-specific costs.

- Review your monthly actuals as soon as you get them. Any deviations from your previous budget plan need to be examined and explained promptly.

Corporate Factors

- This is where the CIO's familiarity with the overall business and the key IT staff's knowledge of day-to-day reality have to be merged. A site may only have two help desk staff, which might look right from the CIO's level, but if the users are complaining and those users are vice presidents, then a review may be called for.

- IT must be able to estimate the direction the various parts of the organization are going and the velocity they have in that direction. Engineering may be growing data storage by 50 percent a year, while Finance is hardly moving. Adding additional data storage capacity may or may not be part of the IT budget process. In larger companies, it tends to be the role of IT to provide storage on demand, but in smaller companies the VP of Engineering may have to request additional storage cost each budget cycle.

- If possible, the CIO should review the business plans for each business area to estimate its future requirements. However, in many companies the business area plans are often generated long after the core groups such as IT and Finance have already submitted their budgets. This is where the CIO's ability to team with peers is critical. The Facilities department can supply information on office and factory space utilization and plans, the HR department usually knows about headcount growth or reductions well in advance, and the financial planning group within Finance usually knows what the business area revenue and expense targets are even if the details have not yet been determined.

- Once collected and stated, the assumptions used should be carefully reviewed internally to make sure they make sense in the context of the current business. If a new or significantly changed future is envisioned, then the CIO needs to review and solicit approval for the new assumptions from the executive team or the CEO.

Expense Budgeting

The major categories in an expense budget are as follows:

- *Contracts and depreciation.* This includes all depreciation in effect over the budget period and all contracts in effect over the budget period.

- *Service delivery.* This includes all of the expenses related to keeping the doors open and the end users working: people, support systems and expenses, and miscellaneous expenses such as spares, repairs, blank tapes, and so on.
- *Service provisioning.* This includes all of the expenses related to provisioning and supporting the systems and applications infrastructure:
  - People
  - H/W
  - S/W
  - Data centers
  - Network links and remote access
  - Security

The following sections expand and provide the rationale for the items in this list.

Contracts and Depreciation

Contracts and depreciation should be simple to account for and itemize for the next budget period. When these items are a commitment from a prior period, they can be automatically entered into the budget. This is the only exception to the rule that all items must be individually justified.

What is important about these items in a ZBB is that they do get promoted, but only at the next period's net level. If a contract ends during the period or some component of the depreciation runs out, then only the net number should be used. You also need to review all depreciation items to ensure that the assets are still in use. Items that have been retired before their depreciation schedule need to be accounted for as an accounting disposal. One item that may or may not be in the IT budget is the local property tax on assets. Even if it is not part of the IT budget, it is part of some department's budget. The asset register must be up to date with all correct disposals in order for the company to minimize this expense.

New capital expenditure will drive new depreciation expense (usually the month after the item goes into production). The list of capital investments, excluding projects and strategic initiatives, should be broken into two portions, the sustaining and the maintenance. The sustaining items are critical to the business and should never be cut. Included would be network ports for new employees, the replacement of hardware that is out of warranty or vendor maintenance, capacity improvements where the existing capacity can be clearly demonstrated to be affecting the business, new software applications that are part of a larger project, or software that is a prerequisite for some other business requirement.

The maintenance items are investments that could be deferred. These might include replacement hardware where the existing system could be utilized until the next budget period, capacity upgrades for future growth and adjustments to low-risk services such as wireless support in a conference room. Knowing what is critical and what is optional is the key to managing IT infrastructure investments.

Contract management can be very complex for an IT organization, but the fundamentals remain the same. Get the best price up front and the best price for the ongoing maintenance and support. If possible, lock in the support costs to a fixed price for two or three years or to a maximum increase amount. When negotiating renewal contracts, you should build into the budget a reasonable contingency for cost increases from the supplier. In all cases, make proposals to the supplier for different or custom terms. The bigger the customer you are, the better chance you have of trimming the bill. You should also review with the CFO or treasurer the plan for cash in the upcoming fiscal period. Your company may have a very low cost of money or a very high one. If cash is tight, then capital investments are difficult and leasing may provide the cash-flow relief the company's treasury needs.

Service Delivery and Service Provisioning

Service delivery and service provisioning are the fundamental expense items required to deliver to the users what IT has to offer. Depending on your business, this could range from delivery 24/7 worldwide to 8/5 locally.

Included would be all expenses related to staff, applications, servers, infrastructure, networking, facilities, consumables, and any additional expenses for the staff in this area, as well as the tools and systems they need to perform this role.

The key questions to ask when planning service delivery follow:

- Have the budget assumptions or philosophy changed in any way such that this group should be planned differently? Unless you are under significant financial constraints, this category usually stays the same at the high level. If there are financial constraints to be considered, then an EL/ML proposal may be required to define the discussion about what can be done at different funding levels.
- Is the right staff deployed in the right places? If not, change!
- Is the value of the services that are being delivered changing? If there is a major shift to laptops from desktops in the company, then remote support will probably have a higher value to the business.
- Is the current fiscal period tracking to budget? If not, then determine what is up and what is down, and why? For each category of expense, you need to understand and model the drivers of cost.

If you can keep these categories consistently defined year over year, then the ratio of these expenses to the served employee base can be meaningful. For example, if the served user base is growing rapidly and the corporate factors stay the same, then a flat budget means that operating leverage is being exploited by supporting more users with the same resources. However, if the goal is to reduce costs in a dramatic way, then the expense base within this group must fall and the assumptions about who does what or who pays for what must change.

This is a difficult area to discuss because it is where most IT contingency money is held. If you have a very transparent company with extreme financial honesty then you have no fears but if you are expected to cover unexpected costs as part of your budget without specific line items then this is the place where the money needs to be. We do not recommend "sandbagging" or having a "loaded" budget, but in some organizations it may be the best way to manage for success within the context of the organization.

ZBB Process Example

Everything discussed to this point is just good practice in budgeting. Where the ZBB process differs from other practices is in the management review and oversight of each and every line item in the budget proposal. An existing-level budget, or EL, can be broken down into the following process steps:

1. All staff positions, roles, and responsibilities are reviewed and approved one at a time for inclusion in the budget proposal. This may sound difficult, but in most cases it is very straightforward. The position will either continue to exist or will not.
2. New staff positions are only proposed with supporting documentation as to why the position is required and how it will be funded.
3. For each and every purchase order planned for the next fiscal period, a corresponding budget line item must be created. The amount of each item must be validated by either a reference to an existing contract, a proposed purchase estimate or an estimate based on the current year actuals or the TTM actuals. For small purchase items such as office supplies, a simple number may be appropriate. Just don't let these items get out of control.
4. Carry-forward expenses such as depreciation require a line-by-line description of the item and the associated expense.
5. Other corporate expenses such as facilities charges, overhead, or shared services expenses each need their own line and their own description.

Once this information has been compiled, the role of the CIO is to examine the rationale used to justify inclusion in the proposal. A solid, intellectually honest argument is needed for each line item or group of items. It needs to be in the context of the budget philosophy, the past actuals, and the corporate factors. Where the item is new to the budget, the business justification and funding strategy must also be reviewed.

It is critical that the CIO and the senior IT managers take the review process seriously. If the IT staff believe that the CIO will not look too deeply into their numbers and justifications, then they will not perform the diligence necessary to give good results.

Here are some key questions:

- Do we really need this item?
- Is the proposed expenditure consistent with past years, or can a calculation be shown to justify the number?
- If we take the line item out, what happens?
- Is this the best price from the supplier, or can we do better?
- Have contingencies been built in to the proposal? Where and how much?

ZBB Result

The result of the ZBB process will be one or more departmental budgets that are 100 percent clean, 100 percent approved and 100 percent understood. Entitlements and fuzzy justifications will have been challenged and either approved or rejected. The rejected items go away unless a realistic justification can be made. The approved items are now ready for executive scrutiny and review. A ZBB is a great tool because it allows the CIO to link the performance and delivery level of a department to the business need. If the CIO has defined the business need correctly, then approval should be easy. If not, the CIO now has the information at hand to either increase or decrease the budget as required.

Conclusion

ZBB is an exercise in knowing the details and being able to discuss each item or group of items in the context of what they deliver to the business. Common sense must be evident in all parts of the budgeting process: Too much detail and the process will never complete; too little and you end up knowing nothing about what the budget is saying. Know the critical influencers of IT cost, keep the executive team informed and involved, be flexible, and treat your budget as the tool you use to align IT with the business.

Your success depends on your ability to deliver a suite of services and capabilities to the business for a known cost with a known benefit. Do this enough times, and you will have earned your seat at the executive table.

Notes

1. Peter A. Pyhrr, "Zero-Base Budgeting," *Harvard Business Review,* 48, no. 6, November to December 1970): 111–121.
2. Peter A. Pyhrr, "The Zero-Base Approach to Government Budgeting," *Public Administration Review,* 37, no. 1 (January to February 1977): 8–10.

Gordian Knot: Centralized versus Decentralized

Pamela Vaughan, Jennifer Diamond, and Dean Lane

The Gordian Knot

A legend of the ancient kingdom of Phrygia tells how in the eighth century BCE, the first king Gordius was crowned because he fulfilled a prophecy by driving his oxcart up to the temple doors. In gratitude to the priests and to the gods, he secured the cart with an intricate knot with no discernable ends, and the cart and its knot were enshrined in a temple. The cart remained on display, and became the center of its own legend and prophecy when sages decreed that he who could unravel the knot would rule all of Asia.

Hundreds of years later, in 333 BCE, Alexander the Great tried his hand at the knot. The story goes that when he could not find the ends, a bold stroke of his sword created them, severing the knot, and indeed, he became the ruler of Asia Minor, as predicted.

"Cutting the Gordian knot" now stands for solving problems by questioning constraints. Some of us might also recognize this idea in the form of Captain Kirk's "Kobayashi Maru," converting a revered and accepted no-win test into a resolvable situation by changing the rules. Still others of us might see it more prosaically as "thinking outside the box."

Defining whether to manage a centralized or decentralized IT is a Gordian knot problem. For decades, organizations have venerated the question, raising it to the level of one of IT's greatest with zealots on both sides. The management debate of decentralized versus centralized business functions has fostered entire lines of academic thought and even political ramifications. The two sides are polarized into black and white.

Black: Centralization

In the world of black, centralization as a method speaks to complete definition and control of IT from headquarters closest to management. The implication is that control and oversight are of primary importance, followed quickly by economies of scale. Advocates feel that processes, technology, and customer and vendor management are all better served under the umbrella of a centralized IT. The arguments for centralization are as follows:

- Improved coordination, standardization, and consolidation of infrastructure and applications
- Significant economies of scale and more efficient management
- Reduction of inconsistent redundancies, better controls, and standardization
- Reduced business risks to company data and systems

In a centralized environment, supporters say, more streamlined and efficient IT services can be achieved, ranging from operating data servers and servicing desktop computers to procurement, development, and data management. Consolidation of knowledge management speeds information sharing among different departments, and standardized consolidation of infrastructure and applications is more cost effective than having a distributed environment.

Centralized IT management allows companies to create consistent and secure technology standards across the enterprise and avoid reinventing the wheel, which becomes inevitable when separate business units devise similar solutions to the same problems.

White: Decentralization

Taking the side of white, decentralization arguments anchor on the elimination of bureaucracy, increased accountability, innovation, and the ability to provide customized solutions. Arguments for decentralizing include the following:

- Greater individual business unit control over their own IT resource use
- Greater scope for motivating and involving users
- More supportive environment for innovation and responsiveness
- More direct business understanding of IT value, costs, and benefits

Generally speaking, decentralized IT proponents see a more democratic environment where business unit leaders see the value of IT as it applies to their own neighborhood of needs and initiatives, better understanding how IT contributes and the associated cost.

Without the dilution of a bureaucracy, the potency of IT dollars for services leads to more involved and responsible decision making. Partnership between IT and business leaders is more intimate, focused on local business issues and solutions, increasing overall satisfaction with IT participation as a corporate citizen.

The World of Gray: Hybrid

Both seem to have the good of the organization in mind, and are trying to create a highly service-oriented IT function. Black and white are both compelling, but the right answer is that the world is gray. The real question is the shade of gray that achieves the right balance. So many factors define what is or is not the right approach for each organization.

Clearly, whole-cloth advocacy of one method over the other just does not have reasonable application in today's business world, but there are leanings toward one side or another that seem to depend on the industry in which the company operates, the regions in which it performs various corporate functions, and even the management style involved. The first task, then, is to objectively define what considerations determine which elements of the IT portfolio of services and processes need to be decentralized or centralized.

Hybrid Considerations

Just about all the factors that would guide these decisions fall into four categories of considerations, as shown in Figure 1.3:

1. Risk management and control
2. Business alignment and responsiveness
3. Efficiency and effectiveness
4. Leadership and innovation

Risk management and control relate to a required level of oversight applied to a function. Centralization lends itself to tighter controls and consistency than decentralization, so an emphasis on risk management and control could count as a vote in favor of centralizing whatever needed the emphasis.

Business alignment and responsiveness is a balancing consideration to risk management and control. Because of the dispersed nature of IT customers, company wide user communities consuming IT as a utility and business unit leaders using IT on a project basis, IT responds and maintains alignment with a leaning toward decentralized agility.

Efficiency and effectiveness point back to that sense of economies of scale, but with an understanding that performance also matters. This consideration is most often associated with centralized functions, eliminating redundancies and streamlining methods. A good CIO remembers that in stark contrast to years ago, when *efficiency* meant linear manufacturing lines and serial activities, technology now permits an extremely efficient distributed process, letting IT bring effectiveness to users' doorsteps if needed. The point of this category has more to do with incremental improvements in ongoing operations.

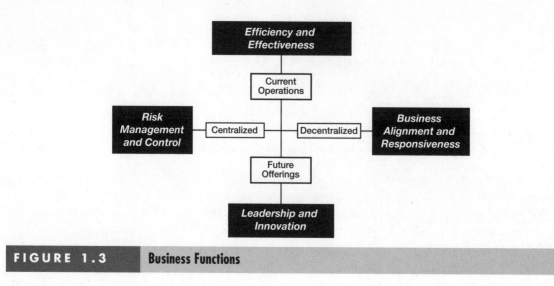

| FIGURE 1.3 | Business Functions |

Leadership and innovation is another mixed consideration. Long thought of as the balancing thought to a robotic drive toward cost reduction, innovation was supposed to come only from being close to the customer and coming up with solutions through immersion familiarity. It is clear now, however, that taking a centralized approach to strategic planning is definitely a part of a responsible approach to designing an optimal IT offering. Again, like *efficiency and effectiveness*, what we used to think of as a stark centralized versus decentralized need is more about what IT is doing, and this category has more to do with future IT contribution.

To test these four categories, consider whether the industry in which a company operates is a determining factor whether to centralize or decentralize. That decision depends on what the company needs from IT, and perhaps the needs of a New York based insurer, for instance, calls out risk management and control as well as efficiency as primary considerations, leaning toward centralization. It may be clear, then, that financial services demand centralized IT.

But it is quite possible that another company in the financial services sector, maybe a national on-line mortgage broker, needs more emphasis on business alignment and responsiveness, with forward-leaning leadership and innovation. The industry is not the determination; in this example, corporate strategy is, and two companies in the same industry need different things. Using these four categories of considerations can help to capture in what way each company's IT needs are different.

Hybrid Components

But while companies need different things based on a set of considerations, making the choices about centralization versus decentralization does not require a *tabula rasa* approach. There are right beginnings, the right family of gray shades, to use. Two main components of hybrid IT models can be launching points:

1. Centralized governance and security
2. Decentralized execution and service

When the realities of today's IT are examined, there is little debate over the need to govern IT through global standards and methods. The IT world changes too quickly and is too regulated to not use a systematic approach to setting rules.

On the operations side of things, a centralized approach to networks, security, architecture, and standards creates an environment in which consistent protection for business systems and information can be relied on throughout the enterprise.

IT leadership also benefits from the centralized nature of IT strategy development and senior management processes by staying close to the forward-looking business strategy of the company. Corporate governance, not just IT governance, is happening more and more on a centralized basis, and CIOs know that the best way to manage an IT budget toward approval is to have it closely tied and supported by fellow C-level executives as part of the overall corporate plan and governance program.

At the same time, the speed of business and the heavy reliance on IT by business users require that IT is accessible and reliable at the immediate business activity level. That means decentralized presence and partnering, replicating the senior management model at the local level. From dedicated analysts assigned to specific business unit leaders as IT liaisons to a universally accessible and possibly even regionally outsourced Help Desk, local presence calls for a decentralized reach. These decentralized functions should still follow the global standards to reduce costs and provide consistent effective service.

Hybrid Benefits

Remembering IT's perpetual requirement for delivered value, the benefits of the right shade of hybrid gray also continue to prove its validity. The benefits to the company include the best of both worlds:

- Globally imposed direction and standardization
- Globally managed oversight and review
- Targeted efficiency and performance
- Service-focused responsiveness and effectiveness
- Business-aligned investment and improvement
- Business-sponsored and co-delivered initiatives
- Business-driven TCO and ROI

By driving centralized definitions and expectations and providing decentralized service and partnering, IT can be a wide-reaching and stabilizing force to implementing business solutions and providing the backbone of business operations. By establishing targeted metrics across IT, proving the benefits and delivered value of the hybrid model is part of doing business. Measurements or indicators might include any of the following:

- Compliance metrics reporting on adherence to standards and methods
- Performance metrics reporting on operating efficiencies and capacity
- Project-based metrics reporting on progress, cost, schedules, sponsorship, and relevance

- Satisfaction-based metrics reporting on availability, responsiveness, and service
- Investment metrics reporting on business value and return on IT resources

Maintaining metrics on the hybrid organization, in addition to providing the portfolio of fact to show the benefits of IT's structure to the company, also allows for tuning or adjusting the hybrid mix, perhaps choosing to move the slider more toward centralized management if an area is suffering from over distributed inconsistencies, or decentralized if more responsiveness is needed in an area that is well controlled. At all times, IT management is ready to respond, which is the true benefit of the hybrid approach.

An Example: Application Deployment

The best way to explain how to operate within a hybrid environment is to provide an example. Looking at an enterprise wide application project, how the process of identifying the need through supporting a new production application is handled shows the migration through centralized and decentralized IT functions.

Beginning at a local level, the business unit defines a business problem that requires an IT solution. The local IT presence, in the form of a business analyst or liaison, assists in scoping the project request and identifying preliminary costs and benefits. Deep familiarity of the business unit's needs and opportunities are strengths in defining the business case.

From the identification phase, the project sponsors and business unit leaders shepherd the project request into the global or centralized project prioritization process, where the entire company's project requests and initiative portfolio are the focus of management attention and decision making. A centralized portfolio management process drives consistency and balances projects for synergies and best use of company resources.

Once the management team approves the project, local IT and business-unit participants form project teams. These are the most qualified resources, experts in the problem and vested in the solution. The sponsors of the project are nearby, staying involved, informed, and committed to the project to participate in the centralized methods of ongoing approval within the global portfolio.

In the course of participating in global approval processes and performing project tasks, the local project team utilizes established standardized methods to enforce control and allow for effective oversight. From project management methods to application development methods, centrally defined requirements increase predictability and decrease implementation risk. Maintaining a centralized approach to continued approval in the portfolio also reduces the risk of lost relevance over time. The project team made up of business-unit participants and the decentralized IT analysts and project specialists use centrally defined rules to execute the project.

The project team interacts with the centralized infrastructure organization to participate in the highly controlled release to production (RTP) process, utilizing segregated environments, administered testing, and scheduled releases to deploy the new solution in a production environment. No longer a local solution to a local problem, the application is part of the global architecture of the company, and has to be administered as such. The

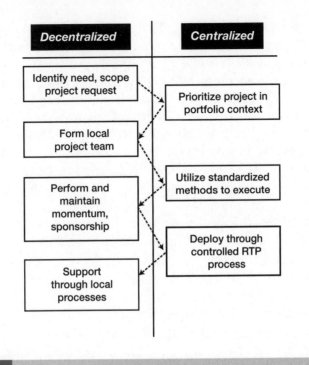

FIGURE 1.4

project team members participate in acceptance testing and appropriate approvals, but the migration itself is a closely controlled and centrally managed activity. Once the application is in production, the service model of centralized administration and decentralized support comes into play, where the users rely on decentralized help desk resources and their local business analyst liaisons for questions or help associated with the new production application, along with any other IT needs they may have.

To get the application project done, the business follows a pendulum through decentralized and centralized activities, using a local sponsorship approach for investigative and collaborative steps, and a standardized collective approach for oversight and control. This process is illustrated in Figure 1.4.

How to Get Started

It is not difficult to see how a hybrid model of centralized and decentralized IT functions can work. The real issue is getting to the right shade of gray from whatever starting point the organization is currently experiencing. A poorly defined or managed transition can hurt credibility and effectiveness severely, and cause unnecessary risk.

When making the transition in IT operating model, the first considerations in the current business environment have to be risk management, security, and continuity. There are many obvious and good reasons for starting here, but a less obvious one might be that a CIO approaching a change in IT structure may find that risk management as a rationale is far more palatable to business unit and executive management than promises of agility and responsiveness. Starting from a responsible position of governance and oversight is comforting to those who may be leery of an IT-initiated change.

This drives right into the second step. A centralized approach to security and a coordinated approach to continuity are both areas that fall into the category of risk management and control. In the course of restructuring IT with risk management and control considerations the process becomes focused towards enlisting business unit leaders to participate in forming an IT governing and advising body.

This body, whether an existing steering committee that is due for a recommitment or a new advising team for IT, serves an absolutely essential role for the CIO trying to revamp the model of how IT does its business. If nothing else, this body is the sounding board and later sponsoring voice for the changes IT needs to make. Selling from the top down will happen from the IT governing body, so its formation and commissioning is essential.

The role of the IT governing body includes the following elements that are critical to an effective transition in the structure of IT offerings:

- Represent the business units to define the proximity needs of IT offerings
- Receive education from IT regarding criticality of IT control points
- Discuss and approve standardized methods and requirements from IT processes
- Serve as the IT portfolio oversight body

There are those who would argue that creating such a body and explicitly granting it these roles removes authority from IT to enact its own practices and, frankly, do its job. They would continue to say that this organization would plunge the CIO into a full-time job of politics instead of administering a critical business function.

The truth of the matter, however, is that most companies have a version of this body already, whether it is performing its intended role or not, and by enlisting its active participation in this way, the CIO guides exactly what the committee does, serving the best good for the company and IT. Instead of leaving potential unhappy customer executives unattended, a good CIO knows to actively enlist potential detractors as newly converted supporters in a systematic and process-oriented way.

Going back to the project example discussed earlier, the centralized tasks associated with approving the project in the context of the portfolio, standardizing methods, and queuing into a consolidated release process all presume that the centralized rules and approaches exist. If they do not exist as yet, the CIO can guide the IT governing body to define these rules, and at that time clarify the business unit roles and commitments within them. It would be the IT governing body of business unit representatives, then, who would decide that it is a business unit leader's responsibility to define the business case for a project, provide ongoing support and sponsorship for it, and fund it. IT cannot alone make such a decree. There are many water-cooler horror stories detailing the career-limiting ramifications of trying.

If the criteria for decentralizing or centralizing a function come down to identifying the best balance between control and service, the IT governing body is the final arbiter of customer satisfaction with that balance. As company executives, they determine the appropriate level of control they require from IT, and as IT customers, they determine the needs they have for access to IT offerings. In the context of these roles, the IT governing body can decide that it is appropriate to outsource decentralized user support in off-shore operations, but maintain a centralized in-house version for quality control and standard-setting for corporate headquarters. The governing body can also decide upon, and enforce, a rule that requires any project with a projected cost of over $100,000 to be presented with full business case analysis to the committee before being considered in a broader portfolio conversation.

By facilitating this group skillfully, a CIO can create a very powerful advocacy group that will be the ongoing sounding board for the decisions regarding other IT functions, and the ongoing sponsors of those decisions throughout their implementation. There is no better example of business alignment, and no better recipe for implementing the right balance of centralized and decentralized IT offerings.

Conclusion: How to Know When the Shade of Gray Is Right

Unlike the absolutes of black or white, there are infinite shades of gray, and the right shade may be valid for the moment only, requiring ongoing tuning of the IT organization to meet current objectives. Having a solid set of criteria to evaluate, a clear basis for decision making, and a collaborative management approach with an IT governing body representing the business ensures that the decisions made to centralize a function or distribute it are based on actual business need. Verifying IT performance on criteria that address each of these areas and collecting the data that supports those discussions keeps the conversation collaborative and focused on the job at hand.

Centralized and decentralized IT can peacefully coexist and flourish under the hybrid organizational model accommodating the best elements of black and white where appropriate. Functions that need to be consistent on a global basis like information security and network design are centralized while functions requiring a close coordination with internal customers such as business analysis and help desk should be decentralized but still adhere to global standards.

The hybrid approach to IT structure rejects overzealous adherence to a single management theory despite the needs of the business or the culture of its management team. By refusing to revere overmuch any one approach, and by establishing a system of proof, acceptance, and advocacy, a CIO can completely redefine the problem, cutting the Gordian knot of old "us versus them" thinking permanently, and instead establishing a new tradition of innovative and collaborative business participation.

Evolution of the CIO

Steve Paszkiewicz

"Change is inevitable. Change is constant."
—Benjamin Disraeli

Driving Forces

As we progress in this first decade of the new millennium, it is important that we understand, in practical terms, how opportunistic business models and a technologically driven workforce have become the most significant driving forces behind the evolution of the CIO.

Today, no single business element is more inherently dynamic than information technology—and every type of business depends on it in one form or another. New innovations in information technology tend to create the basis for still further innovations. Rapid advances in computational power, memory capacities, storage systems, and miniaturization have fueled the demand for new types of business applications, products, and services.

The pervasive nature of the Internet has fueled the proliferation of new networking appliances and handheld devices that deliver converged communications anywhere and at any time. These are dramatically changing the way people work, the way information is delivered, and the way knowledge is obtained.

Over the last ten years, innovations in information technology have, on average, helped to increase employee productivity levels by 2.6 percent year-over-year as reported by Technology, Communications and Information (TCI), a component of GDP indices.

As IT becomes more commoditized, aligned, and integrated within the context of specific business strategies and processes, the primary role of the CIO continues to evolve beyond that of the traditional organizational and systems management of the past two decades. Simply put, the role of the CIO is in a state of change across all industries—in early-stage start-ups, growth-oriented companies, and mature business environments.

In this chapter, we will explore how CIO leadership and effectiveness are moving to the forefront of modern-day businesses and may be *the* determining factor in the future success of a company as today's emerging technologies become tomorrow's new IT infrastructure.

CIO Leadership Characteristics

Companies searching for a CIO may not just be seeking an executive with deep expertise in the application of IT, but rather for an executive who also possesses strong business acumen and broad management skills—someone who has demonstrated the capacity to provide leadership across the entire corporation. In addition, companies most likely will be searching for a candidate with business diversity, having experience in multiple industries, multinational operations, and having managed a P&L operation. In other words, these companies are searching for a candidate with the characteristics, attributes, diversity, and style that are prescriptively matched to meet their unique business circumstances in order to compete in an ever-expanding world market.

This is in sharp contrast to what was expected of CIOs during the 1990s. Then, the focus was centered more on technical planning—establishing and maintaining secure networks and computing infrastructures, managing organizational resources, formalizing internal processes, and developing budgets and procedures necessary to support back office systems in low and medium-mix technology environments. These skills and expertise remain the foundation supporting every successful CIO, but the role is evolving to a much more strategic orientation. Moreover, today's technologically driven, savvy, and conversant workforce expects the company to provide a secure infrastructure for converged communications services, wireless connectivity, and remote access.

The Changing Role of the CIO

In many high-performance organizations the role of the CIO includes responsibilities for business process management and large-scale transformation programs that are designed to advance strategic initiatives across the enterprise. To drive these initiatives, the CIO must possess not only the necessary technical, business, and communication skills, but also the ability to adapt these to an organization's unique culture. It is not surprising that CIOs are being asked to lead these important activities in all but the largest corporations, as (IT) has a rich heritage of being process-centric.

Increasingly, in high-mix, high-volume technology environments the CIO not only determines which specific technologies to deploy that will enable critical business processes, but also how and where these investments in technology may be further maximized and leveraged to create real business value, making contributions to both the top- and bottom-line margins. To be successful, the CIO must thoroughly understand and be conversant with the strategic goals and language of the business, far beyond day-to-day technical operations and other related support activities.

This will require a deep immersion into the business—taking the appropriate amount of time to thoroughly understand all key business processes and functions, assessing the strengths, weaknesses, opportunities and threats that affect each, and how this information relates to the company's strategy, (IT) plan, and more importantly, its financial objectives.

The CIO must develop meaningful relationships and key partnerships with business leaders throughout the company to drive paradigmatic change while advancing business initiatives through the use of information technology. The CIO must anticipate and prepare for some degree of resistance—as transformation programs often engender a wide variety of organizational and employee resistance. Orchestrating change at this level, a CIO will need the commitment and full support of the executive team (CEO and CFO) and the cooperation from members of senior management team in order to achieve the desired outcomes.

Additionally, the CIO role includes the full responsibility for developing and managing capital and expense budgets across the company for all technology-related purchases and the management of important vendor relationships. This, too, is not surprising, as it provides a mechanism for controlling unnecessary expenditure on technologies that may have little value or benefit to the business. It also enables the CIO to leverage the companies purchasing position in terms of a greater economy of scale for software and hardware purchases, while establishing vendor services levels and measurement capabilities for service delivery.

Learning about the Business

Taking time to learn about the business is an essential part of every CIO's job. A CIO must gain a deep understanding of how other parts of the business function—both individually and collectively—instead of narrowly focusing on the IT organization. A CIO must develop a wide-angle perspective of the company to influence future strategy or to affect any type of meaningful change. Decisions that a CIO makes in any one part of an organization—whether process or technology related—often will have a significant impact in other parts of the business, and therefore, must be carefully considered and planned for accordingly.

Enterprise Architectures

More than ever before, the taxonomy between business processes and technology have become highly coupled and intertwined. Changing one often requires changing the other. Business models that depend largely on high-mix technology environments, or those that

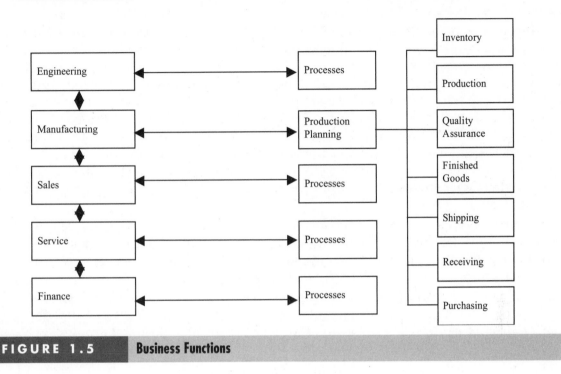

| FIGURE 1.5 | Business Functions |

require a high-volume processing or a transactional set of capabilities, have significantly increased the complexity of managing (IT) operations both inside and outside the firewall.

A few examples of these environments may include online reservation systems financial services management, online purchasing, banking, insurance claim processing, social networking and many others too numerous to mention.

These complexities are manifested as critical information flows moving through and between various application sets, or as business transactions executing in a number of interdependent systems. At some point the data must converge in order to deliver business-sensitive and time-critical information. Few changes, whether business processes or technology related, involve just one functional area or one area of knowledge. For example, consider a business initiative to replace an aging manufacturing system with a newer more technologically advanced system, shown in Figure 1.5.

Although the purpose of the initiative is seemingly straightforward, to "improve manufacturing capabilities," it will involve significant process changes within these and perhaps other interrelated business functions. Understanding how and where important interrelationships exist and the role each function plays in the context of the whole business should be on the CIO's list of top priorities.

In the previous example, a CIO must determine how a proposed solution matches the business requirements of manufacturing, while assessing the potential impact with other cross-functional business processes, systems, and employee resources. The CIO must also decide whether the solution fits architecturally and is sustainable within the framework of the (IT) services, processes, and integration architectures. Communicating the benefits, risks, and value of the initiative with key stakeholders is a prerequisite.

Business is moving at the speed of the Internet. As already described, new innovations in IT are fueling the development of new products and services. Contrary to popular opinion, very few companies today rely solely on single-solution packages, such as an ERP platform to run their entire business operations—as these too have become complex and expensive. The reality is that while single-package solutions may work well for some types of business, they do not work well in other types. This represents something of a reversal of the old 80/20 rule, whereby 80 percent of the customers may be served by a particular ERP package and the remaining 20 percent will not. I see this trend developing even further, whereby businesses continue to move to more specialized niche solutions to meet their unique requirements. Think about the early successes of Software-as-a-Service (SaaS) and aggregation providers.

Today, there are a number of available SaaS products in the marketplace providing relationship management, contact and account management, performance and compensation management, marketing campaign management, facilities management, time and expense management, and many others for businesses.

As SaaS products become more commonplace, they will require greater coordination and interaction between internal (IT) organizations and SaaS providers to ensure that persistent datasets are clean and rationalized for integration and reporting purposes.

More about Cross-Functional Business Processes

A company's success is measured by the speed and value of its cross-functional business processes. With regulatory requirements such as Sarbanes-Oxley legislation directed at publicly traded corporations, cross-functional business processes are moving to the center of Six Sigma, ITIL, and other quality-related programs to enforce regulatory compliance. These methodologies provide a framework to identify inefficiencies and persistent execution problems through disclosure, certification, and audit. Although cross-functional business processes do not appear in any organizational chart, no business can succeed without them. Together, they establish the company's value chain for achieving maximum operating efficiencies between interdependent business organizations.

Business Immersion

After spending the majority of my career working in technology-related and manufacturing sectors, several years ago I accepted the role of CIO at a publicly traded NYSE mid-cap consumer-goods company. The position was appealing, because it provided an opportunity to apply my skills and experiences in a cross-over environment. The primary industry was in home décor / home accent products, which included everything from gifts and collectibles to fine art replications for a well-established and highly recognizable brand. The company considered its core business to be marketing, sales, and distribution of fine art replications; however, it owned and operated significant manufacturing operations and original equipment manufacturer (OEM) product warehouses.

Product sales occurred mostly through several hundred independent retail outlets and through a company-managed Web-based store front. The IT organization consisted of approximately fifty professionals distributed within five technology functions. These included networking, applications development, desktops and servers, and a boutique point-of-sale development team of twenty software developers and quality assurance (QA) personnel acquired through a prior acquisition. The core business utilized J. D. Edwards financials, manufacturing, inventory, purchasing, and order-administration modules, running on an IBM AS400 mainframe environment.

Due to economic conditions at the time, product market saturation, and the cyclical nature of the business, sales had declined appreciably over the previous three years resulting in a significant amount of inventory sitting in finished goods. With increased pressure on stock performance and a noticeable measure of frustration at the executive level, the CEO asked that I take a look at internal business processes to help figure out how to reduce inventories and improve operating margins. My prior experience as CIO with a multibillion dollar contract manufacturing business would be an asset: I agreed to look at all internal planning and production processes and to report back my findings and recommendations to the executive team.

Since its inception, the company had relied on a *make to stock* production philosophy, whereby manufacturing would produce all products in anticipation of future sales. The VP of manufacturing explained that this was necessary, because many of the raw materials used in the final assembly process were sourced overseas. By leveraging economies of scale, bulk purchasing of all necessary materials was essential to obtain the lowest possible cost per unit. In addition, master product plans and schedules were produced for independent demand directly within production planning, as production forecasts were generated without any direct linkage to marketing or sales forecasts for dependent demand.

The VP of sales explained that his organization was not able to produce a reliable sales forecast because it was difficult to gauge consumer interest. He said sales were generally made through impulse purchasing by consumers. The VP of marketing agreed that due to the often-fickle nature of consumers, advanced product market testing through independent retailers was not reliable because product appeal—especially in fine art replications, gifts, and collectibles—did not translate into universal consumer excitement.

In this example, while inventory was certainly an issue requiring immediate attention, it was only a symptom of many larger challenges. Business immersion is about learning how business functions based on your own observations and through the perspectives of your peers from within their functional areas. It involves making an assessment of the challenges and opportunities affecting each, and how this information relates to the company's strategic and financial objectives. It is not about looking at individual tasks or discrete processes that support intra-business functions, as these may be too numerous to evaluate in many types of businesses. However, if these are not working, you will hear about it. Business immersion should not be considered as a one-time event.

Conclusions

The role of the CIO is evolving. The degree of change does vary by industry and market segment. If you are standing at the finish line waiting to see the results, you may be there for quite some time. Emerging technologies must be evaluated from both a pessimistic and optimistic point of view. As history has taught us, not all technological innovation achieves commercial viability. Equally important, CIOs must determine whether a particular emerging technology is a competency enhancer or competency destroyer within their organizations.

Many young men and women are entering the IT profession as computer scientists in a variety of disciplines, from software development to quality assurance, modeling to simulation, applications to databases, networking to security, desktop to server administration, business analysts to program managers. As CIO, you should strive for a level of balance between the younger generation and the more seasoned professionals as you build or extend your organizations. Both groups have something to offer the other.

In my opinion, as the CEO, CFO, and board members gain a deeper understanding of the intricacies of the interdependent relationship between processes and technology, it will further strengthen the position and value of the CIO as a trusted member of the executive team. Finally, if a CIO does not thoroughly understand how the business functions, or is unable to describe it or communicate it, the CIO will not be able to successfully influence, change, or manage it.

Leading IT in a Hyper-Growth Environment

Al Pappas

Introduction

I joined one of the fastest growing enterprise software companies that became the leader in business revenue growth of all software institutions to that date. This company was established in the traditional manner of angel funding in its early stages, then supplemented by Venture Capital after a few years in product development and product sales successes. This company was initially formed by the product developers who had incubated the product and associated strategy in two of the more prestigious universities in the San Francisco Bay Area. I joined the company as their first CIO and discovered that they remained in a "start-up" mode even after 6 years in existence and having been acquired by a major technology company. I immediately began to apply my previous experience with early stage companies by developing an IT strategy and vision with the approval of the C-level executives. In conjunction, I began a recruiting effort to employ the senior IT skilled personnel required to raise the level of the corporation to the next level. The existing staff was dedicated but unskilled in supporting a hyper growth based company and as such relied heavily upon heroics to meet the ever growing demands of the business. The engineering organization represented the largest element of the personnel base and as such had their own dedicated service and support organization and therefore required only minimal IT services and support (i.e. email, telephony, etc.). I recognized that the success of the new IT group was heavily dependent upon the inclusion of seasoned and established IT experienced personnel. I utilized my extensive network to recruit the early stage leaders and senior technical staff. I also hired a dedicated recruiter that possessed IT management experience and therefore enabled us to rapidly select only those that met our rigid criteria for technical and management expertise. This reduced the overall level of hiring manager demands to review the numerous resumes and early interviews required for personnel qualification. The candidates that they ultimately met were well qualified to meet the specific needs of the hiring managers due to the due diligence performed by my in-house IT recruiter. I focused the majority of my attention aligning with both the Chief Financial Officer (CFO) and the various VP's within the corporation. My initial efforts resulted in a 90 day evaluation and a 6 month to 1 year development plan supplemented by an IT Portfolio of projects and key business demands. This was developed in conjunction with the establishment of an IT Steering Committee which included all C-level and senior VP's comprising the Executive Staff. I met individually with each of these members to review their key projects and associated priorities. These one-on-one meetings provided the details required to complete the associated parameters and related project characteristics of the IT Portfolio. The initial meetings of the IT Steering Committee were driven largely by me and the CFO. I used this forum to establish an ongoing review of projects and key IT operational tasks that many deemed critical to the support of the company's meteoric growth. The large majority of this executive staff was never exposed to this type of forum so it was imperative for me to meet with each of them separately to both educate and build consensus regarding both their and other IT projects and associated efforts. The CFO was the most supportive of these activities and I depended upon his tenure and expertise dealing with these staff members since he behaved more as a Chief Operating Officer (COO) than a typical CFO. The IT characteristics noted above addressed my personal experience with a startup like company whereas other more established companies that were found to be in a hyper-growth environment due to acquisition required similar but different actions. The differences are noted in Table 1.3.

The following sections of this chapter are written to portray my experiences with both this hyper-growth company as well as others that fall into similar categories.

TABLE 1.3		
Actions Required	**Startup Environment**	**Mature Environment**
Recruiting	Dedicated recruiter	Depended upon HR
Personnel	Seasoned and experienced	Build from within & recruit
Organization	Rebuild anew	Modify as appropriate
Acquisition	Integrate rapidly	Integrate with due diligence
Alignment	C-level & key VP's	All senior management
Projects	Executive staff meetings	IT Steering Committee
Prioritization	C-level & key VP (1:1's)	IT Portfolio reviews
Business process	Establish new parameters	Evolve with business models

What Is the State of a Business before Hyper-Growth?

Steady State

The steady state of the business portrays modest growth prior to larger scale adoption. This state represented a typical "start-up" mentality and behavior with the majority of investments divided between Engineering development and Sales / Marketing. IT is very minimally invested in and viewed largely as a cost center and thus kept financially constrained. The state of the business evolves over several years from a technology that was not readily adopted to one that eventually becomes the "killer app" that many software companies strive for. The IT team is comprised of a few Java developers and operations personnel that crafted an eCommerce based application for accommodating sales via the internet, internally entered transactions and those received directly form OEM's and distributors.

Stable

The IT systems and associated technologies are adopted from within and based largely on low cost or no cost (i.e. Open Source) tools readily available to most home grown and internally based development teams. The steady state of the business requires the sustaining of this legacy based application to maintain customer order data, retain sales transactional data and provide for minimal support for technical support services. The major sales activities are associated with those high tech companies that were more willing to utilize advanced technologies in their IT environments. These early adopters of technology help define the feature sets that become the precursor to the basic product offered to the general public.

Plodding Along

The IT systems developed are usually supplemented with some lower level or second tier financial systems (i.e. Great Plains, Quick Books, etc.). This period continues to minimally enhance systems and operational environments based upon sales and headcount growth only. Most investments continued to be limited in IT, Facilities, HR, etc. and the majority of budgets are allocated to product development (i.e. Software Engineering) and sales through major channels or the early adopter communities.

Warning Signs of Hyper-Growth Approaching

Sometimes There Are No Warning Signs

In many instances the warning signs remain under the surface since hiring and associated budget increases are not forthcoming. This period may also be categorized by increased investments made by either the Venture Capital community, Angels or founding personnel. Early adopters are usually proclaiming the praises of the new product or services in all avenues possible. This includes their peers in related industries. Analysts begin to call out the innovations and benefits to the market place and incorporate their thoughts in major industry articles, symposiums, presentations, etc. The attentions of larger corporate giants in a similar or related industry begin to evaluate and investigate the products and services to determine their competitive benefits and associated market attractions.

"Landed" Sales Begin to Rise, "New" Customers Increase

Sales to both existing and new customers begin to increase. There becomes more recognition in the marketplace that this product is right for the times. This is usually driven by the need to reduce costs of existing products and services or improved performance extracted from existing products. The number of partners as identified by new business alliances, increased numbers of OEM's or resellers join the ranks of sales and support channels increases dramatically.

Product Delivery Begins to Fall Behind in the Scheduled Delivery of Products and Services

Product delivery with expected new or enhanced features usually drives the adoption by new and existing customers. Early adopters are suddenly supplemented with the next wave of corporate users. These are driven by successes defined by their peers in the IT environment or more importantly by either cost or technology based factors. The technology factors are associated with the need to utilize or supplement existing technologies and require the use of these new and innovative products and services for further advantages.

How Do You Know When You Are in Full-Blown Hyper-Growth?

You know that you're in a hyper growth environment when all business areas are struggling to support the demands placed upon them. This is initially true for both Engineering (demands for new features sooner than practical) and Sales (booking and delivery of products and services sooner than possible) but then is also evident by Legal, Marketing, Technical Support services, etc. Other key characteristics are definitely evidenced by the IT organization. This becomes obvious as more IT services are needed sooner than normal and the need to enhance or support legacy applications come under substantial strains.

What Are the Issues/Problems?

The major issues and problems surround the need to accurately determine priorities from the various end user and related business partners. This becomes more evident when the business models are based upon dependencies with existing resellers and OEM's. The needs to service these business partners with collateral, early versions of the product or service becomes outstripped by the personnel available or the time required to educate and support these various partners. IT becomes the limiting factor for these hyper growth environments since the need to replace, enhance and supplement all elements of the business are constrained. This is also true for Facilities and Human Resources functions since they also are pushed to provide additional space and personnel to meet the growing technology and business needs.

What Stresses Does It Place on IT and on the Rest of the Business?

The obvious stresses placed upon IT begin with the lack of a strategy and direction for supporting a hyper growth environment. The need for a CIO or relevant IT leader to establish a collaborative vision with the various C-level leaders is paramount. This will enable both the CIO and their respective peers to participate in the needed prioritization and planning required to meet both current and future demands. These business leaders must partner with IT to clarify both their business and personnel needs to work towards a model that becomes acceptable to both their organizations, their business partners and ultimately the end users and customers of the business.

Human Resources

Shortage of People to Get Things Done and Multiple Open Requisitions

The obvious trends from a Human Resources (HR) perspective are the large number of open requisitions being requested and the lack of clarity associated with the specific timing of these needed personnel. Usually, these open requisitions are established when the obvious pain points for support are beyond meeting current requirements. Most key people have more than likely stretched to their limits from both working hours per week level and a lack of skill level available to perform new functions (i.e. Sales Tracking, Customer Marketing coordination, etc.).

Watch for Fatigue and Burn Out in Employees

The burn out factor for existing employees is portrayed by the large number of backlog demands from all areas. For IT, this results in their inability to properly prepare for new employees introduction into the company (i.e. Computer laptops and desktops not available during their first day in their new office or locations). This is exacerbated for those usually remotely located from the home offices since these personnel may not have adequate IT resources or services for initial and ongoing support. The IT employees feel enormous pressure and lack of confidence since they've had a history of performing minor heroics successfully but now are unable to multiply that level of performance across all areas of corporate growth.

Process and Procedure Breakdown

The typical scenario for many hyper-growth companies is to avoid the establishment of established best practices for business processes. This is not unusual and requires that the CIO team with the executive members to approve both the review and incorporation of these processes in order to improve operations of the overall corporation. As such, the CIO must act as the Chief Process Officer (CPO). This is usually supported by the senior IT staff most likely in the business applications domain. The handling of new sales and customer support services are the areas that are most likely to be impacted but this will also have a ripple effect into Finance, Facilities, HR, etc., as well as IT.

Shortcuts Are Sometimes Taken to Achieve Goals

Taking shortcuts to achieve goals becomes the mainstay of hyper growth environments. This becomes the case for almost all business functions and is therefore a driving force for IT organizations as a mantra to follow. This behavior has huge implications for both personnel behavior and customer expectations. Many examples can be portrayed but the most obvious occurs in the areas associated with IT Service Desks and IT Help Desks.

These personnel are usually stressed to the highest level to support both new and existing employees and may not have the benefit of using established Helpdesk systems for both tracking and recording services needed and provided. Most typically, are dependencies upon homegrown open source tools that are developed during the early stages of company development but are retained through periods of high growth. These systems and applications are never designed to accommodate the needed data required to monitor both performance and customer satisfaction but become a request tracking service with minimal tools required to drive improved customer satisfaction.

Another example of shortcuts is associated with the lack of established and documented business processes. This has more far reaching consequences since this level of immaturity limits the ability of both the IT organization and its internal customers to apply best practice models for optimizing, scaling and improving the effectiveness of all employees in the enterprise.

A Mentality of "It's Good Enough," along with "Fix It Later" May Set In

The early stage companies are usually very anxious to get some IT services and functions in place and therefore limit the investments required to build infrastructures and systems for scalability and longevity. Therefore, a "good enough" mentality becomes the prevalent strategy with the implication that IT will "fix it later" when time permits. The truth is that there will never be enough time to fix it later since demands for newer and faster services will typically relegate those early systems to the back burner to meet the most current and pressing demands.

Strong Management Needed to Avoid Chaos

The CIO and the senior management staff must establish a clear strategy and associated timeline to develop or improve both original and legacy based systems. This requires that the CIO establishes a vision and a tactical plan for all IT based systems and applications that are directly tied to benefits and requirements required by the corporate customers. The IT Portfolio is one mechanism that enables both the planning and monitoring of this strategy and tactical project plans. In addition, the CIO must establish a methodology for monitoring both the actual and perceived performance of the IT organization. This will require the incorporation of agreed to metrics and the use of Key Performance Indicators (KPI's). These measurement tools should become the models for determining customer satisfaction, meeting expectations and servicing of a diverse and usually demanding employee base. I strongly suggest that these metrics be initially applied for the use by the IT organization until refined and established then is shared with the internal customers for their review and ongoing monitoring. Perception of the IT organization at the executive levels is also a KPI that the CIO should review and sustain since most executive's perceptions will become their reality regardless of IT metrics reported.

Budgets and Spending

Budgets and associated spending are always critical for any IT organization. The overall personnel, consulting and capital spending are the most obvious elements that comprise most IT departments budgets and are usually established annually but adjusted quarterly or semi-annually based upon business performance. Partnering with the CFO to arrive at an acceptable budget model for IT is key to reaching agreement on the spending details and associated model. I personally advocate a corporate model that addresses all IT infrastructures and a shared model with business owners for specific business based applications. The allocation of these funds would then require approval from both the CIO and respective business owner if properly allocated during the budget planning stages.

Officially the Budget and Spending Must Remain under Control

The agreed to budget becomes more of a guideline than a restrictive limitation within a hyper growth environment. It's usually driven by approved headcount and projects that may or may not have been fully quantified during the annual planning stages. Therefore, it's critical that budget parameters be loosely addressed to meet ever changing business demands. The criteria most readily applied are associated with overall sales and approved headcount. These usually expand substantially beyond original planning levels and are key parameters used by the CFO and the executive staff to support hyper growth business demands. The IT budget can then be directly tied to business imperatives that are approved by the business owner, CFO and the CEO depending upon the established approval levels developed. In reality, there is a loosening of both so that goals can be met in a timely fashion.

Money Becomes Less of an Issue than Time

A hyper growth environment dictates meeting of business needs in a timely manner more so than maintaining compliance to budget parameters. This is especially true if overall profitability exceeds planned expectations. The CIO must closely align IT services to match the overall business needs driven by increased hiring, added business facilities and new customer support initiatives. Time becomes a key factor in product development, customer services and sales support which are especially pressed during the hyper growth period.

The Internal Customer

The internal customer is the key driver of IT demands. The typical internal departments (Finance, Sales, Support, Marketing, etc.) are also driven by the external customer and associated market dynamics. They expect that the IT organization is addressing their internal operational needs to manage their technology based operations.

They Will Be Facing Hyper-Growth as Well (So Can't Baby-sit Their IT Items)

The IT items that they depend upon as basic necessities are typically:

- Desktop support
- Communications (telephony and network)

- System and storage support
- Corporate applications (email, MS Office, ERP, CRM, etc.)

They will always have their own unique applications tools and report generators that may initially have been purchased and deployed by their staff but then expect that IT will adopt the support role for these non-standard or customized applications or systems. This is especially true in technology based development environments that are populated with unique engineering personnel.

Important to "Over-Communicate" (Keep Everyone on the Same Page)

Communication at all levels becomes a paramount strategy and mantra for all IT personnel. This is especially true for the CIO and associated staff. It's imperative that the CIO fosters strong and ongoing over communication through the helpdesk, internal website and periodic corporate updates. This level of communication serves to reduce the angst felt by many internal personnel that they are left to their own devices and that a team of people (namely IT) are there to support them and enable them to become secure, stable and productive in their respective areas.

Priorities Change Quicker in a Hyper-Growth Environment

Priorities are like the time of day! They get set in place but then are constantly changing. This is especially true for the hyper-growth environment. The CIO and the executive staff attempt to establish clear priorities for themselves and their business partners but the likelihood is that they will evolve very rapidly due to external customer demand and the ongoing learning that all elements of the organization must adjust to. The IT Steering Committee is one element for tracking and reviewing priorities but they usually become guidelines at best due to the need to perform cross corrections in the business. This is especially evident when acquisitions and mergers are introduced into the business.

Need to Be Extremely Agile

The IT organization needs to be structured and prepared to react to ongoing changes in priorities and established plans and schedules. This is especially true for the IT operations organization that's constantly dealing with changes in the corporate infrastructure. Working with the CFO (and the associated administration areas) becomes critical in these cases. The CIO may or may not be included in the early due diligence associated with acquisitions and as a result must be prepared for the inclusion of whole new business units and associated personnel into the current environment. The CIO and associated senior staff should establish a series of best practices that would be adhered to to accommodate the integration of new entities. This would include:

- Network connectivity
- Telephone connectivity
- Email service
- Helpdesk services
- Server and key systems support

- Basic applications integration
- Others as driven by the business

Can't Be Offended When the #1 Priority That Everyone Is Working on Shifts and There Is a New #1

The CIO and the associated IT organization need to be in tune with shifting priorities. This may seem like the standard practice during the period of hyper-growth and would appear that there are several #1 priorities being addressed concurrently. This is very typical and must be managed by communicating these facts to both the executive staff and the IT staff in a consistent manner. Everyone needs to be on the same page when priorities are evolving and the business owners expect that all of their needs are definitely the #1 priority. All key players must realize the culture and dependency upon the IT organization during these periods and judiciously use the resources of both full time employees and consultants when required to fill the ever expanding demands upon IT.

Hardware

Lead Times Seem Longer and Can Become a Gating Item If Not Managed Properly

Hardware suppliers may become a pacing item for many services. This is especially true when depending upon the availability of Personal Computers (PC's) and Servers for both new and existing employees. An inventory of spare PC's and Servers may be necessary to accommodate the unexpected increase in both hiring of new employees and deployment of new and additional IT based business applications.

Must Have Standing Contracts Set Up with Vendors So They Can Respond Quickly If Needed

Standing contracts with Hardware vendors is a must for all products. This should incorporate both the provisioning (i.e. Inclusion of the base Operating System software and key applications) and a committed delivery of this inventory in a fixed period following order placement. Most PC and Server vendors (like Dell, HP, etc.) will provide service and provisioning contracts for limited extra costs to ensure the receipt and maintenance of business.

Keeping All Servers in Synch (Patched to the Same Level, etc.) Becomes More Difficult

It's an ongoing challenge to ensure that all servers are maintained and in synch. This may usually be accommodated by deployment of unique server maintenance tools provided by key vendors in this space (Altiris, HP, etc.). The various IT server administrators must maintain a current patch level for all servers and coordinate their update with the business and IT application staff to ensure compliance with the latest accepted and user tested versions.

Software

Greater Coordination among Systems That Interface with Each Other Is Necessary

The coordination of various software versions of key systems and business applications become a key concern during the hyper growth period. The deployment of these systems that may interface between business areas and geographical regions are especially vulnerable to appropriate confirmation of operational functionality. This is true for both operational (i.e. telephone, PC operating systems, server operating systems) as well as business applications (i.e. ERP, CRM, reporting systems).

Watch for Shortcuts, Like Developers Gaining Access to Production

The IT organization must establish and ensure that both regulatory controls and best practices for production systems and business applications are followed diligently. This is especially true in order to maintain compliance with mandates established by SOX, HIPPA and other governmental, health care and financial bodies. Many of the software development teams within IT (and possibly others) that support existing business applications have access to development environments but are usually asked to monitor production environments to evaluate both performance and production usage problems. Read Only access is the standard for these type of scenarios and the temptation to provide them with production access should be avoided at all costs. These production access areas must be segregated by technical personnel (i.e. DBA's separate from developers) and maintained in that manner to avoid the introduction of new code functionality before having been approved by the business owner and associated quality assurance (QA) teams.

Quality Assurance Will Need Assistance from the CIO to Hold the Line

Most CIO's and senior IT management recognize the need for QA to prevent untested and unapproved code functionality for going to a production environment. In many instances, the CIO or their designee should retain final deployment approval where QA plays a key and determining role. This is also supplemented by user acceptance to ensure that the key business owner requirements are developed and functional to the level required to support appropriate business operations. The QA team needs to be authorized by the CIO to perform those level of tests and evaluations based upon the functional requirements developed by both the business analysts, project managers and developers as defined in both the functional and development specifications developed and agreed to with the business and technology owners. This assistance comes in many forms but ideally is prevalent within a Change Management or Product Release and Approval process that was developed and chaired by the CIO and his designated reports.

Hyper-Growth Subsiding

The determining factors associated with the decrease in hyper growth are as distinct as the business or technology area of the enterprise. The most obvious indicator will probably be a decrease in new Sales revenue or new account establishment. This usually implies that either the market has reached a level of saturation or maturation that neither of these two factors is increasing but begins to level out.

What Are the Pre-Cursors to a Decline in Hyper-Growth?

The specific pre-cursors are then based on the change in sales revenue, new account establishment, a higher degree of competitive options in the market, a decline in overall business activity and reduced demand attention by customers and analysts. This may be accompanied by either an equity event (i.e. an IPO, an acquisition or other related activity) which may eventually be followed by the departure of the key personnel responsible for either the product or market development of the product or service offered.

What Issues Does this Create for IT and for the Rest of the Business?

The major issues created for IT is usually a reduction in project and support demands and reduction in associated open requisitions. This is also true for the rest of the business but may precede IT in direct impact especially in sales, product development and support. The IT organization has longer term efforts in place and the associated planning cycles may require more evidence and redirection by the CEO and associated business leaders before the CIO is exercised to reduce either the number of projects in the pipeline or eliminate the needs to enhance or improve the overall performance of the key components of infrastructure due to diminished growth.

Summary

In summary, leading an IT organization in a hyper-growth environment requires constant vigilance and coordination among all key C-level and associated senior leaders of an enterprise. This must also be accompanied by a strong ability to manage the evolution and associated leadership of the IT personnel. There is no panacea for this environment but experience in similar situations with the use of key CIO Advisory Boards and associated thought leaders become a key component for ensuring success.

SECTION 2
Customers/ External

Vendor Management

Cliff Bell

Introduction

Vendor management is all about a relationship. The cliché "You only get out of it what you put into it" is as true with your vendor management as it is with any relationship. The relationship could also be viewed as a dance. You only get good at dancing when you can connect with your partner and move together. In vendor management, this means that must get value from the relationship and the vendor must get value. If either one of you feels that the relationship is one-sided, then you both will suffer. Symptoms of this collapse are lack of involvement unless there is money involved, a lack of follow-up on issues, a lack on your part to extend new opportunities to the vendor, and so on.

You Must Decide How You Plan to Use Your Vendors before Determining How You Will Manage Them

If you wish to terminate an employee, then you typically can make this kind of a change in two to four weeks, assuming that you have been diligent about documenting the issues leading to such a decision. However, if you are upset with a vendor and you wish to terminate the relationship, then most likely it will take you months or sometimes years to remove this relationship, particularly if it is significant. I am not talking about someone who provides temporary resources. Think about replacing your ERP system, your e-mail system, or your global wide-area network (WAN).

A typical IT budget contains 60 to 70 percent of the budget in support of outsourced services. I include WAN costs, depreciation costs, maintenance costs, software costs, consulting, phone charges, and so on in this figure, as depreciation and maintenance are in support of outside services. This means that employee costs are only 30 to 40 percent of your costs. As a CIO, you job is to manage the money. So, in theory, a CIO should spend roughly two-thirds of his or her time managing external relationships.

Given the impact of vendors on your budget and on your time, it becomes easy to understand why you need to take relationships with your vendors as seriously as you do your employees. If you consider the impact that a negative reaction from a vendor can have (production is down, vendors blaming each other, etc.), then you have all the more reason to make sure the relationship is solid.

Managing vendors is more than just managing costs. This chapter will discuss negotiating techniques. But more importantly, this chapter will give you guidance about setting up your relationships to be a more positive partnership.

Best of Breed

If your goal is to build a best-of-breed solution, then you will most like need to consider the integration components of your solution. During the Request For Proposal (RFP) process, be sure to understand the interface components of the products you are considering, the skills of your staff, and customer references.

As a best-of-breed choice, your vendor relationship becomes most critical. The biggest risk you face is that something will be broken between two of your vendors and each of the vendors will be blaming the other. The key point to remember is that while your two vendors are blaming each other, your system will be down or, at a minimum, impaired. This situation is known as *the man in the middle,* and is more common than one would think.

The best way to minimize the risk that you have is to have one partner that supports both products. For example, purchase both solutions and the integration from the same VAR. By doing this (and purchasing support through the VAR), you ensure that you will have support. Another advantage of using a single source is that you can focus building the relationship with one vendor. I highly recommend that you develop a relationship consistent with the solution's impact to your business. It is not unusual for me to have a relationship with the executive vice president or even CEO of a solution provider. And by relationship I do not mean having their business card. I mean that I will meet with them once per quarter to discuss the relationship. For lesser relationships, I will delegate the relationship to one of my directors.

The fact that you have chosen best of breed does not mean you should remain passive during the implementation. You will also need to make sure your team is involved in the implementation. Also, make sure that you are required to sign off that all training of the solution has been given to your staff.

Minimize the Number of Vendors

Minimizing the number of vendors is one strategy to improve the overall price of IT services. This strategy only works if you take a long-term perspective and continue to manage the relationship. I only enter into this type of relationship when I have access to multiple levels of management and multiple VPs. The reason for multiple relationships is that for many companies, there are multiple sales channels, and you need to be connected to all of them.

For example, one VP may control the hardware sales and the other VP may control software sales. Sometimes you need to explain to both of them the value of the total deal. Compensation plans can be complex and sometimes inconsistent across a company. This can be just as dangerous of a situation as the *man in the middle* discussed earlier in the chapter. In this case do not get trapped between two VPs. The reason for having both of them involved is that you often can build win-win strategies across the divisions and they can go to their management to increase your overall discount. I've been known to go to the CEO or president of the company and ask why the company is making it difficult for me to do business.

It might at first seem strange that you are managing two different parts of one organization that is supposed to serve you. However, remember that as a CIO, you are often managing across VPs in your own company to find common ground. So, if this vendor is important to you, it will also be worth you time managing across the VPs. Inside or outside your company, important relationships need to be managed for your success. I usually find I am rewarded with better service from my vendors with this approach just like I am rewarded for making two internal VPs understand each other's situation.

The advantage of this strategy is often the reduction of interfaces. By outsourcing your solution to a single vendor, you also ensure that the interfaces are included in the solution. The reduction of interfaces simplifies all future upgrades and also simplifies testing because you usually get certification from the vendor that the interfaces are compatible. But the most important reason for reducing the number of vendors is the reduction of scope that your technical staff has to understand.

Imagine the scenario of one vendor for routers, another vendor for your switches, and a third vendor for your VOIP PBX. In order to implement VOIP, you have to configure priority packets in all three vendor products with three interfaces. With a single vendor, the configuration is usually consistent, but at a minimum it is supported across the technologies. For large complex environments, the savings by selecting best of breed may outweigh the cost of having expertise in multiple vendor solutions.

Selecting the List of Vendors

I will be assuming that you have a clear idea of the requirements. Requirements definition will be covered in a different chapter. But suppose you have a great set of requirements. Where do you find the solution providers? If you follow a traditional approach, you would get access to Gartner group, Meta group, IDC, or similar organization that classifies the various vendors into the categories. In many cases, you can buy an annual subscription to these groups or you can purchase specific industry reports. You should check with your marketing department, as it might have already purchased one of these services. You can often visit the offices of some of these groups and do the research without charge.

For the more adventurous, you can look at leading-edge technology journals to see if there is an open source alternative supported by a vendor. These can often be lower-cost alternatives that also offer similar features to some of the vendors in the *magic quadrant*.

Peer Recommendations

Another source for vendors is to get recommendations from peers. This is one way to get inside stories about how a solution performs in real life. This is always a good idea. At a minimum, it expands your personal network of contacts. But be careful. If you ask for recommendations, you should be prepared to give recommendations. You do not want to be known by your peers in the industry as a *taker*. This is another example where it is often better to give than to receive.

You can often leverage your experience implementing a solution that you have done in a different group or company. It might feel a bit like déjà vu, but in this case it could be a good thing to leverage your past life experiences. My only caution would be to make sure that you do not force-fit a solution. Remember the adage that "everything looks like a nail when all you have is a hammer." Using prior experience can reduce costs for your company because you can leverage relationships from the past, reduce the training costs, and eliminate some risk to the project.

Negotiating on Price and Value

There are two opposing types of negotiators. The first type is the person who views negotiation as a war. For the record, I am not one of those who see negotiations as a war. In fact, I feel that a warlike approach may allow you to win in the short term, but once you have purchased the solution, the vendor will be doing what it needs to do in order to gain back the margin. And the vendor will often leverage the fact that it will be harder for you to switch once implemented and will thus increase your prices on subsequent upgrades, and so on. Like they say, if you live by the sword you may die by the sword as well.

My strategy in negotiating is to find a situation where your strategy and your supplier are mutually beneficial. When negotiating the vendor relationship, remember that it should be considered a long-term investment. Once a vendor is selected, getting rid of it is at a minimum expensive and potentially career threatening.

Responding to Adversity

My first test of a new partnership is to see how they respond to adversity. I try to create a situation of adversity during the negotiating. I tell my potential partners that I am going to stress the relationship. During the sales cycle, vendors often try to make things easy, and they try to say yes to everything. But you need to know if a critical problem occurs during the project that they will be there for you after they have been selected. It is a parallel perspective to knowing who your friends are in a crisis. Examples of what I will do is change the scope of the project (watching their faces to see if they are professional), is to go through detailed reviews of resumes of people being proposed for the project before I sign the contract. If the vendor responds to you honestly during this part of the proposal, then you can be more assured that the vendor is also interested in a long-term relationship that is mutually beneficial.

Vendors as Team Players

A parallel to this testing adversity is to access how much of a team player the new partner will be. The best thing to do in this area is to check their references. Be sure to ask questions about how much teamwork they had with the reference's company. Make sure it was not just one person, but was consistent across the company. You will rely on this vendor to train your staff, and you need to make sure it will work to that end. You do not want to be locked into the vendor for basic support (unless it is a support contract). To test the vendor to see how it will partner, check to see if it has existing marketing initiatives. I have found that the better companies and sales representatives search out spiffs the company is pushing so that a win-win can be found. For example, is there a marketing plan for early adopters of a technology that will reduce your costs? If the perspective vendor brings this to you without asking, then you know that they have been listening to you and want to solve your needs as best that they can.

What Do You Have to Offer?

There are three questions you need to consider:

1. Do you give references?
2. Are you an early adopter?
3. Is there an opportunity to have a strategic relationship with the company?

On the subject of references, my strategy is to always give references, for several reasons. I want my relationships with my vendors to be excellent and built on trust. If I am not happy with the service, then I need to tell the vendor and make it better. Also, if I am going to invest in a vendor and use its product, I want to be sure than I am proud of the work we did together. There is no excuse for not doing a project well. Projects are team efforts and I feel that it is important to set a high standard. In my case, that standard is making sure the products and services that are used are worthy of a reference.

If you have an issue with a vendor, then resolve it. This is no different that the process you should have for employee corrective actions. You need to have the same attitude about your vendor relationships as you do about employees. So I make sure my team is proud of what they have done with our vendors. And I reward my vendors by giving references.

Again, the strategy is not that much different than you have for employees. If you find an employee doing something right, make sure your reward them. Make sure that your vendors are performing for you, and reward them by telling others how they helped. Your vendor will remember and will do an even better job for you in the next project. Everyone excels thru positive re-enforcement. It does not matter that they are paid by another entity.

Every CIO should decide when or if they are willing to take a risk on new technology. I do not recommend you take technology risks for technology's sake, because your first priority should be to be a businessperson. Assuming that you have a good business case for taking a chance, there are other advantages for leveraging the newest technology. One major advantage of new technology is that it may offer business functionality critical to your company's success.

I have implemented a project before where the beta software was used at the beginning of the project because the feature set was critical for the business. In this case the software went to production release prior to the end of the project. During this project, we had to manage the risk that product bugs would create for the project team. In addition, we had to manage the overall risk to the project that the software would not be ready in time for us to go live. During this project we had meetings with the vendor VP every other week to make sure these risks were reduced.

Related to the functionality advantage, you can often get a price advantage. Most vendors are looking for early adopters to provide customer references and will often give price discounts in return for early adoption. This also means you often get access directly the developers of the product and you are also most likely to have the vendor's best implementers on your project. Lastly, by being an early adopter you have the advantage of developing relationships with senior management. The relationships with senior management could be very important to you if you should have a crisis at a later date.

Another consideration for a CIO is to determine if this vendor partnership is a strategic relationship for the company and not just IT. If you are in the high-tech business, there are often opportunities between the product you are implementing and your company's product. If this is the case, then you can often bring an improved business relationship to your company. This added business relationship provides the CIO the opportunity to shine as a businessperson, not just as the person who delivers solutions. These opportunities can often lead to added responsibility beyond IT.

This just does not mean that your company product can somehow be related to the vendor's product. For those of you not in high tech, you can leverage your vendor relationship to drive innovation in your specific industry vertical. Perhaps your involvement on a customer council can lead to feature for your industry that helps position your company as a leader in your industry.

How Flexible Are They?

Flexibility can be the difference maker. Does the sales team work with you to solve things creatively? Is it supported by management? If the sales team is supported by its management, then this often means that it put the customer first (as a company). It also means the vendor is personally engaged in your business, not just looking for a quick sale!

Two-Pocket Theory

This is one of my favorite negotiation efforts—not because it is especially good for pricing, but because it helps me determine who is a good partner. I have discovered over time that if I am pushing hard for a closure of a deal, I will tend to get feedback from the salesperson at some point that the price limit has been reached. This is usually a judgment call on your part, or sometimes the salesperson can tell you that the company just cannot discount more based on the criteria of the current deal. Usually during negotiating, I try to find out about the likes and dislikes of the salesperson and their management. Do they like sports, or food, or ballroom dancing?

Now, right before I close the deal, I will ask for one more concession. I will ask the salesperson for a celebration event (or two) based on mutual likes and dislikes. I may go golfing with the senior management of the vendor to strengthen the executive relationship, or I may ask for a large dinner at the conclusion of a project paid for by the vendor. I call this the two-pocket negotiation, because usually a company has a product price list and a separate marketing budget or expense budget for the salesperson. By taping into an event that the salesperson likes, you gain a better relationship with the sales team. Often, the sales team only gets to go to these types of events when a customer requests them. The goal of the perk is not to get the perk, but to improve the relationship. You need to know that if a crisis occurs, you can call on the vendor's sales team for help. A shared experience is often enough to create a bond that can be used later in a crisis.

It may seem odd to use a two-pocket theory in negotiating, and I do realize it is a bit unusual. However, I have been put in situations where I needed to break a contract. Often, I have been able to make the changes to a contract without threatening legal action. I have leveraged my personal contacts to explain the business problem I have. Good vendors recognize that I am trustworthy, and they want my future business. I have been told more than once that our team-building events were one of the major reasons management was willing to renegotiate. You can give bonuses to your employees, so it really is not that unusual to create a similar event with your vendors.

A word of caution: Be sure that you are not violating any company policy in doing any of the team-building events. I keep a log of events and reviewed them with my boss prior to the event. I also keep these agreements in writing. I do everything above board, because I also want my management team to trust me. When my management team sees me building good relationships, then it also realizes I do the same with them. Two-pocket theory takes a potential adversarial situation and creates an opportunity for teamwork.

Meetings during Implementation

I will just touch briefly on meetings during implementation. At a senior level, you can create a vendor council that meets on a regular basis during implementation. Vendor councils are usually only necessary when you are using multiple critical vendors for a single project. The goal of the vendor council meetings is to make sure all of the vendors realize that they are responsible for the success of the project. These meetings are usually held once a month. The attendees to the meeting are usually the project manager/director, VPs from the various vendors and the CIO. It is similar to a steering committee in that you are making sure the senior executives are aligned on the goals. In this case, however, it is a council made up of vendors and not a council made up of your internal management team.

The Ongoing Maintenance—How Often Do You Meet?

Given the premise of treating your vendors similar to employees, it would then make sense to meet with them on a regular basis. As the CIO, you cannot meet every vendor. But just how often should you meet with the vendor base? And what types of forums are the best for such meetings? What I have done in this section is to make a distinction between my strategic vendors and my nonstrategic vendors. Key criteria that make a vendor strategic are size of budget, risk the solution can cause to the business, relationship of this vendor to your IT roadmap, and other key criteria you may wish to add.

Ongoing Meetings with Strategic Vendors

With strategic vendors (top five to ten), I usually try to meet with their management team or the representative at least once a quarter, but if any activity is taking place I will want to meet with them monthly. I like to combine the meetings with a customer event. By doing the combination meeting, it also gives me a chance to network with my peers. In fact, a vendor who schedules meetings for peer networking purposes has a chance of getting more business. I am likely to learn something applicable from my peers. Since the peer group shares a common connection to the vendor, it is likely to able to get my business. This can often save me the time of going through a detailed RFP process (particularly if this is an enhancement) and results in a faster delivery to my internal customers.

I also appreciate vendors that expose you to its executives. This gives you the chance to meet with people who you may be negotiating with in the future, and also can give you a sense of how the management thinks, which says a lot about the culture of the company.

Ongoing Meetings with Tactical Vendors

I also meet with my less-strategic partners at least once a year. An example of this is my computer notebook vendor. Notebooks are primarily a commodity, but it is still important to meet with the vendor on an annual basis. You learn what changes have occurred in the industry and also what changes have occurred in the vendor-supplied solutions. I mostly want to learn about any new partnerships that could result in a new bundled product offering. I have found that I could get a bundled discount from my vendor for Virus software that was cheaper than my negotiated price if I bought with each computer. This is just an example of how a regular meeting can result in looking at old problems in a new way.

How Do the Teams Work Together?

I provide feedback to the sales team on a regular basis on how their team works with the permanent staff. I do this because I want good working relationships across the organization. Just because they are a vendor does not change the fact that many problems within IT are related to working together as a team. Over the years, I am finding less and less technological hurdles as reason for project delays. Most slippage in projects comes from interpersonal relationship challenges. For this reason, I am vigilant to communicate with vendors early and often to ensure that the team is highly motivated.

Do You Treat Vendor Employees Like Your Employees?

This is not meant to contradict legal terms that are required to separate employees and contractors for employee benefits. It is more to the question of whether you include them in team meetings, off sites, status meetings, company meetings, and so on. My general rule is that I try to include my consultants where I would include my employees unless I feel that some form of inside information or employee-relevant meeting is taking place (quarterly earning call, for example).

My reason for including vendors as employees is that they are often able to understand business problems and can develop good relationships with different parts of the organization. Sometimes employees feel limited to "doing it the way we always have." Because vendors have different experiences, they might lead you to finding a new and creative way to solve a problem. Vendors often come up with creative solutions primarily *because* they were not used to doing business the same way. When a vendor can make significant insights, however, it is good to have an employee around who understands those insights and how they can be put to use in the company.

Future Projects

Success breeds success. If you have a positive outcome with a vendor, it is almost natural to think of that vendor for the next opportunity. The teams know each other and the vendor has knowledge of your business. You can also sometimes ask for a discount for its services because you are now doing a higher volume of work and you have reduced the cost of sales for the vendor. It never hurts to ask. It is also a good idea when negotiating with a vendor to tell that its success will result in future project possibilities.

I always recommend that you tell vendors you will reference their products. It is always good to position your implementation so that both of you want a successful implementation. Having your vendor motivated by having a potential reference means that it will put the best resources on the project and work hard to meet the requirements on time and within budget. Of course, if success could be guaranteed just by offering to give a reference, then life as a CIO would be simple. But alas, there are many factors leading to success that are covered in other chapters in this book.

Summary

Relationships matter in the final analysis of business. The fact that IT is on the buying side of the relationship does not change the fact that relationships matter. The longer you are in IT management, the more sales organizations will build a reputation of what is like to work with you. Just like you talk to your peers to find out how to work with your vendors, sales teams talk about you! All those Customer Relationship Management systems we have been implementing are filled with words about you. Your choices in managing vendor relationships affect the words in those systems.

Information Technology for Small to Mid-Sized Companies

Doug Harr

Introduction

This chapter will focus attention on how to efficiently and effectively provision information technology solutions and services in the lower range of the small- to medium-size businesses (SMB) marketplace. For purposes of clarity, let's consider small business to be start-up or small enterprises that are earning anywhere from $0 to $75 million in revenue. Medium-sized businesses, then, might be considered to be earning anywhere from $75 million to $150 million in revenue.

The SMB marketplace is often defined to include companies making up to $500 million or $1 billion in revenue. From my experience, however, companies of this size have a radically expanded set of requirements for IT infrastructure and business applications. They typically will have already made huge investments in computing infrastructure, and the focus for any IT chief information officer (CIO) or other IT management personnel coming into such a corporation will be to understand the path this large enterprise has followed to get to where it is today, and how to either stabilize their solutions or move the company back in the right direction.

An additional topic that we will not review in this chapter is the wholesale outsourcing of IT to a third party. While this can be an effective strategy for selected large corporations or companies with serious IT requirements, it is not a strategy I find advisable for smaller businesses. So, while CIOs in large corporations can benefit from an understanding of what follows, we will focus our attention on start-up and small companies earning between $0 and $150 million in revenue, where IT management is compelled to make key decisions differently early in the life cycle of a business. In the notes that follow, I will be advocating what we have done at Ingres Corporation. All IT functions are either outsourced, open source, or both.

Recent History of Computing

During the last two decades, when computing for business expanded into the industry we see today, companies who required automation to schedule and monitor production, take and fulfill orders and manage financial records turned increasingly to packaged business applications to provide these capabilities. This was particularly true for discrete manufacturing and services businesses, where productivity tools with relatively standardized sets of features could be applied broadly across a range of companies. Some software makers targeted broad ranges of prospects with enterprise resource planning (ERP) and customer relationship management (CRM) packages, which could be implemented in a broad range of companies. Others focused their software on specific vertical markets, such as insurance, banking, and heath care. Yet others focused in on a specific area of enterprise computing to meet challenges for specific departmental computing requirements, such as human resources automation or professional services automation.

In addition to these business application solutions targeted to departmental computing needs, there has been tremendous growth in application software targeted toward specific utility needs or to end user computing requirements. We now see utilities specifically for messaging, collaboration, e-mail, and calendaring. There are also targeted applications for document or knowledge management, as well as routine and advanced reporting for the business hoping to aid in establishing *business intelligence.* This utility and collaboration software touches nearly every worker in the enterprise, and has been aided by similar developments in consumer-based products on the market.

By the end of the 1990s, with the emergence of the Internet, there was a burst of activity focusing on extending these older technology solutions to a new Web-based sales and services channel. While many of these software makers have utilized the Internet as only a means of advertising company wares, most companies with a tangible product have been able to sell directly to their customers leveraging the Web as a new sales channel. The growth of the Internet has also spawned entirely new businesses whose proposition depends fundamentally on Internet-delivery mechanisms, rather than just a means of advertising or as a sales channel. The older core business application providers rapidly began to migrate their platforms to be accessible via the Internet, and to take advantage of Web-design principles to extend their business applications to all employees, customers and vendors of their target market.

Since the end of the century, there has been a drive to extend delivery of both traditional and new market software services via the Internet. In the past, *time-share* models of computing did exist whereby a software distributor might host and run your software as part of its service. Alternately, some *application service providers* would host and support software made by other firms, hoping to bring efficiencies to the market.

With the emergence of Web-based computing, the ability to provide solutions via the Internet, over standard browsers straight to a desktop computer, and subscribe to these solutions has revitalized this space. This is now commonly referred to as the *on demand* software or *software as a service* (SaaS) market. While industry experts used to debate build versus buy decisions, we can now also subscribe directly to targeted solutions, many of which are very extensible.

During this same period, there has been an additional drive in the market toward nonproprietary, *open* software solutions, which can be shared widely. These are currently referred to as *open-source software*. Individuals and companies can now obtain open-source software free of charge and deploy it without support if necessary. Open-source software runs the gamut between small utilities developed by moonlighting engineers, to enterprise class software, certified and supported by successful software companies. Increasingly, business is turning to these open operating systems, utilities, and applications for inclusion in the enterprise.

At this point, computing technology in its various forms has come to touch every possible function within the corporation, and users of that technology range from someone at the front desk greeting visitors on up to the CEO. Although computing has become ubiquitous in business, providing IT services that are secure, reliable, recoverable and auditable, it has also become more complex and expensive. The means by which these services can be provided has developed to the point where IT professionals are left with a dizzying array of choices when considering how to meet the needs of a particular business in a cost-efficient manner. IT professionals in small companies particularly face this challenge: How can a new IT team and its leadership set a proper strategy, then select and implement solutions to meet growing business needs? It is the intent of this chapter to provide guidance to answer these questions.

Getting Started

For the sake of this chapter, let's anticipate that you have been hired to run the information technology (IT) department for a new company that has a defined product and target market. Your title will either be chief information officer (CIO), or the VP or director of information technology. You will most likely report to the chief financial officer (CFO), chief operating officer (COO) or the chief executive officer (CEO). You have a number of peers also new to the company heading finance, sales, marketing, human resources and engineering/production. So what comes first?

The first step in your new role is to learn as much as you can about the business objectives for the company and the strategy by which the leadership team intends to accomplish its goals. Ask for meetings with the other key executives. Collect presentations, charts, and documents pertaining to their business plans. Plan to ask open-ended questions to find out what you can do to best assist the other executives, both personally and for the departmental functions they own. Find out how much each executive knows about IT and technology, and what predispositions are based on their past experiences. What software and services have they used, including their favorite phone and laptop? What messaging and e-mail applications do they enjoy, and what enterprise business applications were effective in their past? Find out just how quickly they are expecting to roll out each type of functionality. Finally, determine if they, or someone key on their staff, should attend your infrastructure and application planning meetings.

Count on this—the management team at your new company will want to have basic computing capability implemented directly upon your arrival:

- Desktop or laptop computers
- Access to the Internet, via cable or wireless
- Printers, copiers, and faxes
- E-mail and shared calendaring
- Basic accounting and business software applications

This list will, of course, depend on your specific company, its industry, go-to-market strategy and other factors. But in general, you must determine what decisions have already been made in these areas, or others you have determined to be of import, and what has been done to date. This is the second area for your initial research. It is almost never the case that an IT leader at a director, VP, or CIO level has been hired during the first year of a company's existence, unless the Internet is used as an integral part of the product or service offered by the firm. More often than not, you will inherit decisions made by others while the company was being built. Some of these will have been made in haste, others after careful research. Try not to be too dismissive or dogmatic as you discover these. Offending those involved in past decisions only sets them up as hostile to the decisions you will make in your new role, and you will want and need their support. Instead focus on the end goal: What application and services portfolio is required by your company given the strategy and objectives the other executives have shared with you?

The Application and Infrastructure Technology Portfolio

The next step will be to depict the main building blocks of a portfolio of infrastructure and business solutions required by your company. A workable diagram is likely to look something like Figure 2.1.

The foundational layer will be your data center. Next, layer on voice and data networks, to carry phone and databased information between local and regional workers and out to customers and partners via the Internet. Follow this with a number of servers, storage and recovery devices. Connect this via a layer of personal computers, PDAs, and related computing platforms. Finally, you can deploy business applications, collaboration tools, and reporting and business intelligence functionality. After all of this time, energy, and capital you should have created value for the organization.

The decisions you will need to make to support your portfolio can be broadly divided into two primary areas: infrastructure and applications. As you approach the decisions outlined in each of the following sections, you will face a fundamental question: What infrastructure and applications will you install and support within your facilities, and what personnel will you hire on a full- or part-time basis to support those installations? In the SMB

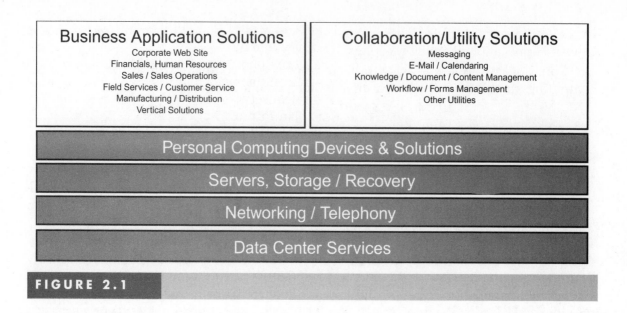

FIGURE 2.1

marketplace, nearly everything shown in Figure 2.1 can be outsourced, or provided on a rental basis by subscribing to products or services in the SaaS marketplace. Even equipment that must be on site, such as personal computers for each employee, can be leased and supported through third parties. Taken to an extreme position, it is possible for a company to provide computing services almost entirely through virtual IT strategy. Given the possibilities in the marketplace since the turn of the century, sourcing becomes one of the most important strategic decisions to make for every company.

Infrastructure

For a smaller company, the list of requirements for infrastructure and the roles required to provision, implement, and support these can be overwhelming and costly. The infrastructure for data center services, networking, telephony, servers, and storage will require hundreds of thousands of dollars in capital. In each of these areas, you need to decide what will be installed on site at your facility, what will be done by your full-time personnel, and what will instead be provided by others.

Data Center

For just about any type of facility larger than a leased executive suite there will be a small room where the most basic IT services can be supported. Typically, the minimum requirement is considered a *wiring closet* where telephone and network lines terminate, and where it is possible to set up a small stack of server and storage equipment to support file sharing and printing services. All wiring from desktops and cubicles, provided there is traditional cabling to reach these workstations, will terminate into this closet. If traditional telephones are to be provided, there will be one cable for each phone and at least one cable for each workstation computer coming into this wiring closet (more often, there will be three to four data cables per office or cubicle). For wireless data services, in order to provide access to the network and Internet within the facility, plan to provide at least one wireless access point to the office area. Plan to purchase and install at least one UPS power conditioning and backup device for this closet. Unless the environment is particularly hot, this minimum configuration will not typically require any special air-conditioning services, other than a fan to move out warm air.

If your requirements go beyond basic telephony, networking, and shared file/print services, you will be faced with decision to build and maintain a data center. For the purposes of this discussion, consider that this data center might contain servers for engineering services and business applications, which are not satisfied by the personal computers used by company personnel. You might have many servers required for the company's engineering function, and if you plan to install your own business applications, these also will require dedicated servers and related services. You will have storage, backup and recovery devices to protect and recover these services in case of data loss or disaster. If your facility has no existing data center, and after research, you decide to build your own, plan to utilize outside expertise to build it out. Your vendor will aid in arrangements with the owner of your facility, and will assure compliance with local and state ordinances. An additional benefit is that it will typically already have established relationships with vendors specialized in flooring, air conditioning, power conditioning/assurance, and fire-retardant equipment.

A clear alternative to building out your own data center is to co-locate your servers and related equipment with a data center services provider. Co-location services can be as basic as renting a site where simple *rack, power, and air* is provided within a cage or small cubicle. On top of this, qualified vendors can add services to help you manage the equipment that may include monitoring, maintenance and backup and recovery services. Finally, larger facilities can provide you a second site where additional equipment can be placed and managed to allow for recovery of your services in the event of a disaster at the primary site.

Before you travel this path, sit back and carefully consider whether the engineering services and business applications really need to be purchased and installed by your company. The data center decision is completely dependent on decisions you will make regarding the rest of the IT portfolio. After all, the infrastructure exists only to support access to collaboration and business applications, most of which can be provided via Web-based services. So ask yourself: "Can these services be rented elsewhere?" or possibly "Are there hosted business and engineering applications that would meet the company's requirements?" If your company employs software engineers as part of the product or solution you sell, be prepared for the "I have to be close to my servers" argument. It is typical and understandable for engineers to want equipment close and accessible, but there are managed services providers who can accomplish the same mission. In conclusion, for the SMB market, at this juncture, it is advisable that you co-locate servers and services that scale beyond the simple wiring closet model.

Networking/Telephony

Networking and telephony decisions rest on the facility and data center location decisions already discussed. In the minimum configuration of a wiring closet, you will provision a phone switch, a firewall, and router/switch devices to connect the office together and to the Internet. At the time of this writing, it is becoming possible to combine networking and phone services through equipment that allows voice traffic over the data network (VOIP). While debates abound as to whether this method is yet more cost-effective than traditional telephony services, it's only a matter time until we utilize software-based phones via personal computers or lightweight portable VOIP phones in all businesses. Although there is a bit more configuration to accomplish this, if you opt for this route your wiring closet just got a bit more compact and you have one less vendor to deal with.

One debate you will face is whether your company should sign up to corporate cell phone and PDA accounts with selected vendors. In the SMB I recommend against this. While it is possible to get discounted rates, it requires at least dozens of employees to subscribe to the same service in order to get the discount. Many employees will be reluctant to switch to a corporate provider, and in general, employees will constantly be moving in and out of the service. Vendors will require some minimum spend level for these agreements, and if you fall below that usage you still pay the base fee.

Additionally, you will need someone in purchasing, accounts payable, IT, or some other function to manage the agreement to assure your company meets minimum usage levels. The alternative to all of this is to have employees expense to the company any business use portion of their cell phone or PDA. Another way to handle this is to establish a set-level fee similar to a car allowance. This way, the company pays a fixed amount per month to cover telephony charges, based on level of type of position. These alternatives represent the most cost-effective model for managing telephony fees for employees in the SMB market.

There are creative things that can be done to reduce cost and complexity of providing networking and telephony services. There are companies where network access is nearly 100 percent wireless, and the phone service is provided by public Internet-telephony solutions, or simply via each employee's cell phone. Some companies have launched a business phone service that just accepts voice mail, or that is picked up by an answering service and routed to the employee via Internet or cellular phone. I recommend anyone in the SMB to spend some time researching the state of the market in these areas before you make purchasing decisions, and lean heavily toward a more wire-free and virtual strategy for providing networking and telephony services.

Servers, Storage, and Recovery

In the area of servers and storage, there are continuing developments that enhance our ability to provide computing power and related storage for more uses, with less equipment. When computing was born, computing power rested within large shared mainframe systems. Over time, the mini-computer and microcomputer age expanded exponentially the number of physical computers and storage devices to be managed. We are coming back to a more rational era, combining the best of both worlds: centralized shared computing power and storage resources, with powerful local and personal computing equipment for individual needs.

For servers, *virtual machine* technology is allowing for the shared server with many uses, all in one or few central chassis. By deploying fewer physical servers, you centralize what was once distributed, which generally leads to improved manageability. Manufacturers are at the same time offering centralized servers, which can be loaded with dozens of sharable computing units, referred to by some as *blade servers*. At this stage, in the SMB marketplace the most likely outcome is that you will use two to four CPU utility servers with several uses for each, utilizing local or shared storage.

With respect to storage and recovery, storage, which is sharable over the company network, is readily available and benefits from efficiencies in management and support. At the same time, local storage, which can be purchased along with a server, is inexpensive and manageable. Recent innovations provide backup and recovery options that allow for disk-to-disk backup and recovery, with disk-based failover sites in case of disaster. Some of this innovation is being driven by the availability of inexpensive shared storage that can be used for backup space locally and regionally. Rentable backup sites where data can be stored elsewhere without tape are also now available. Although it is still likely you will need to procure tape-backup solutions, it is now possible and almost affordable to provide these services all based on disk storage, which will simplify your stack of required solutions by removing tape drive systems, tape media, backup software, and offsite storage services.

In the small wiring closet model, you can end up with a simple configuration of a single server and locally attached, inexpensive storage for file sharing. This stack may extend to a basic collaboration utility, such as a portal-based or wiki-based intranet utility for departmental and project team collaboration within the company. This will suffice for most new companies in the SMB. Beyond that, I recommend taking up the strategy of setting up shared servers utilizing virtual-machine innovations, and protecting your data with sharable disk-based backup and recovery solutions. For a time, you may still need to rely on locally attached storage for first level storage, and shared storage for staging backups, file shares and collaboration; however, we are close to a scenario where servers, storage, and recovery can be provided in a sharable model at the right price for the SMB, significantly reducing complexity and management requirements.

Personal Computing

At the time of this writing, there are a few interesting strategies that can be taken relating to provisioning and supporting personal computers. Although prices have come down on desktop and laptop computers, you may wish to look at leasing programs for this equipment. This can be an effective way to spread the payment for these systems evenly over their useful life. If this is considered, look for vendors who will also manage the delivery and replacement of these systems. The traditional way to provision personal computers is to purchase these systems and depreciate them over a two- or three-year period. This requires the cash up front, with the expense amortized over the useful life of the system via a depreciation schedule. In either model, you will need to plan on a refresh of these systems, replacing them every three to four years on a rotating schedule.

While the company is small, say up to 200 employees in one or two regions, it is most likely that you will employ one or two systems administrators to handle day-to-day support of personal computers, along with light data center services. The advantages to having someone in the office are huge, in that personalized desktop support is more effective for maintaining employee satisfaction than other outsourced help-desk models. The disadvantage is that your already stretched administrators will need to deal with virus management, malware protection, backup strategies, and a host of other disciplines related to PC maintenance and support. The state of the practice in this area is evolved enough that a few sharp and talented internal IT personnel can provision and support what is needed.

For managing personal computers, it is possible to obtain a hosted service that will install, manage, and maintain all the software required, along with a ticket or phone-in based help-desk solution. As an alternative to on-site staff, or once the company grows to a certain point, the hosted and managed solutions become a viable way to provision, support, and manage personal computing devices and to gain some economies of scale. Although there are many considerations that will affect your decision in this area, in general, for the SMB, I recommend starting with local administrators for desk-side support and then consider moving to hosted providers once you see that the company's hiring plan will expand help-desk demand beyond the means of a few administrators.

Software and Utilities

For each server and for managing and monitoring server and network equipment in your infrastructure, you will have choices as to operating systems, databases, and monitoring and management solutions to deploy. Although there are vendor-specific proprietary options for this software, there are also many offerings based on the open-source model that will solve nearly all requirements within the infrastructure. At Ingres Corporation, we deploy enterprise class Linux from RedHat and Novell, along with our own open source Ingres database, Nagios, for monitoring, and other open-source tools for managing the complete stack. For SMB in particular, I recommend evaluating open-source tools and utilities for building and managing the infrastructure effectively and at a low cost.

Personnel

Often, systems and network engineers and administrators are the first IT professionals hired into the company. To augment these personnel, an entire industry exists ready to provide engineering consulting services for infrastructure. Most often, these are temporary services, while on-site staff are hired and trained, but it is also common to find long-term hourly contractors filling roles within IT Operations to provide these needed services. Regardless of your overall IT strategy and application portfolio, you will have some of the following roles filled by full-time employees (see Table 2.1).

TABLE 2.1	
Typical Title	**Role**
IT Operations Manager/Director/VP	This management resource is responsible for all the technology and infrastructure required to support the company's applications. The person in this role will typically set the roadmap for these solutions. In the SMB, this resource typically provides or contracts others for technical architecture, and the role itself might be filled by part of the CIO's daily efforts.
Network Administrator/Engineer	Network engineers configure, provision, and support networking equipment including firewalls, routers/switches and cabling necessary to connect all employees to computing resources, and connect all needed resources to the Internet and external resources and international sites. This expertise is required for telephony solutions that utilize the network, and at times network administrators also support any internal phone switches and related technology.
Systems Administrator/Engineer	Systems engineers size, scope, provision, and support servers, storage, backup and recovery solutions required for all computing needs. This same group will typically provision and administer e-mail and collaboration platforms. Database administrators can be said to live within the ranks of these engineers.
Help-desk Administrator	Personnel dedicated to help desk functions are required once the applications and solutions deployed create support requirements specifically to manage level-1 type of support. These help-desk personnel also provide desktop support for people experiencing issues with their personal computing devices. Most commonly, in the SMB market, the systems administrator and help-desk administrator roles are combined.

These are the primary roles typically required by an enterprise seeking to utilize information technology. The roles are described broadly, as IT professionals tend to have skills across these general categories. I know an exceptional help-desk administrator, for instance, who can also set up the networking gear for a new company. It is possible that in your new company, there are one or two generalists who have taken on the roles above to get things started. Depending on the size of your company, and on your strategy for providing all infrastructure required, you might actually be employing only one or two people in operations, particularly in a situation where, if you have a data center, it is co-located with a managed services provider.

Business Applications and Collaboration/Utility

Business Applications for ERP/CRM

As stated earlier, an entire industry has been built to provide either custom or configurable business application solutions to the market. Although in specific vertical markets, custom-built software is required to meet specific business requirements, it is more common to find that your business can take advantage of configurable and extendable packages of software with broad functionality.

In the last several years, there has been consolidation in the enterprise software market, yet no one platform model such as SAP or Oracle seems able to provide software to cover all services required by the business in a cost-effective and efficient model. In the SMB marketplace, you will be considering alternate players in the market who provide traditionally licensed or SaaS offerings for their software solution. At the time of this writing, several new companies are rapidly expanding their hosted, Web-based portfolio of solutions, and are vying for position to take on the giants of corporate computing. I recommend strongly considering the hosted SaaS models in the SMB market.

Although there are a few emerging solutions that advertise broad functionality across the ERP and CRM spaces, most of the recent SaaS offerings focus on a specific targeted offerings:

- Salesforce.com targets CRM-oriented sales force automation, service management, and marketing solutions.
- Netsuite, Intacct, Compiere, and others target traditional ERP financials, distribution and/or marketing applications.
- OpenAir, Quickarrow, and others target professional services automation (PSA) solutions for consulting and field service organizations.
- ADP, SuccessFactors, and others target human resources information systems solutions (HRIS).

Because many of these companies are newer players in the applications market, it is important to spend time doing traditional due diligence as to the fit of the product to your company's requirements. Next-generation enterprise software will certainly not have all the bells and whistles of the established players. In fact, some capabilities that have been considered baseline or standard functionality in ERP/CRM packages, might not yet exist from the new provider. Be prepared to decide carefully what functions are really critical, and which are more on the "nice to have" list. It is important to understand what the roadmap of the newer products is, and how missing functionality might be provided. Salesforce.com is an interesting example of a newer player in the CRM market. Certain functions that would have been typical for CRM in the prior generation's offerings are missing. However, Salesforce is a leader in best practices for extending the product either through light configuration or through extensions already integrated and available from their partners. It is as important as it has ever been to understand the capabilities of the vendor and the application with each solution considered.

Another factor to consider is that to the extent you need to deploy multiple applications to solve the problems tackled by the entrenched mega-suites, you will need to integrate the solutions. Preintegration is one of the advantages to an application suite available from one vendor. However, the newer players know this, and have integration built into their suites, including pre-integration with other popular solutions in the new market. Spend time reviewing the integration capabilities to ensure you don't end up in an extensive custom integration project.

There are several other considerations to make when determining if specific application requirements can be met with SaaS solutions. These include ensuring that the fee arrangement allows for both expansion and contraction of your use of the application. You clearly will pay additional fees to add users to the application—make sure you will also be paying less if you remove users from the application. Also, ensure you have provisions in the agreement for cancellation with an appropriate notice period, and that you have an established method for getting your data back from the vendor. The next chapter in this text is dedicated to the SaaS marketplace and covers these topics.

Collaboration

Collaboration applications and utilities can broadly be defined as solutions that allow all employees, people in specific departments, project teams, or similar groups to work together with some form of computing-based support. Employees will collaborate in this way with other internal personnel, or with vendors and partners outside the company. In this broad definition, e-mail, calendaring, and conferencing applications promote collaboration. The company intranet and project management software solutions promote departmental and companywide collaboration. In this area, you will have to decide whether to build out your data center and on-premises infrastructure or look to SaaS offerings to supply needed tools.

For e-mail, calendaring, and conferencing, it is now not only possible, but also advisable that SMB-level companies look to hosting providers or SaaS solutions for this service. At Ingres Corporation, we initiated a search for a hosting provider for Microsoft Exchange. There were several providers on the market that offered shared or dedicated environments to provide all needed e-mail and calendaring services, as well as support for PDA devices. All were under $15 per mailbox per month to provide all capabilities needed for these key computing functions. There are other providers with proprietary e-mail and calendaring solutions, such as BlueTie, that also do a fine job providing subscription-based platforms. Conventional wisdom seems to be that security or performance issues will invalidate hosted or SaaS solutions for e-mail, but these issues can be mitigated by the latest technology. You will face a similar decision regarding voice and Web-based conferencing. There are dozens of providers to consider here, and no compelling reason in the SMB market to install and support your own tools for these services. Having said that, negotiate price carefully; user-based telecom fees can be high, and hosting providers may ask for minimum fee clauses.

Collaboration will also encompass capability to share knowledge, organize it, and work together on shared tasks. To the extent that the need for automation at your company is basic, then with a single server you can support all centralized file management and intranet requirements utilizing a standard directory structure and a bit of open-source software in the category of *wikis*. In order to evolve to the next level of computing in this area, there are collaboration portal or content management suite offerings from Microsoft, BEA, and others that you can use for more advanced document management, project management and other collaboration needs. At the time of this writing, basic file sharing and collaboration tools exist in the SaaS marketplace, but it has not yet been common to rely on these as a replacement for the intranet. At this juncture, it is most likely that your basic file sharing and intranet tools will be on premises or in your offsite co-location facility, but keep a close watch on this space.

Personnel

Project managers, business analysts, and application developers are involved when you implement and extend business applications or integrate the various solutions that had been selected for the company. Consultants from the software vendors or from services and

TABLE 2.2	
Typical Title	**Role**
Business Applications Manager/Director/VP	This management resource is responsible for the business applications (ERP, CRM, HRIS, PSA, etc.) deployed by the company and for all internal and external resources required to deliver and support them. In the SMB market, the person in this role will typically set the roadmap for these solutions and act as an application architect, and very often this becomes another part-time role for the CIO.
Business Analyst	Business analysts (BA) are required to translate business requirements into functional designs, which can be delivered by application developers, database administrators and similar personnel. The BA may also directly configure applications and deliver reporting or other custom components of the solution. The business analyst should also document procedures and deliver or assist with training for each department supported.
Software Developer	Developers are required who can write extensions to application solutions, either by extending the application, customizing it or by creating new point solutions to work with the applications. Multiple types of developers may be required, based on the work to be delivered. It is most common in the SMB market to work with outside services to provide software developers.

accounting firms can be utilized to install, configure, and extend these solutions. They can supply temporary business analysts who can translate business requirements into the configurations needed for the software, or for functional designs, which would then be handed off to temporary software developers. They can also provide temporary database administrators to manage the information underlying the applications. All of this can be marshaled by project management from within your company, or in partnership with a temporary project manager from one of the contracted firms.

In the meantime, companies will typically scramble to supply both the project management role and business analyst roles wherever possible, from their own ranks. IT will typically seek to hire these roles, or recruit for these within the ranks of sharp people already working in the departments affected by the new computing solution. The best business analysts often have already been administrators or managers within finance, engineering or operations functions, and are ready for a challenge different than managing those daily activities. Some will vote to leave these analysts in their respective departments, and some will move them into IT. In either case, companies typically hire personnel listed in Table 2.2.

Conclusion

At the end of the process of developing and gaining approval for the company's IT strategy, you will have developed a diagram to depict your application portfolio recommendations, along with a budget for these solutions and some type of timeline for delivering them. One example of a portfolio diagram is shown in Figure 2.2.

To support your conclusions, prepare a budget that will show both capital and expense needs by quarter. For your list of capital, you will typically list any equipment costing more than $1,000, including networking gear, servers, storage and software, to the extent that any software you deploy is paid for by an up-front license fee. Your list of expenses will then include any training fees, consulting services, hardware or software maintenance, telecom fees, and, to the extent that you have utilized SaaS solutions, the quarterly fees for

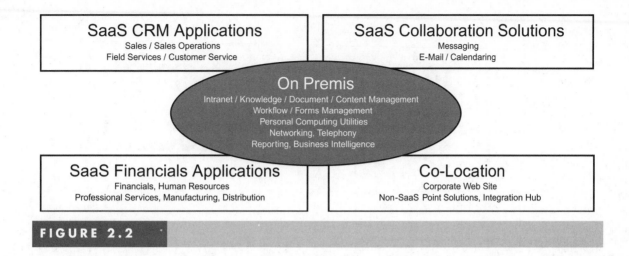

FIGURE 2.2

those. Organize this list not by vendor, but by business solution or service area, so management can understand for each service, the associated cost. This will require that you apportion the cost of any shared infrastructure to the solutions on top of that infrastructure. Although some estimation will be required to do this, it will be well worth the effort.

It will take at least your first quarter at the company to assemble this strategy, and most likely will take the second quarter to refine it into a complete strategy, which can be used as the basis for your technology and services roadmap. Your number-one criterion for selecting the solutions in the application portfolio is that each solution provides the best functional fit to current and expected business requirements. After that, consider that how the solution will be delivered is the second most important decision. The example portfolio above depicts a heavy reliance on SaaS solutions for components of the architecture. This is my recommendation for SMBs, with the understanding that your company's particular circumstances may prohibit you from utilizing the SaaS delivery model for specific applications and services. This will all depend on what solutions fit and whether any of these are also provided via the model. The portfolio and sourcing diagram in Figure 2.2 is very close to what we have done at Ingres Corporation, with the knowledge that this model will provide the best solutions to our company at the right price point.

Software-as-a-Service (SaaS)

Dani Shomron

Introduction

Software-as-a-Service is a disruptive technology that will have a great impact on the IT business and presents challenges that are radically new and that exacerbate the problems that the CIO is dealing with currently. But SaaS could also create an opportunity for IT to grow from a (seemingly) ineffective cost center to a proactive technology strategy center, from deploying and maintaining software to a service-centric entity, supporting the business goals of the enterprise.

The Milkman

Say you need two bottles of milk each day for your household. To achieve that you have to build a cowshed in your backyard, (for two cows; one may be sick) provide feed, heating, vaccination, periodic veterinarian checkups, shed cleanup, and of course, milking the cows each morning. Find this ridiculous? Doesn't sound very economical, does it? But, isn't this the reality in the enterprise software space? If a company needs essential software to run its business (e.g., CRM, business intelligence, portfolio management), doesn't it need to spend hundreds of thousands of dollars (or millions) on the licenses, and then much more on an implementation project that may take three or twelve or thirty-six months? And when that is done, a dedicated team is needed to maintain the hardware, databases, and application. And we don't want to even start on upgrades, which are always a painful and resource-intensive process.

Now imagine that a milkman knocks on your door and offers you the same milk for the price of the product plus a margin, allows you to choose how many bottles you want each morning, and leave all the worrying about producing the milk and delivering it to your doorstep, to him.

Makes sense, does it not? This is exactly what is happening in the enterprise software space and it's called Software-as-a-Service (SaaS), or on-demand software. (This is also known as subscription software, utility computing, managed services, hosted software, server-side computing, or the now-forgotten application service provider.) The Gartner Group declared 2006 to be the year of SaaS and had previously named SaaS as one of the top five technologies for 2005 and predicted that it will account for 50 percent of software licenses in 2008. Saugatuck predicts that SaaS adoption will grow to 47% by the end of 2007. ("SaaS 2.0: Six Key Trends for 2007," Saugatuck Technologies, Dec 27, 2006.) Almost all Venture Capitalists today are demanding their portfolio software companies offer a hosted solution.

But if the milk is absolutely essential for your household, you need to have a solid belief that the milkman will get the bottles to you doorstep every morning, and that the milk will not go sour. The milkman may say: "I may be sick some day, so if you want to make sure the bottles are there you should pay a premium price; then I will hire another milkman to cover for me." Also, in your backyard, you may have manufactured chocolate milk and yoghurt and now you will not be able to get it through this service. Some milkmen will give you a sad look and shrug their shoulders, others will get you the yoghurt, but at a higher price; but the smart milkman will provide you with the right ingredients to make your own milk products.

This analogy holds for SaaS. The higher the service level agreement (SLA), the more you are expected to pay. On-demand vendors typically offer the equivalents of silver, gold and platinum customer agreements, ensuring higher levels of availability, performance, security and add-on services. Smart vendors will allow the customer to configure the software to their specific needs.

A Disruptive Technology

SaaS is one of the hottest trends in enterprise software. Eight out of the ten fastest-growing software companies in 2005 offered a SaaS model.[1]

Even though the SaaS model primarily targeted the SMB market, the adoption rate in the large enterprises was much faster. This could be explained by the fact that in larger corporations, this new model allows business units to consume services independently, at a low entry point without the need for IT intervention. In the smaller enterprises the decision to consume a new service will be made by the CIO, and that involves fear of losing control and naturally takes more time. A line of business in a large corporation will be able to make a quick decision to purchase a service and pay for it without consulting IT or affecting the rest of the business.

AMR states that 40 percent of companies are using hosted applications, growing to 49 percent in the next twelve months. The Gartner Group predicts that large enterprises will use hosted applications for 25 percent of their applications by 2010, while IDC predicts that the SaaS business model will grow by 21 percent Compound Annual Growth Rate— CAGR to $10.7 billion from 2005 to 2009. According to a McKinsey & Company survey (Software 2006—Unifying the Ecosystem, presented in 'Software 2006' Sandhill conference, Santa Clara, April 4, 2006), there has been a huge jump in CIOs who are considering adopting Software-as-a-Service applications, from 38 percent in 2005 to 61 percent in 2006.

There are now thousands of SaaS applications for almost every function within the enterprise, including CRM, Accounting, Mail and Messaging, Web conferencing, Security, Groupware, Workforce Management, Marketing, Manufacturing, Travel and Human Resources to name but a few.

Principles of On-Demand Software

Software-as-a-Service has two main ingredients:

1. The software is hosted by the software vendor (or channel) and is accessed through the Internet via a browser.
2. The software is leased on a periodic basis, with varying pay structures.

The first component means that the enterprise consuming the service does not need to install and implement the software in-house, and therefore does not need to maintain the uptime, availability, performance, and upgrades. All these activities are the sole responsibility of the software vendor (or channel).

The major impact of the first component is that for simple, stand-alone applications the time from purchase to utilization could be measured in hours to days, while for the more complex, integrated systems, the time to utilization could be measured in weeks to months, whereas in the on-premise model, the timetables are measured by months to quarters (in some heavy, enterprise systems it might take years to implement).

The second component means that the enterprise does not purchase the software, but rather, consumes it as a utility with a pay-as-you-go, or pay-per-usage policies. The cost structures vary between yearly subscriptions, monthly, or actual usage. Some vendors will charge as low as a few dollars per user per month. For more complex systems, the providers may charge for a set-up fee, but these costs are usually negligible compared the cost of the license for the same software.

The major impact of this component means that the cost of entry is very low, maintenance costs are almost nonexistent and that *capital expenses* (perpetual license) can be turned into *operating expenses* (subscription).

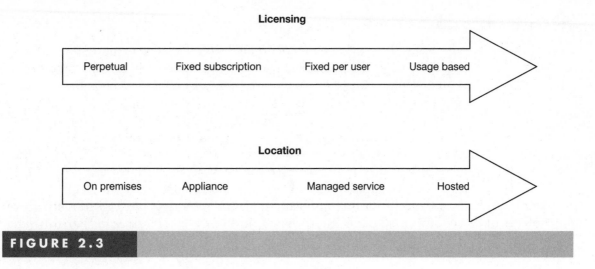

These two characteristics are not discrete but exist on a continuum, and combinations of the two vectors are common, as shown in Figure 2.3.

Historic Perspective

Software-as-a-Service is not a new concept despite all the hype surrounding it. One can trace its roots to the early days of computing.

Timesharing and ADP

The idea of utilizing a single, powerful mainframe computer to serve multiple, geographically dispersed users, was conceived in the late 1950s and first implemented in the early 1960s. *Timesharing* was developed and implemented in numerous operating systems, and is still in use today (e.g., UNIX).

The idea of outsourcing a crucial business service—payroll—dates back to 1949 with a small company *Automatic Payrolls*, which later became known as the giant *Automatic Data Processing* (ADP) specializing in administrative functions services, catering to more than 570,000 clients.

The Internet Revolution—Early SaaS

Software-as-a-Service has been around since the early days of the Web, although the term appeared only around 2004. The early search engines, AltaVista and Yahoo!, provided a service over the net without the need to install software in house. That was followed by the multitude of Web portals that provided a myriad of services (weather, stock market, health, etc.) by simply having a Web browser and access to the Internet. Hotmail is an example of an early SaaS product that replaced the need for maintaining a complex mail exchange service in-house.

ASP and the dot.bomb

Toward the end of the 1990s the *application service provider* (ASP) scene exploded with thousands of software vendors, technology enablers, service providers, and hosting facilities to allow any company to consume almost any software that was otherwise available as an in-house product. The idea was compelling and is still valid (as this chapter suggests). The ASP market evaporated with the collapse of the dot-com bubble in 2001, and very few companies survived. There are a number of reasons why the ASP model failed. Most of the applications offered as an ASP were simply HTML versions of client-server programs that did not have multitenant architecture or service-ready features, suffered from poor performance, and were difficult to scale. Most of the ASP offerings were delivered by service providers that had no expertise in the application. The high-speed Internet infrastructure was not yet in place, and finally, the enterprise IT and CFOs were not ready for this new business model.

Enabling Technologies and Market Trends Leading to SaaS

When the bubble burst, what was left in place was billions of dollars worth of high-speed connectivity, but rapidly shrinking budgets for IT departments. CIOs were expected to deliver more with less.

A new generation of net-native, multitenant, service-ready applications came on board, which were written from scratch to support a service model. These applications were feature-rich and comparable to their on-site competition. Software vendors started to host their own applications, offering a high level of expertise and fast problem resolution. The few ASPs that did survive had a number of years to learn the lessons of the past, and test and perfect the model. This includes architecture and features, but also the business model, pricing and sales of the service.

As confidence in the ability to deliver a solid service grew, business units in many enterprises started testing out essential but noncritical applications in the on-demand model. As the entry price was low, and since no infrastructure, installations and maintenance were necessary, there was no need for IT approval, and in many cases IT was not even notified of the subscription contracts.

Rationale for SaaS

Although referenced in the previous sections, the rationale of SaaS is covered in this section from the points of view of the provider (the ISV) and the consumer (the Enterprise).

The ISV Perspective

- *Simpler development.* There is only one platform—the one the ISV is hosting—so development tends to be simpler. No need for consideration of multiple databases, Web, and application servers. The development cycles can be reduced to new versions every few weeks instead of once or twice a year.

- *Simpler testing and problem resolution.* Since only one instance of the application is running, it is simpler to test that environment instead of spending a large portion of the tests on any number of combinatorial configurations. Bugs are easily reproducible and fixes can be tested in-house.

- *Recurring revenue.* Predictability in the revenue stream is easier to achieve.

- *Economies of scale.* The cost of adding a new customer is negligible if an operation is built properly; therefore, profits could grow at a much faster rate than the perpetual model.

- *Shorter sales cycle.* The low entry price and faster implementation lowers the risk of consuming the service. This model also allows business units to consume their own service without involving IT. For these reasons the decision cycle for the purchase is much quicker.

- *Reduced implementation costs.* Since there are no (or greatly reduced) implementation needs on the customer side, and no need for in-house upgrades, the traditional role of professional services is no longer needed.

- *Access to new class of customers.* Lower entry costs and minimal maintenance costs allows small and medium-sized businesses to use the software that was previously out of their reach.

The Enterprise Perspective

- *Consumer, not manager, of the software.* The enterprise that uses the software has to do just that—enjoy the advantages that the software offers without the need to become an expert in managing it. That is the main reason why so many lines of business have adopted the model—they do not need IT to set up and maintain the software.

- *Managed risk of software deployment.* Very few unknowns exist in this model. The cost, the time for deployment, the resources needed are all small and quite predictable.

- *Time to value, faster ROI.* Whereas with the former model, the time it took to implement a software product was measured in months or sometimes years, with the SaaS model it is usually measured in days or weeks.

- *Testing and scale-up.* Consuming a service does not mean a major commitment to the ISV. A department can test drive the software with only a few seats for a limited time. If it is successful, the business can gradually add more users as its needs demand.

- *Lower upfront costs.* The entry price is low, and no major commitments to infrastructure or software licenses are needed.

- *Reduced TCO.* According to Gartner, the annual cost to own and manage software applications can be up to four times the cost of the initial purchase. Companies may spend more than 75 percent of their IT budget just on maintaining and running existing systems and software infrastructure. With SaaS, the service provider maintains the software, so no costs are associated with maintenance.

- *Avoiding the upgrade nightmare.* In the traditional model, major potential disruptions in the service and the costs associated with upgrades may cause the enterprise to postpone the process or sometime skip a number of versions, even though important features are missed. In the SaaS model, upgrades are (in theory) transparent to the business.

The SaaS Landscape

What does the landscape look like today, and who are the players in the market?

The Providers

The independent software vendors (ISV) and their channel partners are the first link in the chain. They need to build and host the software that would be service-ready, scalable, secure, and reliable, with high performance rates.

Note that as SaaS is growing in popularity, the traditional, large, on-premises, enterprise ISVs want in on the game and are starting to offer their on-demand versions. It is important to be able to differentiate between the pure-play SaaS providers—those companies that offered their solutions as a service from the onset—and those companies that are providing a half-baked solution, only to be able to claim that they also offer on-demand. Many of these large firms are not structured to provide a service, and in those cases there will be a constant struggle within the company between the advocates of SaaS and the old timers who want to continue doing business the traditional way. In some cases, they will offer a partial solution or a slimmed down version; sometimes it will be a single tenant, non-scalable product.

The Consumers

The consumers of these services are the second major players. These would be either the IT organizations in small, medium, and large enterprises and in many cases independent lines of businesses within the corporation.

The Aggregators

A growing trend in the on-demand business is *SaaS Ecosystems* or *SaaS aggregators*. Known examples are AppExchange from SalesForce, Jamcracker Service Delivery Network (JSDN) and NetSuite (NetSuite started out with a sleuth of homegrown services but is expanding to allow third-party providers to integrate to its platform). These vendors provide an SaaS integration platform (SIP) to allow other vendors to offer their services through a common interface, aggregating multiple providers in a single portal.

An important group of players that are now becoming more prominent are the service providers, namely the Telcos and ISPs that are beginning to offer their clients a full array of SaaS offerings.

The Enablers

In order to be able to provide these services there are many companies that act as *SaaS enablers.* These are the hosting and bandwidth providers, which allow ISVs to host their servers at their facilities. As few software vendors have expertise in the operations of a 24/7 critical application, many hosting providers offer additional services such as monitoring, application management, help desk, and first-tier support.

Then there are software companies that produce platforms for SaaS to run the operations support systems (OSS). Functions such as access, provisioning, delegation, metering, branding, and reports are all part of the OSS.

Another class of software vendors offers SaaS integration platforms, targeting mainly the ISPs and Telcos.

Challenges for IT

The disruptive trend of SaaS is creating an unwarranted headache for CIOs, exacerbating issues they are already contending with.

The major impact of the SaaS trend is that this model allows for business units to contract and consume the services independent of the IT department. Because the infrastructure demands are minimal and because the upfront costs are a fraction of any IT project, a business unit can circumvent IT altogether and start consuming the service without even informing IT. In some instances, IT finds out about the new service only when the help desk receives a call regarding an issue on that service. How does IT chargeback for services incurred due to an SaaS engagement if it has no control on who is using the service, or how much?

Since IT has little control of the services consumed by the various business units, a number of problems present themselves.

Loss of Control

To begin with, a mind shift is required of the CIO to become a manager of services, providers, and SLAs rather than a manager of software.

Since the vendors are typically not selected by IT, but rather by the business units, this adds to a high vendor complexity. IT has been gravitating toward fewer vendors to provide more solutions, and of course IT controlled the vendor selection process. All of a sudden, there are multiple vendors popping up who have not been scrutinized by IT.

Moreover, multiple business units could contract separately from the same provider, adding to the confusion and lack of control. IT cannot enforce policy across business units with each one acting as a separate customer vis-á-vis the provider.

Single sign-on (SSO) presents another control issue. Since each software vendor provides a unique login for its customers, users within the enterprise will have different login IDs, hindering the efforts for SSO in the enterprise.

Another issue that touches on security and compliance as well as control, is the fact that IT has no ownership of the data, as it is scattered all across the Internet cloud.

Security

As mentioned, IT has no control of what information is delivered outside of the enterprise's premises. Even if IT is involved in the process, it may have qualms about sensitive information residing at another company's database. What happens when an employee leaves the company? IT has little knowledge of which on-demand applications the employee has login to. If the former employee ends up working at a competitor, he or she may still have access to business sensitive information. How will IT de-provision access if it was never involved in provisioning it?

Hidden Costs

Although the upfront costs are minimal and maintenance costs are nonexistent in most cases, the accumulated costs over time, when the number of users of an application runs into the hundreds, may end up being more expensive in the long run, than the purchase of a perpetual license for the enterprise. The problem is that these costs usually creep up on the enterprise bit by bit until a substantial body of users is already hooked on the product.

Since business users are typically the ones that sign the subscription agreement, without IT's involvement, many questions that should have been asked are not brought up, as these users are not equipped to ask the questions. The business may end up paying a lot more than was intended as storage needs were not computed, and mobile device access was not discussed. The business user may not be aware of the heavy price of exit charges that may result from either scaling down the number of seats, or from exiting the contract at an earlier date.

Another cost that is not advertised by many SaaS providers is integration with back office systems. Although early hosted solutions mainly provided peripheral systems, more and more SaaS solutions are exceedingly becoming core and need to integrate with the other solutions, whether on-site or other SaaS products. These integration projects are no different than the traditional on-premises integrations and would be offered by professional services or third-party integrators.

Customization is another hidden cost. Most SaaS products allow an ever-growing ability to mold the product to the customers' needs. This configuration, which is done by the customer, should be calculated into the overall costs. IT may be requested to perform a customization of a product that it did not even know was consumed by the business users who don't allocate sufficient resources for administration and management.

One of the merits of SaaS is that fact that the customer does not need to deal with upgrades, which are done seamlessly by the provider. Although the smooth installments of bug fixes and added features are a great plus, when it comes to major upgrades, this may become a serious problem. If the user base in a certain company is not prepared for the upgrade (the provider's timetables do not necessarily sync with the customers'), it might affect business continuity. Say processes have changed due to a new feature set, or that certain functions have been pushed to a new tab. That could affect a workforce that did not get proper training.

Governance and Compliance Tracking

IT cannot enforce policy across business units with each one acting as a separate customer vis-à-vis the provider. The services may provide business processes that satisfy end user needs but fail to comply with company policy and government regulations. Maintaining internal controls as prescribed by Sarbanes-Oxley is hindered by the following:

- Inconsistent access policies that leads to security vulnerabilities
- A large portion of SaaS deployments that IT is unaware of
- Usage data that are incomplete and unauditable
- Inability to run analysis and reports across applications

Ensuring Success of Implementation

Opportunity for IT

Although SaaS introduces a set of new challenges to IT's mode of operation, the CIO should view the SaaS model as a great opportunity to shift from the reactive role of IT to one that focuses on high-value activities that support the business goals of the enterprise. Now IT can free resources devoted to application-hosting operations, and function more as a consultation group to help business units derive more value from technology to accomplish their objectives.

SaaS Taskforce

The importance of the involvement of IT in the process of selecting, negotiating, and purchasing the on-demand service cannot be overstated.

IT should create and lead an SaaS taskforce within the enterprise and require a commitment from the business units to work through only this group when considering a SaaS purchase. The process will be perhaps slower than dealing directly with the vendors, but the benefits should pay off: The taskforce would offer a professional group that has the ability to test the technology, perform due-diligence on the vendor, evaluate backend integration, examine the service level offerings, and negotiate better prices. In addition, working through this group will ensure a measure of control, consolidated licensing, and vendor management.

The taskforce should be comprised of dedicated IT staff with know-how in the areas of vendor management, procurement, and performance testing, as well as named members of the business units that would either be permanent members or join the team in an ad-hoc fashion regarding a service relevant to their business. This team should also meet on a regular basis to discuss procedures and process, to examine new offerings in the market, and to review existing SaaS implementations and work out problems across the enterprise.

For a successful implementation, several areas should be examined. These are discussed next.

SAS 70

Statement on Auditing Standards (SAS) No. 70, Service Organizations, is an internationally recognized auditing standard developed by the American Institute of Certified Public

Accountants (AICPA). An SAS 70 audit is performed by an independent auditor and results in an SAS 70 report, which the SaaS vendor could provide to its customers for their audits. SAS 70 does not imply any standards, nor does it come with a stamp of approval. It merely outlines the practices of the vendor with regard to the service it provides. SAS 70 Type II includes detailed testing of the service organization's controls over a minimum six-month period. Since it does not dictate best practices, rather sketches out the existing practices, many SaaS providers do not feel compelled to undergo SAS 70 auditing, especially if they provide utility SaaS solutions, though enterprise SaaS solutions providers will feel more obliged to do so. If a provider does have the Service Auditor's Report, do not accept it as a stamp of approval; rather, scrutinize it to ensure that it complies with your standards of security, privacy, reporting and so on.

SaaS Gateway

Once a service has been approved for consumption, it should appear in the IT Service Catalog as a service offering, no different than other application offerings.

An employee or business owner should be able to select the service and register through the catalog to ensure a uniform provisioning and de-provisioning, control, and compliance.

IT should strive to get an SSO solution from the vendor to enable an SaaS portal for the company so that all traffic is initiated through a single gateway and can therefore be tracked and monitored.

Backend Integration

Is the suggested software a stand-alone system, or does it need to integrate with the back-end legacy software? What are the resources and skill set needed to accomplish that? Does the provider have a professional services team to make that happen, or does IT need to provide the skill and manpower? What assurances are given that upgrades will not trigger another integration effort?

Service-level Agreement

It is imperative that the SaaS Taskforce take a careful look at the offered SLAs and dive into the details. Here are some items to look for:

- *Availability.* Many ISVs promise the five nines (99.999%). In simplistic terms, that comes to about one hour of downtime per year, but the interesting question is, what does the 100 percent mean? Typically, the commitment means uptime minus the planned downtime, which may be periodic, and/or preannounced. A two-hour monthly planned maintenance time will account for another twenty-four hours of unavailability. Also, definition of *availability* might be tricky, as the application may be up, but major functionality may not be available.
- *Performance.* Determining performance is a nontrivial task as it may mean different things to different people. It might be measured in number of concurrent users (how

do you defined concurrent—logged in or running a business process?), number of hits per given time period, transaction response time (e.g., 95 percent transactions respond under five seconds, while 99 percent respond under ten seconds), business process completion time, number of database connections, and so on.

- *Support level.* One should scrutinize the policies and practices of the provider's customer support. Do they provide 24/7 coverage or only 12/6, or business hours only? Do they allow phone contact as well as e-mail as well as a Web-based contact? Does the vendor publish its SLA numbers on the Web? Look for response time to answering the phone, responding to an e-mail, and its commitments to timely problem resolution. Negotiate the advance warning time for unplanned downtime and how soon the vendor would inform the customer following an outage.

- *Escalation.* Ask to see the vendor's *escalation procedures.* Look for problem and severity classification. Verify that issues are being escalated through a defined tier structure, based on this classification. Check customer notification policies and procedures (e.g., if an event occurs and unplanned maintenance is required, how early can a notification be sent to inform of that unplanned maintenance beforehand, or how soon will a notification be sent following an outage?).

- *SLA breach.* What penalties or reimbursements are associated with an SLA breach? Ensure that the penalties are clearly defined and that those penalties are significant enough to guarantee you are getting a premium service. These terms are typically negotiable.

Note: A service level commitment, or SLC, is the *nonbinding* version of an SLA. Verify what is being promised versus what happens when these promises are broken.

Exit Strategy

The more successful the SaaS implementation, the more difficult it would become to disengage from the service provider. As the number of users in the enterprise grows and volume of the data at the hosted end expands, the reliance on the ISV deepens. Any number of events may warrant a break in the service. The provider may go out of business, or be acquired by a larger company with different goals, or IT may want to switch from one service provider to another. The enterprise may want to regain ownership when a significant volume threshold is reached (there may be a point where managing the service becomes more cost-effective than outsourcing it). That will amount to a licensed version of the application.

It is imperative to demand a clear exit strategy from the SaaS vendor, and it is essential that before a contract is signed, a clear data migration path must be established and verified to ensure that the vendor does not create a dependency that cannot be broken.

Costs

Read the fine print on the agreements. Verify you understand the exit costs and the price for scaling down or early termination. Calculate storage needs and verify whether there is a premium price for storage over-consumption. Find out whether training is included in the subscription price or is an add-on. Try to include it in the deal.

As an organization representing the enterprise, the SaaS taskforce could negotiate for volume discounts. With many vendors, paying upfront for the annual subscription may cut costs by up to 15 percent compared to month-by-month payments.

For integration projects, look for professional service firms outside of the vendor organization that might perform the job at a lower cost. Satellite firms that do just that typically surround large SaaS providers.

Conclusion

Software-as-a-Service is reality that is growing in prominence because the time-to-value and cost-effectiveness to the business units is irresistible. It cannot be ignored or wished away, as it tends to come in through the back door. For all the fears that the CIO might have of losing control, of lesser security, it should be embraced and seen as an important step of evolving the IT into a proactive, service-centric function that aligns the technology with the business goals. With outsourcing, managed services, offshoring, or SaaS, IT should accept the shift from managing tangible assets to adopting a new paradigm of managing services for the enterprise and be willing to compete with external service providers on their terms.

To ensure a successful implementation of SaaS at the enterprise, the CIO should take the initiative and deploy an SaaS task force that will provide a measure of control, governance, and compliance for an IT landscape that will only grow in its complexity in the coming years. By getting involved and leading the initiative, IT can utilize this powerful sourcing method to benefit the company while safeguarding its assets.

Note

1. "50 Fastest-Growing Software Companies for 2006," *Baseline*, 29 (2006).

eCommerce

Gordon Jones and Tony Young

eCommerce Explosion

eCommerce[1] is exploding at a phenomenal rate as shoppers gain more confidence buying goods online. In fact, comScore Networks[2] reported 2006 online shopping increased 24 percent since 2005. Sales in the last two months of 2006 grew 26 percent compared to the same period last year.

If online shoppers encounter problems or have a bad experience, they are likely to turn to a competitor site or abandon online shopping entirely. According to Harris Interactive[3] 40% of online consumers are doing just that. In today's online world, the demands on a CIO are increasing. Online customer loyalty is low, and business can slip away with the click of a mouse.

This chapter explores the issues and concerns that CIOs must address to mitigate eCommerce risk. For example:

- Does your company have the appropriate governance processes in place to support your company's eCommerce initiative? Do you have the necessary funding and resources to scale with the projected growth of eCommerce transactions?
- Are you structured optimally to support the organization?
- What are your key IT operational metrics and necessary change management procedures?

- Are your systems reliable, scalable, and secure, and can they be easily modified for additional functionality?
- Do you have the people, processes, and technology in place to support eCommerce transactions 24/7, 365 days a year?
- What kind of architecture/legacy systems are you connecting to? Are you positioned to leverage nascent technology such as Web services or service-oriented architecture (SOA)?
- What key metrics do the business units need to measure success?
- Can you measure the cost per transaction for eCommerce?

Governance, Funding, and Organizational Structure

Who owns eCommerce in your company? Organizationally, where does it fit within the corporate structure, and who funds it? To succeed at eCommerce there must be full agreement between all executives and appropriate governance and adequate funding approved.

For Web-centric business models such as eBay or Amazon.com, ownership is likely to be at an executive level—President or COO—and the person may oversee functions other than traditional IT (e.g., customer service, product development). In a bricks-and-mortar business using eCommerce to augment the business, ownership and funding should be with the business users and the executive-level business sponsor, responsible for profit and loss, not the CIO. The CIO should be the key advisor on how to best exploit and provide technology to achieve eCommerce goals, but not the decision maker related to eCommerce development initiatives.

Once ownership is established it is imperative that all parties with a stake in eCommerce have a strong voice in establishing the governance processes and the necessary funding for eCommerce. Although the business users may have a plethora of ideas on how to use eCommerce to improve the business, the CIO knows which technologies to use, how to use them, and when to retire them. The CIO can advise on the best technology investments to make and the processes that need to be in place, and can ensure that the company understands its risks.

In most companies, IT investments are mainly infrastructure related. As Figure 2.4 depicts, only nine percent of an IT budget is truly strategic, as related to the financial services industry. Although eCommerce may be a strategic part of your corporate strategy, the technology that enables it and gives you a competitive advantage is generally short-lived.

For example, the first airline that enabled passengers to reserve and buy tickets online had a competitive edge. Today, most airlines offer these services. Some airlines let passengers shop on the Internet while in the air, and this may be perceived as a competitive advantage. The real question is, how long will it last, and when will the competitors match the offerings?

The strategic value of eCommerce belongs to business users as well as providing the funding. The IT staff should act in a support role, conducting research such as *make versus buy*, ascertaining detailed costs, and writing technology proposals. Ultimate accountability for expected business benefits must be with the business sponsor.

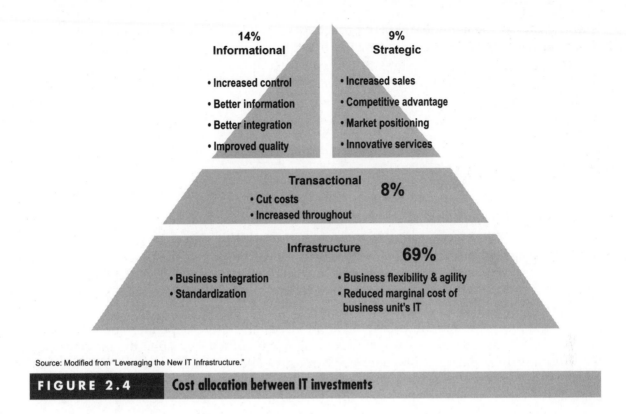

Source: Modified from "Leveraging the New IT Infrastructure."

FIGURE 2.4   Cost allocation between IT investments

The needs of eCommerce will fluctuate and so should its funding, which should not be appropriated based on fiscal budgets or automatic percentage increases. Investments should be sought on a case-by-case basis, depending on the ROI. If a business initiative is proposed that is expected to increase revenue, then as part of the approval process the sales budget numbers should be revised upward accordingly.

While the eCommerce initiative is driven by the business, it is important that the executives and the team fully understand and endorse how the IT staff is organized and the skills sets required to support eCommerce. It is important that the business users know who is responsible for each aspect of eCommerce. Who do they contact regarding each of the following?

- UI (user interface) issues
- SLAs with IT and dependent processing partners
- Customer service issues
- User requirement changes
- Business initiatives—priority settings
- Incident management
- Metrics

The organization structure will vary depending on the unique demands. In some companies, the CIO has the responsibility for engineering the eCommerce offering. In these situations, then, the CIO should consider this as a product-development group rather traditional IT, and the importance of a strong, independent QA function should not be underestimated.

The demand for talent is competitive around the globe, and top talent demands salary premiums. The CIO's balancing act is to determine in which positions more seasoned/expensive staff need to be recruited, versus those positions that can be filled with less-expensive labor.

Operational Metrics

Ultimately, your company and its trading partners want the same result: a perfect online experience for customers. It is imperative that the metrics truly reflect the actual experience.

Most companies recognize the importance of availability and fast response times. When issues occur, staff must be available 24/7 to receive immediate notification alerts. If corrective action is not taken within minutes, then sales will be lost, as online customers may click over to a competitor.

As eCommerce transactions become more global and more dependent on processing partners and their systems, measuring *actual uptime* is difficult. Despite the fact that you may rely on third parties, the customer cannot be disrupted if your supply chain of resources has an issue. For example, if you rely on credit card processors and you cannot complete a transaction due to their downtime, you have impacted the customer experience. Uptime must be measured from a customer experience perspective.

How do you compute uptime? What demands can you place on global dependencies that have not invested in redundant data centers, so one can go down for routine maintenance? What steps can you take to avoid losing the customer? For example, can you construct your eCommerce back-end architecture with asynchronous processing so the transaction is captured and held in a suspense file until the partners processing systems are operational?

More experienced eCommerce companies take operational metrics a stage further and define whether business transactions are correctly processed and effective:

- Can order details be taken with payment information?
- Did the customer receive up-to-date inventory levels? Were they accurate?
- Was the product shipped when promised?
- Was the payment transaction validated by the issuing financial institution?
- Was the customer satisfied with the complete transaction and the experience?

The challenge of the CIO is to *capture the complete customer experience* with operational metrics, irrespective of the trading channel or combination of them. Customers do not care if it was a back-end system that was down or that inventory levels reported were inaccurate. They simply know *and remember* that the shopping experience on your site or with your company was disappointing. For example, this holiday season an online customer used a trusted and reputable eCommerce site to shop and compare a particular brand of sandals.

She chose a pair, entered the payment information, noted the expected date of arrival, and confirmed the sale. A few minutes later she received an e-mail from the eCommerce company confirming her order. Two days later, however, she received an e-mail from the actual store that was shipping the sandals, stating they were not in stock. There was no apology, no mention of the credit card charges being reversed, and no offer of compensation for the inconvenience. The customer never received an e-mail from the original eCommerce site where she placed the order.

Every phase of an eCommerce transaction must be discussed with business users and partners, and proper controls must be built into your processes. For example:

- If customers are downloading software, intellectual property can be transferred within seconds. Do your processes ensure that payment is confirmed before final delivery?
- If an order has to be sent to a warehouse for goods to be picked, did the picker retrieve the goods promptly?
- If the order is placed online, but the customer wants to pick it up at the store, is the inventory reserved so that it is not taken by a local shopper?

Ongoing trend analysis metrics and mandatory operational weekly meetings with all key personnel present are vital. This is the time to discuss any adverse customer experience reports in detail. The discussions reflect on *what* went wrong, *why* it went wrong, and *what steps* to take to ensure the problems do not happen again. Any imminent changes and associated risks are discussed and evaluated by all the dependencies or processing parties. Ongoing trend metrics ensure that all parties continually strive to improve their processes and technology and adhere to change management procedures. This weekly data and discussion should include:

- Achievements and observations
- Issues and problems to be resolved
- Action plans for the coming week

All trend analysis is shared between all processing parties and business users to verify when tangible processing improvements are realized.

Costs Per Transaction

As more and more business transactions are handled via the Web, it is becomes increasingly important to collaborate with the CFO to compute the cost per transaction. For example, in some companies the value proposition may be to offer the lowest prices (e.g., Wal-Mart). For these companies to be cost-effective they must attain high transaction volumes using the lowest-cost transaction method, which may be taking orders via the Web. Understanding the actual costs per transaction per given volume is imperative to accurate predict full operating costs.

Fixed Costs

In consultation with finance staff, agreements must be made as to which costs will be fully loaded into fixed versus variable and to which cost center these amounts will be charged. Fixed costs typically will include hosting centers (facilities, utilities, hardware, software, supplies and operational costs), networks, and security. The depreciation amount related to all the equipment and software licenses purchased to date should be computed in the fixed costs.

Variable Costs

These are the actual costs that will be incurred once a certain threshold has been exceeded, The CIO must be aware to what extent the current systems and software can scale and at what point of transaction activity processing degradation will occur. The investment necessary to scale to the next level should be known and executives should know in advance when the condition will occur and if funding is necessary.

Business Metrics

Business metrics will vary depending on your business as each company has slightly differing go-to-market objectives. Business metrics should be predefined and part of governance.

Figure 2.5 shows a few questions and metrics to consider.

Systems Reliability, 24/7

The *DNA* of all IT staff must be committed to be on call 24/7, 365 days a year. Every minute an eCommerce site is down could result in a significant revenue loss for the company.

When Severity 1 or 2 issues occur, immediate alerts must be sent to IT support personnel, network engineers, database administrators, and so on, as well as pertinent trading dependencies. The challenge with many of these outages is pinpointing the exact issue. A team, therefore, should be deployed to triage the issue and resolve it as quickly as possible. Merely rolling back to previous versions could have a negative impact on customers if it happens during peak times and the rollback time is lengthy.

It is also important to alert all trading dependencies because the problem could lie within one of their processes or systems. If a particular expert (on your team or within your trading dependencies) is on vacation, you need to ensure back-up personnel are available as well. For example, a few years ago a financial institution called a Severity 2 late on a Friday afternoon. Immediate alerts went out to executives, support personnel, and technical staff, as well as key processing parties. The problem was found with a processing partner and a code fix was available within a few hours. When the code fix came, the people responsible for QA of the code at the financial institution were not available over the weekend, which jeopardized its ability to meet the service-level agreement (SLA).

Customer Acquisition

Questions to Consider
- Is your current value proposition compelling?
- What does it cost to drive a viewer to the site?
- What is the acquisition cost of each customer?
- What promotional initiatives are planned? How effective were previous campaigns? Are the optimum affiliates/marketing partners in place?
- What is the status of online customer profiles? Is there segmentation analysis of customers who buy through different channels: Internet only, Internet and catalog, or bricks and mortar?
- Can we segment target markets?
- What is the demographic reach?
- Are leads and applications managed effectively across channels?

Metrics to Consider
- Reach
- New customers: company or selling channel
- Percentage booked via channels
- Acquisition cost
- Customers acquired via third parties
- Look-to-book ratios (conversion rate)
- Advertising effectiveness

Cross Sell and Retention

Questions to Consider
- Is cross selling strong enough for unified products? (e.g., Amazon)
- What is the balance between product push versus relationship versus quality focus?
- Is there an effective measurement of attrition and reasons for leaving?
- At what transactional step do most customers abandon the site? (e.g., shipping)
- What is the current process of forming and managing partnerships?
- Are there comprehensive data-mining capabilities?
- Are there customer profitability models?
- Are we contacting management across channels?

Metrics to Consider
- Attrition rate
- Lifetime revenue/profit per household
- Acceptance /conversion rate
- Customer satisfaction
- Partnership ROI
- Abandonment points

Channel Integration and Optimization

Questions to Consider
- Is there a seamless synchronization and integration of channels and processes?
- Is there a unified view of the customer and common identification?
- Can updates be done in real time regardless of the source channel?
- Is there one common database? If not, frequency of synchronization? For example, can a customer register online but drive to the store to inspect the goods? (e.g., baby car seats)
- Is there a common architecture and proven software to exchange data across channels?

Metrics to Consider
- Customer satisfaction
- Channel costs—individual and total
- Synchronization cycle time
- Transaction mix by channel
- Average selling price (ASP) by channel
- Customer/household—revenue and profit—total and via channel
- Functionality gaps by channel

Integrated Fulfillment and Transaction Processing

Questions to Consider
- Are systems and applications secure, highly reliable, and scalable throughout all channels?
- Can we support multiple platforms?
- Are disaster recovery plans current and tested?
- Have all payment vehicle options been evaluated?
- How up to date are inventory amounts? Are these shared between the channels? Can inventory be booked via the Web and picked up at the store, leaving the amount reserved and not preempted or taken by a shopper in the bricks and mortar?

Metrics to Consider
- Availability
- Security audits—Gap analysis
- Scaling costs per transaction threshold
- Postmortem results on dry runs
- Mean time to recover
- Percent accuracy on cycle counts
- Fulfillment accuracy

FIGURE 2.5

Although many large eCommerce players are building in redundancies by clustering their systems to systematically minimize failures, you are still likely to have single points of failure. Some of these companies may be your trading dependencies or processing parties to your trading dependencies, so it is important to understand the systems and processes of all parties involved in a transaction.

The CIO has to continually ensure that all dependencies are accountable. Although SLAs are an acceptable practice within most organizations, CIOs should really consider this a basic requirement. The onus is on the CIO to ensure the eCommerce site and its dependencies have as clear and flawless engagement model as possible.

Architecture and Technologies

Over the past three decades, several technologies have emerged with promises to revolutionize the notion of distributed computing. Yet, many of these technologies were only moderately successful, as they lacked consistent standards and protocols that inhibited adoption. As a result, IT organizations built tightly coupled systems that became brittle over the years.

A service-oriented architecture (SOA) is an architecture that organizations use to build loosely coupled infrastructures. SOA helps businesses develop and manage their IT systems through reusable technologies and presents information previously stored in legacy applications as Web services. SOA defines how Web services will work within the enterprise.

A Web service is a service that is published and consumed by calling programs. For example, a Web service can be a calculation that automatically converts currency, or a service that calls back-end programs and returns data from various systems.

The ability for companies to electronically interact across enterprises with suppliers, partners, and customers is critical to business success. Consider the role of a supplier in an eCommerce relationship. Some eCommerce sites serve as storefronts but never participate in the warehousing or supply of products. This is the responsibility of the manufacturer or distributor. In order to build loosely coupled systems that can extend across suppliers, eCommerce providers can publish and consume Web services supporting inventory allocation and logistics.

SOA also makes it possible for two programs, perhaps written in different languages and running on different operating systems, to communicate with each other using open standards such as HTTP, XML, and SOAP.

Figure 2.6 shows a service-oriented architecture for integrating both internal and external services. Typically, there is a messaging layer, also known as *enterprise service bus* (ESB), which consists of a standards-based infrastructure that distributes messages across services, provides data transformational functionality, and accesses services.

Integration is inherently asynchronous, with a sender simply posting a message on the messaging layer and the service processing it at a later point.

Services typically expose their interface using Web services such as XML over HTTP using the SOAP or REST protocols.

REST and SOAP are two competing technical approaches to building standards-based Web services. In REST, parameters are passed to a Web service using key value pairs in the URL. A SOAP message is an HTTP document that consists of zero or more headers and a

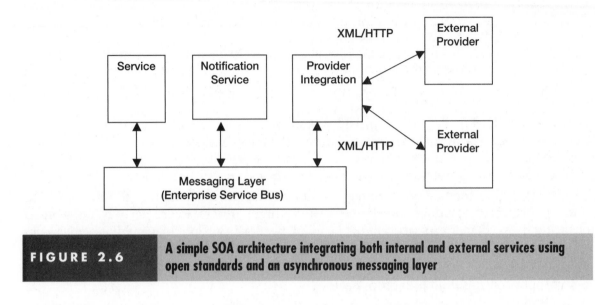

FIGURE 2.6 A simple SOA architecture integrating both internal and external services using open standards and an asynchronous messaging layer

body that contains XML. The headers allow transmission of metadata information regarding transactions, security, reliability, policy, or other optional parameters.

SOAP leverages W3C Web standards including WS-Security, WS-Reliability, WS-Transactions, WS-Policy, and other Web services standards. SOAP is particularly suited for large applications that need these advanced capabilities built on top of a SOA infrastructure. This additional functionality, however, comes at a cost—increased complexity, decreased interoperability, and slower performance.

REST has seen a wide level of adoption for services that tend to be simple, require a high degree of interoperability between multiple platforms, and require fast performance.

In the online world, customers have grown to expect innovation. Using SOA to build services can lead to loose coupling between systems and can make it more flexible to make changes and reuse services. This improves your time to market and gives you a competitive advantage. In the future, successful eCommerce solutions will enable new products to be introduced overnight.

According to industry analysts, over half of organizations are starting to define the role of Web services within their organization and are experimenting or deploying them. If you have not defined the role of SOA in your architecture, you should start through an evolutionary approach. First set expectations as to where most other organizations are, and then show how your organization can start with SOA.

Despite the popularity of SOA, you should use cautious optimism in your approach as tools, protocols, and standards are still evolving. For example, there are at least 56 standards espousing SOA, no consistent security standards for Web services, and numerous vendors still promoting their agendas.

There will always be new technologies on the scene—Web 2.0, mash-ups, blogs, wikis, RSS, and others. The question is, how do you innovate using these new technologies? Can they give you a competitive advantage or keep you in the game? Is the potential investment worth it?

Summary

In many industries, eCommerce has become a baseline expectation. If done correctly, it can improve sales, increase your customer base, reduce costs, and give you a competitive edge. But it will fail without proper governance and funding, effective metrics, or the right people, processes, and technology.

Governance and funding are essential for eCommerce success. Although many people will influence its success, the crucial stakeholders are the business sponsor and the CIO. The business sponsor is responsible for the expected business benefits and funding. The CIO helps establish governance processes and metrics to ensure a complete and satisfying experience.

Operational metrics are imperative. Operational metrics must capture the complete customer experience, including dependencies on trading partners. Every party responsible for ensuring the customer experience must be available 24×7×365 in the event of an emergency.

Remember, customers can exit the site with the click of a button. As a result, *every phase* of an eCommerce transaction must be discussed with business users and dependencies with proper controls built into processes.

With effective alerting, issues can be addressed immediately, before escalating into larger problems. Ongoing metrics and weekly meetings ensure that all parties improve their processes and technology and adhere to change management procedures.

Gathering the right *business metrics* can help business users identify the right customers, push the right products, and give the customers the right information at the right time. This ultimately ensures that the customers are completely satisfied with their eCommerce experience.

The onus is on the CIO and the IT staff for eCommerce to work 24/7, 365 days a year. All systems have points of failure, and they should be well known with documented remedies in the event a failure point is compromised.

A *service-oriented architecture* and Web services can help you innovate. Using SOA to build services can lead to loose coupling between systems and make it more flexible to make changes and reuse services. This improves your time to market and gives you a competitive advantage. Technology continues to evolve in the marketplace. The CIO must consistently evaluate new technologies and adopt the ones that can cost-effectively lead to a competitive advantage.

Notes

1. For the purposes of this article, eCommerce is defined as conducting business transactions on the Web and does not necessarily refer to Software as a Service (SaaS) or merely having a Web presence for information or data capture.
2. comScore Networks, *2006 ends the year with a surge in online sales* (accessed Jan 4, 2007).
3. Harris Interactive.
4. Peter Weill and Marianne Broadbent, *Leveraging the New Infrastructure: How Market Leaders Capitalize on Information Technology* (Harvard Business School Press, June 1998).

Outsourcing/Offshoring

Sam Gill and Dean Lane

Introduction

One day in the early 1980s, my boss called me into his office and assigned me a project to find a vendor overseas that would help us become more price competitive with our products. With a background in purchasing, I considered myself very familiar with finding vendors to subcontract some of our work. I quickly learned that I was not familiar with finding vendors overseas and establishing long-term relationships with them. Thus began my education and long journey into the world of outsourcing/offshoring.

What follows are some of the best practices that I have learned and utilized over the span of 25 years. These practices should help anyone either currently engaged in, or contemplating a move to, outsource/offshore some of their development activities. Outsourcing emerged a few millenniums ago with the production and sale of food, tools and other household appliances. As soon as small communities began to form, people with specialized skills began to trade with each other for goods and services. Though outsourcing and offshoring have been around for millenniums, it had not been a common practice.

Even in the industrial age very few companies outsourced any of their operations. Companies in the 1800s and 1900s were vertically integrated organizations, taking care of their own production, mining, and manufacturing from raw materials to finished goods as well

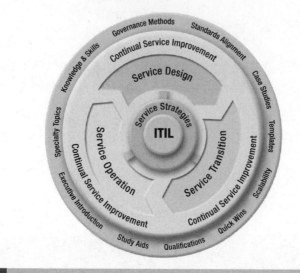

| FIGURE 2.7 | ITIL service life cycle |

as then shipping the goods to company owned retail outlets. The industrial revolution did bring about specialization contracting, especially in the service industry. As a result, it brought about a large scale growth of outsourcing of services such as insurance services, architecture and engineering services, an in our era, software. Many articles have been published on outsourcing and offshoring, but they have been focusing mainly on the economic and managerial aspects. In this chapter, we will present a survival guide for outsourcing and offshoring for an IT manager.

Outsourcing and offshoring is, and will remain, a very hot IT management topic, as evidenced by the latest version of the IT Infrastructure Library (ITIL) (www.itil.org). Version 3 of ITIL now includes a *service life cycle* (see Figure 2.7). This version presents service strategies for outsourcing, insourcing, co-sourcing, and shared service models.

This introduction to the survival guide focuses on the process of selecting, establishing, and maintaining outsourcing/offshoring. In the discussion of each phase in the survival guide, we will focus only on the important issues that need to be addressed. We have developed a methodology of exactly 158 steps required to select a *third-party service provider,* but a detailed discussion of each activity is beyond the scope of this presentation. What is important is to ensure that the initial steps are taken properly to move your firm in the right direction.

Finally, a comment on the use of the terms: To *outsource* means that you will select a vendor that will perform part of your company's business process in order to allow you to gain effectiveness and efficiency in the delivery of your product or service. *Offshoring,* by contrast, means that the vendor you select would be from a foreign country rather than a domestic partner. In general, both outsourcing and offshoring can be viewed as part of creating a virtual organization that would allow a company to extend its core competency and use other domestic and foreign resources to deliver its products and services.

Business Strategy Phase

Any outsource or offshore effort needs to begin with a clear understanding of the business strategy behind it. The importance of protecting the core competencies of your business cannot be overstated. The most likely candidates for outsourcing are business processes that would allow a company to deliver its products and services more efficiently. While cost is a major driver for outsourcing, it is not the only one. Consider a company that needs to expand its product line but lacks the internal resources to implement its plan. In a recent study, the top four reasons for outsourcing were identified as: cost reduction, productivity improvement, faster turnaround, and better quality.

The survival guide to outsourcing consists of several phases. Some of the phases are optional. Determining if a phase is necessary depends on the merit of the project and whether the correct solution is outsourcing or offshoring. In the first phase of the Survival Guide, the business strategy phase, there are four important tasks:

1. Select consultant as a guide.
2. Create business requirements.
3. Establish goals (objectives) for the outsource/offshoring project.
4. Develop requirements for the outsource/offshoring project.

A good outsourcing plan begins with defining the reasons why a company wants to outsource. Since a company typically has not had much experience with outsourcing, even less with offshoring, it should hire an experienced consultant to guide it through the process of identifying its strategy and, in particular, the business requirements and the goals for the project.

The consultant will guide the company through the implantation of all the phases of the Survival Guide. In particular, the consultant will encourage you not to engage an offsite vendor until you know which outsourcing model is right for you and that you should be prepared to reorganize your staff to make it work. The consultant will also emphasize the importance of establishing an intellectual property hierarchy, so that you know what to outsource, and equally as important, what not to outsource. The consultant should also explain that having a clear vision of how you will control quality is key, and that if you are doing this just to save money you will probably fail. Finally, the consultant will explain the importance of acquiring expertise to get it off the ground in the right way, by hiring the right consultant and by understanding the stakes of a failure. It is very hard to re-implement if you fail the first time. Figure 2.8 identifies some of the drivers that push firms to sourcing processes.

Who is a good consultant? Obviously, it should be a person with a track record on helping companies make the right decisions and successfully implement them. And you should be aware that simply because someone once outsourced or offshored a small project does not qualify the person to guide you through the vendor selection process, especially when dealing with foreign companies, countries, and their laws.

Business Drivers
Focus on Core Competencies
Align IT Strategy and Business Goals
Build Global World Class Processes
Improve Overall Competitiveness
Capitalize on E-Business Opportunities

Industry Drivers
Obsolete Contracting Approaches
Changing Success Criteria
New Forms of Competition
Innovation Becoming a Differentiator

IT Drivers
Improve Service Levels
Enhance IT Effectiveness
Supplement IT Resources
Shorten Implementation Time
Mission Critical for Business Success

Onsite–
Offsite
Sourcing

FIGURE 2.8 | Sourcing drivers

Analysis Phase

The second phase in the survival guide is the analysis phase. In this phase, there are five activities:

1. Determine tasks.
2. Define who will do what.
3. Select model.
4. Establish provider qualifications.
5. Define role and responsibility of independent consultant(s).

There are various models that can be pursued, as shown in Figure 2.9.

An inexperienced consultant will tell you about all the models that exist. In reality, there are only three models—everything else is a one-off or enhancement to the three major models. The first model, *outsourced,* is engaging a vendor to perform the work. The second model, *hybrid,* can be thought of as a joint venture where the contracting firm and the vendor both own and share in the risks and profit. The third model, *wholly owned,* is the equivalent of a *maquiladora* in Mexico, where the contracting firm owns the foreign entity and holds it captive to perform only its work.

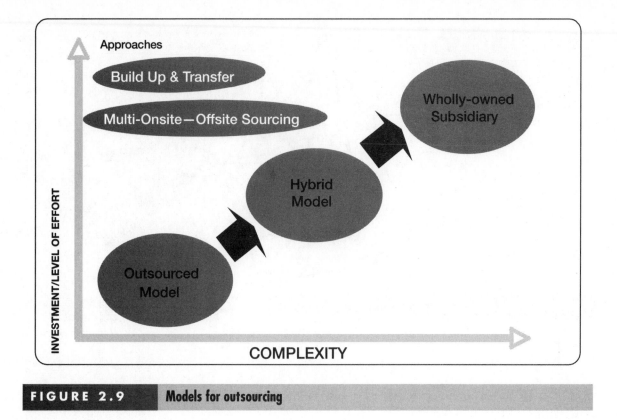

FIGURE 2.9	Models for outsourcing

Preparation Phase

The next phase is preparation. The seven activities in this phase are a key to a successful implementation:

1. Determine what to outsource/offshore.
2. Define intellectual property hierarchy.
3. Determine evaluation criteria.
4. Create a request for proposal that provides a quantitative basis for the first cut.
5. Create a single evaluation template to be used at each site visited so the second cut will be quantitative as well.
6. Develop a slate of providers.
7. Define baseline contract from which to begin negotiations.

Figure 2.10 details some of the criteria that can be used to evaluate the potential companies with which to partner.

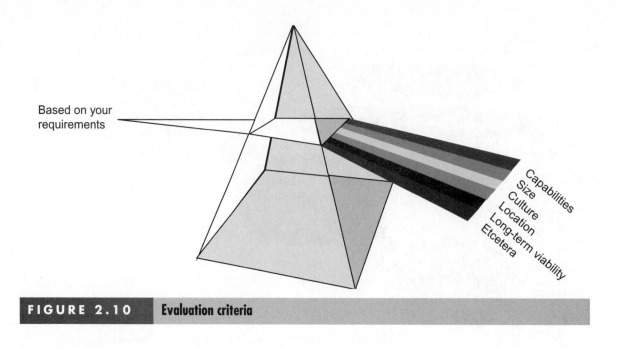

Based on your requirements

Capabilities
Size
Culture
Location
Long-term viability
Etcetera

FIGURE 2.10 | **Evaluation criteria**

Communications with Country (optional)/Company Phase

After the preparation phase, you must start the activities associated with the communication and engagement of vendors both domestic and foreign. In this phase it is important to build on the track record of your consultant and pursue the following three activities:

1. Create a letter of introduction, asking for presentations and responses.
2. Establish dates of visit and schedule to meet with companies.
3. Locate and ensure that independent validation and verification consultants are available for interviews.

Estimation Phase

The next phase of the survival guide deals with how to understand and prepare for the ramifications of working with an outsourced vendor:

1. Determine infrastructure.
2. Determine service requirements.
3. Define communication needs and initiate telecom contracts.
4. Evaluate rate structure (pro forma and negotiable vendor rates).

This is the phase in which a knowledgeable consultant will point out all of the hidden costs associated with outsourcing or offshoring. If your company is limiting its options to outsourcing, your consultant should be competent in this area. When performing offshoring, your consultant should be well versed and have demonstrable experience.

Contracting Phase

Once the estimation phase is complete, the focus should turn to contracting. In this phase, there is a need to address the following eight activities:

1. Conduct evaluation of providers.
2. Conduct risk analysis.
3. Interview independent consultants.
4. Create short list of providers.
5. Designate preferred offshore service provider.
6. Select offshore consultant to perform IV&V (independent validation & verification).
7. Create a management go/no go presentation. (Even if this is just a formality, it should still be conducted. Sometimes it is called a status report to management.)
8. Negotiate contract.

There are many risks associated with introducing change into an organization—even more so when the organization is expanding its scope to becoming a virtual organization. You should consider these risks so as to mitigate them:

- Correct engagement model
- Right vendor and consultant
- Determining what to offsite
- Hidden costs
- Contractual framework
- Relationship structure
- Knowledge transfer /retention
- Intellectual property
- Cultural differences and morale

Knowledge Transfer Phase

Once you have engaged a vendor, the real fun begins. Now, you must make sure that you are setting up the system to succeed with adequate bidirectional communication and knowledge transfer. In particular, you must make sure that you have planned and implemented five activities:

1. Provide training.
2. Provide documentation.
3. Implement software.
4. Test software.
5. Release software.

Measurement Phase

In any vendor relationship, issues and conflicts will arise that at some time will make you regret the decision you ever made to pursue this effort. It is important to keep these setbacks in perspective and keep a current tab on the relationship by establishing and monitoring a service-level agreement (SLA). In this phase, there are four important activities:

1. Define SLA metrics.
2. Monitor provider.
3. Provider performance.
4. Evaluate service.

Ongoing Management Phase

The final phase of the survival guide addresses the issues of how to keep the effort under control and ongoing. There are six activities in this phase:

1. Correct organization structure.
2. Manage resources.
3. Develop processes and procedures.
4. Manage requirements (change control process).
5. Communicate procedures.
6. Review contract for renewal.

Summary and Conclusion

In this presentation of the survival guide, we have attempted to present a comprehensive picture of all the activities involved in undertaking such an endeavor and bringing it to the successful and fruitful outcome of achieving the desired business goals. We have tried to

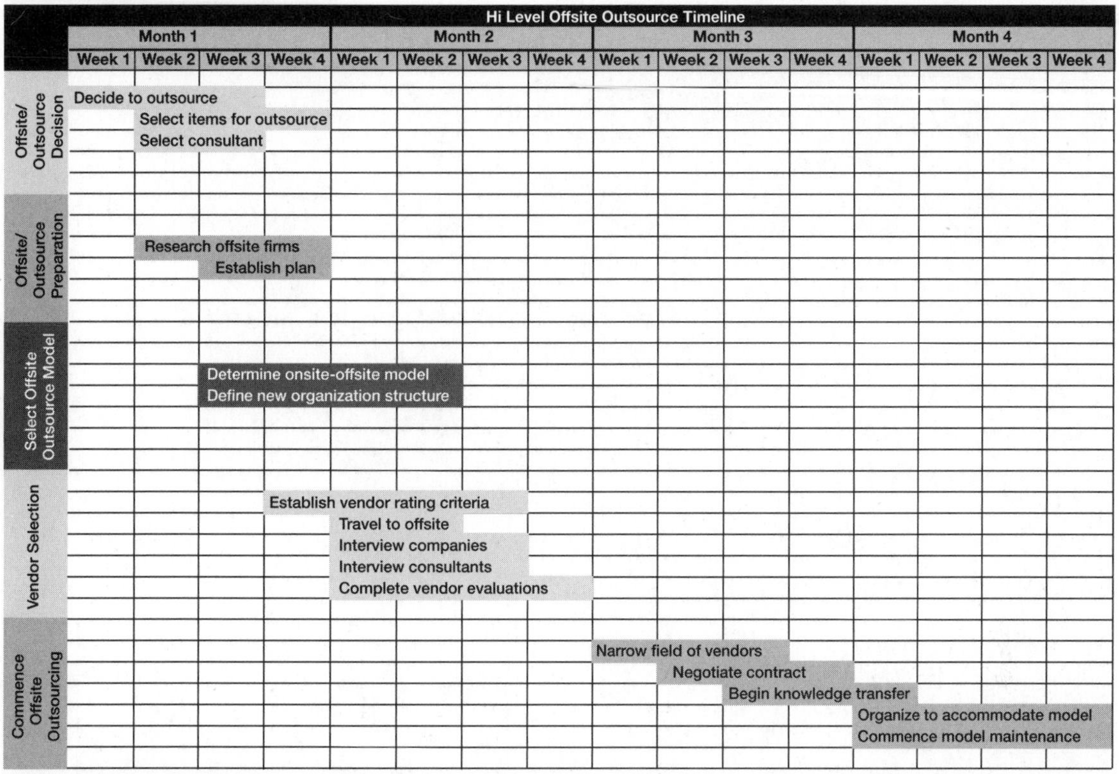

Hi Level Offsite Outsource Timeline															
Month 1				Month 2				Month 3				Month 4			
Week 1	Week 2	Week 3	Week 4	Week 1	Week 2	Week 3	Week 4	Week 1	Week 2	Week 3	Week 4	Week 1	Week 2	Week 3	Week 4

Offsite/Outsource Decision
- Decide to outsource
- Select items for outsource
- Select consultant

Offsite/Outsource Preparation
- Research offsite firms
- Establish plan

Select Offsite Outsource Model
- Determine onsite-offsite model
- Define new organization structure

Vendor Selection
- Establish vendor rating criteria
- Travel to offsite
- Interview companies
- Interview consultants
- Complete vendor evaluations

Commence Offsite Outsourcing
- Narrow field of vendors
- Negotiate contract
- Begin knowledge transfer
- Organize to accommodate model
- Commence model maintenance

FIGURE 2.11   Outsourcing/offshoring timeline

avoid inundating you with too much detail, while still giving you a flavor of the intricacies of some of this process.

The phases of the survival guide should be customized to each instance, to meet the specific requirements of each effort. Figure 2.11 shows an example timeline for one such effort.

The purpose of the survival guide is to share with you the best practices that will allow you to minimize risk and add predictability to the outsourcing/offshoring effort, based on our experience of having performed this process since the early 1980s.

The important take-away from this chapter is that offshoring is an unstructured problem, meaning that unless you are a consultant who assists companies with this activity, you will not undertake this effort more than once, possibly twice in your career. Like buying or selling a home, it is important to engage an experienced professional to assist you through the process.

SECTION 3
Internal Process

Teaming with Internal Customers

Stuart Appley and Ron Sha

Introduction

Of all the characteristics that differentiate a successful CIO, one of the most important is the ability to understand that IT is a service organization, and that all the wonderful and exciting new technology won't matter unless your customers are happy. Understanding and teaming with your customers is critical to a CIO's long-term success.

The steps involved in teaming with your customers, and building a successful relationship, are broken up into the following:

- Process and standards
- Winning over the business
- Marketing IT
- Portfolio management and the IT steering committee

Process and Standards

The need for standards grows as an activity becomes more complex. Establishing processes and policies allows an organization to have a consistent operational environment for all to follow.

With a well-established process, activities can be controlled, measured, and improved. This helps an organization to achieve its goals more efficiently and effectively. Issues can be identified and corrected sooner, thereby improving the overall operational efficiency. Ambiguity is minimized through the application of clearly identified and approved procedures. Emotions are controlled and everyone involved is working from the same page. Friction is minimized and productivity is enhanced.

An organizational benefit can be derived from setting up a policy enforcing IT standards throughout the organization. The policy should encourage discussion at all levels and between subdivisions on priorities, cost savings where feasible, and the sharing of limited resources. As an IT leader, it is important to get to know the current positions, responsibilities and the capabilities of others in the organization. Policies on processes and standards allow the entire organization to improve on efficiency and predictability. Predictability in IT is highly desirous. Consistency with respect to on-time delivery develops trust in the end users (customers) with respect to time-frame commitments, thereby allowing for improved future planning.

Having a consistent global IT standard enables IT staffs to be more efficient. For example, if a company allows employees to use Lotus Notes and Microsoft Word to create documents, IT staff would have to support two platforms, while employees may encounter difficulties or find it impossible to share documents.

A few *best practices* for IT processes, standards and policies are as follows:

- Security policy
- Change management
- Problem escalation and notification
- Service-level agreements

Security Policy

The security policy document describes the measures to ensure computer systems and their data are adequately and securely protected. These measures ensure the continuous control, integrity, availability, and confidentiality of data. The policy should cover but not be limited to the following:

- Physical security
- User access controls
- Password standards
- Password protection guidelines
- Network security
- Server security
- System monitoring
- Extranet connectivity

All new systems have to go through a security review with the IT department. The reviews are to ensure that all access matches the business requirements in the best possible way, and that the *principle of least access* is followed.

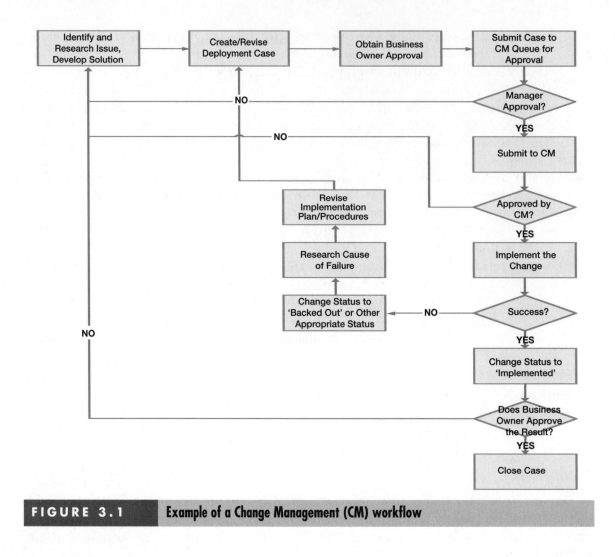

FIGURE 3.1   Example of a Change Management (CM) workflow

Change Management

Change management policy ensures that all configuration, application enhancements and changes, equipment maintenance, and installations are completed and documented, as required through the change management process. The change management group approves all actions globally, which impact or change the production user/customer environment. This is detailed in Figure 3.1 above.

Problem Escalation and Notification

The purpose of the escalation procedure is to provide a framework for managing information technology escalations in a rational and predictable manner so that impact to business users is minimized. Problem management requires forethought, careful monitoring, and

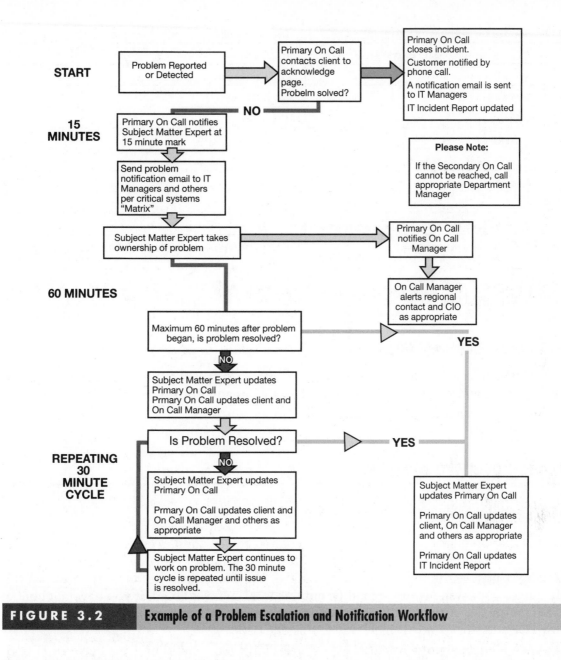

FIGURE 3.2   **Example of a Problem Escalation and Notification Workflow**

follow-up evaluation to reduce risk and negative impact to the user community and to increase the business value of information technology resources. The procedural guidelines given for escalation management ensure that standardized methods and procedures are used to alter the production environment in order to minimize the risk of negative impact.

The benefits of an escalation management procedure are improved system reliability and availability, increased control over availability, and improved communication and tracking. Figure 3.2 is an example of problem escalation and notification workflow.

	Service Description	Service Levels
Help Desk Services	**Coverage: Telephone and Web**	
	Application support hours	24/7 On Call Support
	Technical support hours	24/7 On Call Support
	Business support hours	12/5 Local Time
	Holiday coverage	Yes
	Responsiveness: Telephone	
	Average speed to answer	60 seconds
	Abandon rate	< 10 percent
	Responsiveness: Other Access Channels	
	Web/E-mail-based support response time	Response within 60 minutes maximum from Web/E-mail system delivery of each request

FIGURE 3.3	Service-level agreement for an IT help desk

Service-Level Agreement (SLA)

Service levels usually state measurements and required levels of performance that, if not achieved, can have a critical, adverse impact on a company's business or its operations.

Figure 3.3 is an example of IT help desk SLA.

Winning over the Business

Building a Relationship

The most important aspect in teaming with your customers, and in essence *winning over the business,* is to build a strong relationship with them. Nothing else you do matters if IT and the various business units do not work together. All the greatest technology in the world only makes your systems run smoothly, but this is taken for granted. If you have not built a rapport with the business leaders, all that smooth-running technology is meaningless. Many IT leaders have failed solely due to this one issue.

When we talk about a *relationship,* we are talking about building trust between IT and the business, and doing the steps necessary to ensure that the executives value what IT does. There are four important steps that can help the IT organization accomplish this goal:

1. Understand the business.
2. Use ongoing face-to-face meetings.
3. Listen to business users problems.
4. Have IT get business training.

Understanding the Business

Since IT is only successful if it is truly aligned with the business, and the only way to accomplish this is to fully understand what the company does, then it becomes imperative for the IT team to learn all it can about the company that it represents. Again, this sounds simple, but how can you align IT with a business that you don't fully understand? Find out the hurdles the company faces. Is there a way that IT can help overcome these hurdles? Who are the key customers? Who are the key competitors? What's the short- and long-term business plan? What are the external factors that are affecting the success of the business? Get as much information as possible and become an expert on your company's business.

Face-to-Face Meetings

Face-to-face meetings are a critical first step in winning over the business. You cannot build a relationship without spending face time with your customers. For IT, the customers are the other departments within the company. One reason many businesses don't understand what IT does is that there is no one on the IT side who is willing to sit down and communicate with other departments on their level. By setting aside time to meet with all the business leaders, and as many people in your organization as you can, you show the business that you care what goes on and that you are there to listen.

Many times you'll face leaders who say they are too busy and that they don't have time to meet. Be persistent. I always try to have regularly scheduled meetings with my peers in each of the business units.

In addition to regularly scheduled meetings, ask to sit in on staff meetings. You may already have IT relationship managers or business analysts from your organization that are doing this, but it's helpful if you can participate from time to time also. There is no better way to understand the business than to listen in on staff meetings.

Listening to Their Problems

One tactic that can be used in getting to know the business better is to ask the leaders about their problems. Ask what keeps them up at night. It's amazing what issues you'll find out, and this can become the key to helping you understand how IT can help solve business problems. Always focus your efforts on the business issues facing your company.

Have IT Get Business Training

When I first started as an applications manager, the very first thing I did was to spend some time with our phone reps, listening in on calls made into our sales department. I spent most of the first week getting training by listening to calls, understanding what questions we were being asked and how to use the customer look-up and order fulfillment system. I now try to have all of my new employees go through something similar that is meaningful for whatever company I work for. Provide your IT employees, especially the business relationship side of IT, with hands-on training. Nothing will get them up to speed on the business faster.

Communication

One of my previous bosses, a mentor in my early CIO career, always told his direct reports to "overcommunicate, and when in doubt, communicate it." I preach this today with my employees, as I've come to understand that there is rarely a downside to this. This doesn't mean that you bring up every hiccup or blast an e-mail about every IT concern, but that you make sure you err on the communication side when dealing with your business users. When you know in advance that major systems will be down for maintenance, communicate it. Communicate it more than once, so that everyone knows. If you face unexpected downtime, as can happen with emergency repairs, make sure that your key users are phoned. Don't assume everyone will read e-mails. Here are four simple tactics that you can use to increase your communication with the business:

1. Use IT quarterly/monthly newsletters.
2. Send periodic briefs on security best practices.
3. Ensure that the users are aware of business-value application upgrades or enhancements.
4. Provide consistent and advance notices on system downtime.

IT Quarterly/Monthly Newsletters

A periodic newsletter is a common way to increase the communication between IT and the business. The newsletter can mention some recent projects successes that included IT and the business, as well as talk about new technologies. If it's all about technology, the users will be less interested. Include tips and tricks on MS Office or other internal applications that users may not be aware of. Point to news articles that speak about technology in your industry or technology review articles from industry publications, and discuss how the technology can help business to be more competitive. Include some information about consumer technology that they can relate to as a way of grabbing their interest. Just being consistent in getting out a well-rounded and quality-looking communication will put IT in a positive light.

Communication on Security Best Practices

Use different communication channels to preach security best practices. Whether this is done in the IT marketing newsletters, personal e-mails from your staff, or all of the above, use this type of communication to remind everyone on the dos and don'ts of security best practices. This is a good avenue to communicate with your users, while at the same time increasing the security education of your company.

Communicating When New Systems or Processes Go Live

Communicate on new system implementations. It's amazing how many times you hear from people who say they didn't know that a system was upgraded, or that a feature was added. This shouldn't happen. Ideally, you target your communications for new features or systems to only the affected users, but in smaller organizations, it's OK to inform more people than needed. Again, when in doubt, communicate it. Make sure that senior managers of the business units that are affected are also made aware, even if they don't use the system themselves. It's another way to let them know what's happening in IT that affects them.

Advance Notice on Downtime

Everyone in IT understands that some downtime is a way of life in technology, even if just for periodic maintenance or patch upgrades. However, it's the one part of IT that affects business users the most and can ruin any goodwill built up between IT and the business. To help keep the relationship, a smooth communication process on downtime is essential. For maintenance events, advance notices should be sent out, with a reminder as the time nears. For emergency events, the urgency of the notices depends on the application in question, but high-priority notices should usually be sent out when necessary. If it's e-mail or another application that senior management uses, some sort of personal notification or phone call is usually a good idea. You don't want to overburden people with notices, but they'll also appreciate a consistent notification process. Again, when in doubt, communicate.

Project Management

Progress and Project Review

With projects, it is critical to ensure that your customers are informed of the progress on a regular and consistent basis. A periodic project review will inform the customers if the project is on track and in tune with business requirements. It is easier to correct or change requirements *during* the project development phase than at the end of the project development cycle.

With a regular project review, issues can be discussed and corrected. It also ensures that the business requirements are still valid. Regular project reviews also ensure that the business owner is engaged throughout the project, and viewed as part of the project team. As much as possible, minimize interruptions and complications to existing IT while working toward completion of new projects. Allow for time to solve unforeseen complications so that these complications do not sidetrack the project's objectives.

For large projects, it is beneficial to subdivide the project into smaller groups of deliverables, which can be monitored and measured as part of regular project review meetings. Usually, these deliverables should be completed within a month or quarter. The review process illustrates if the project is on time and on budget, and at the same time if it still meets business expectations (as business strategy/requirement may change while the project is being developed). It is critical to manage the scope of the project to avoid constant changes, which may cause major delay and cost overrun.

In many organizations, IT has a reputation of not delivering exactly what is needed and taking too long. IT is a powerful organization, often overlooked, providing information to all levels of the corporation. The CIO must recognize the value of IT—particularly the timely dissemination of information. This will enable the CIO to be assertive, which, in turn, will provide senior executives the data required for subsequent planning.

IT leaders must adopt a business language and approach and consider the pressures that users are under to meet time and fiscal goals. IT management must continuously provide leadership, innovation, and imagination to the whole team.

Not Just Say No

Not only must IT staffs have good technical skills but also, it would be useful for them to have good interpersonal skills, such that they could practice the art of diplomacy. If it is not possible to honor a customer's request (due to policies, standards, or technology limitations), it would be much better if an alternate solution is offered to solve a customer's need, instead of just saying no to the customer. If no alternative is possible, IT staff should explain the reason why the request cannot be fulfilled.

Take Care of Low-Hanging Fruit

Often, there are many small tasks that IT may not have time to take care of, even though it may only require a minimum effort to do so. Too many of the small, neglected tasks can cause inconveniences and frustration to the end users. Usually, these tasks may not be important enough for the end user to escalate the problem. If IT periodically takes care of these minor tasks *(low-hanging fruit),* the end users are appreciative, you build good will, and customer satisfaction improves. When other problems arise, the end users may be more receptive to new issues and allow the time for IT to resolve them.

Marketing IT

Typically, one of the hardest things for an IT person to do is to *market* him- or herself to the rest of the company. However, studies and personal experience have shown that the business is usually unaware of exactly what IT is doing. Marketing, which can go a long way in helping the relationship between IT and the business, can take on many forms. It typically comprises two areas: Demonstrating to the business the value-add that IT brings and general technology education.

Demonstrating Value-Add

In demonstrating the value-add that IT brings to the table, you need to provide everyone with an understanding of what you are working on, in business terms. Without this, many people view IT as a black hole. It's generally accepted that 50 percent to 85 percent of IT projects support day-to-day operations, or "keeping the lights on." Yet, many users of a company have no idea what is involved in the projects that affect them daily. Some of these projects (e.g., the implementation of a network tool to monitor bandwidth utilization) don't necessarily need to be communicated to the user base as a whole. However, there are many projects where the user community should know and understand, so they get a sense of what takes up more than half of IT's time.

The next section of this chapter will go into more detail on project and portfolio management, but there are a few ways to communicate the value-add that IT brings to the business:

- Dashboard
- IT newsletter, or annual report
- Technology-related training and classes

IT Metrics

METRICS AGGREGATES			PRIMES
Financial	IT Spend as % of Revenue	IT Internal Cost Allocation	IT Cost per Person Served
	IT Utility Spend as % of IT Spend	IT Personnel Cost Allocation	
Portfolio	Types of Projects	Value of Projects	% of Projects Delivered on Time with Quality	IT Enablement Towards Company Goals
People	IT Staff Allocation	Results of Annual IT Survey Customer Sat		
Systems and Applications	Mission Critical Services Availability	Mission Critical Application Availability	Mission Critical Systems Response Time	Data Integrity for Mission Critical Applications, Data Integrity Incidents
	Help Desk Resolution Time	Number of Security Incidents	Core Network Availability	

FIGURE 3.4 Dashboard example showing IT metrics

A *dashboard* and a *newsletter* are two very different approaches. A dashboard is more of *pull* mentality, where information is presented on a company intranet or some portal, and you tell everyone to view the information when they can. Even when monthly update notices are sent out, this type of communication is not as effective when delivered to the company as a whole. A dashboard is better for metrics that are more snapshot oriented, and to a smaller subset of the company. Figure 3.4 is an example of a dashboard. This chapter doesn't go into the metrics part of IT, as there is a lot that could be discussed about which groups to measure and what metrics to use, but the use of metrics is a good example of demonstrating to the business how IT is doing via a dashboard. Every item may not always be positive, but just the transparency in what you're showing helps build credibility with the business and senior management.

An IT newsletter is a more effective way of communicating to the company as a whole, and it can be used for many types of IT news. You can speak about not only general IT projects (e.g., office upgrades), but also business application updates and IT education. This type of marketing can be done in a quarterly newsletter to the whole company. You can also use an IT newsletter to highlight key business projects that are happening. However, no matter what the topic, you must speak to the business in its terms, and explain to business users how IT helps them be more productive, increase sales, or enhance customer satisfaction.

Another way to demonstrate value-add to the business is to provide training and classes for some basic technology that everyone uses. For example, we all take for granted the Microsoft Office suite, even though almost every individual in your company uses it.

You could organize and provide training for new employees and power users. Organize training for e-mail, another commodity application we provide our users. There are new tips and shortcuts in every version, so if you investigate some common tips that your users can take advantage of and pass those tips on in a newsletter or short training program, you will have an opportunity to add value. Make sure that any training you provide is tailored somewhat to your business processes to get the full benefit. You can also organize brown-bag lunches so that users can ask basic technology questions regarding security or other items they don't normally question. There are many topics you can use, but just by opening the lines of communication and making the IT organization available, you can take a step in helping other departments better understand what IT does and how IT helps a company grow.

Portfolio Management and the IT Steering Committee

IT serves many types of customers within an organization. These can be defined as executive leaders and regular day-to-day end users, and they can be broken up in the following way.

- Executive leaders
  - Steering committee
  - Business division leaders
  - Functional groups leaders
- End users

The most powerful customers are the executive leaders. Usually they are part of the IT steering committee, which approves the funding and decides on IT strategy. Most IT employees usually work only with the end users and often are eager to satisfy them. It is important to remember that IT priority and funding are defined by the executive leaders, who could prevent IT from fully satisfying all of the end-user needs.

Governance

Using the IT Steering Committee

The IT steering committee's primary goal is to ensure that IT strategic direction and project prioritization are aligned with the business strategy. IS steering committee meetings should be held on a regular basis (minimum quarterly) to review and approve IT strategies, project prioritization, policies, and investments. The committee usually is composed of senior management such as CIO, COO, CEO, CFO and functional leaders. Since IT supports multiple functional groups, every group believes its projects are most important. If the prioritization of IT projects cannot be mutually agreed upon by the various functional groups, the IT steering committee will play a pivotal role in deciding which projects are more important, or may decide to allocate more funds for IT to perform the additional projects.

Giving Each Business Unit a Voice

To effectively use portfolio management as a business alignment tool, you must give each business unit a voice in deciding which projects are added to the queue, which projects are funded, and what the business value is for each project. Having the business participate in a steering committee also gives it input into determining which projects should be worked on. More importantly, it provides you with a partner on the business side who can help fight for each project's funding.

IT supports the entire corporation. The CIO must view requests from horizontal versus vertical points of view to ensure that any new project can be easily integrated with other systems. The CIO must act as a change agent and coordinator with other functional groups to ensure that all are involved. Strong leadership is critical in resolving conflict and self-serving interests. Lastly, the CIO must work with all functional group leaders to ensure that a global project represents all functional and regional business requirements.

For example, an organization needs an HR work-flow system. Without a collaborated effort, a functional group in the United States might develop a solution for U.S. use, while Asia and Europe will develop one for their respective region. Each region views its systems as best. If the three regional groups worked together at the beginning under a strong CIO leadership, the development could be consolidated to meet all regional requirements. There may have to be some compromise in some of the regions, but in the end, the company will have one global system. The CIO must take on the proactive leadership role to bring all business groups together to build and develop business systems.

Portfolio Management

A well-defined portfolio management process is essential in trying to align your IT organization with the business. Portfolio management is a way of looking at all projects in the IT organization as one or more groups of projects, or *portfolios*. By looking at the projects in a portfolio view, you have the ability to assign and align each project to set business objectives, which is the ultimate goal in aligning IT with the business. Used right, the project portfolio will become more than just a list of projects. For each project, a successful project portfolio will include a business sponsor, priority, project type, business value, and business objective. Additionally, you can use the portfolio process as a way of measuring the success of each project by creating a success factor for each project, and measuring this factor during and after the project is completed.

Project Sponsor

Each project should have a key business sponsor. This should be the business representative who will help provide direction from the business side, and more importantly, the businessperson who should help fight for funding.

Priority

It's up to you to assign priority levels that make sense for your organization. You can use numerical assignments (1, 2, 3) or descriptive (high, medium, low). No matter what scale you use, ensure that the business users have a say into this priority. This input should come from the senior business management and functional leaders that participate in the IT Steering Committee.

Type

You can break the projects into three types:

1. Run
2. Grow
3. Transform

Run is for those projects that are needed to keep the business running (that "keep the lights on"). *Grow* is for projects that will help the business grow in some manner. *Transform,* which may or may not apply to your company, is reserved for those projects that will have a real transformation impact on the business. Typically, companies initially find that 80 to 85 percent of all projects are under the run type. The goal over time is to decrease this percentage so that more of the IT projects are geared toward enabling the business to grow projects, rather than just maintaining the status quo.

Business Value

These values are a way to group your projects into generic business propositions that can be used to demonstrate what the IT projects are being used for. Values might include effectiveness, efficiency, revenue improvement, employee satisfaction, customer satisfaction, cost reduction, and mandatory (regulatory), for example. You don't need them all, but you should come up with a list that makes sense for your company so that you can easily categorize your projects into business values. I have successfully used these value groups in the past.

Business Objective (Company Specific)

Ideally, you are able to apply a real, company-specific objective for as many projects as possible. These objectives should be in company terms and should make sense to management. Some examples are to increase contact network, improve investor relations, reduce product development time, improve operational profitability, and enhance research capabilities. These are only examples, but any objectives need to make sense to you and your organization. If you can come up with four to six objectives that you can apply to most of your projects, you'll go a long way in getting management to understand what IT is working on, and the value that IT brings to an organization.

Deliver

Expectations

A couple of notes as it relates to expectations whenever you discuss your IT projects with management: You lose credibility fast if IT is always late and continually underdelivers, so always remember that it is best to underpromise and overdeliver on your projects. Expect projects to take longer and cost more money. No matter how good your team is, things happen that are out of your control. Additionally, understand that the estimates provided to you by your team are usually aggressive and not always accurate. Business priorities change, and external factors can wreak havoc with your portfolio. Factor those in and set expectations accordingly.

Commitment and Delivering

The CIO, by job title, exudes an aura of limitless knowledge. It is necessary for the CIO to anticipate where current developments are heading, and how problematic areas can be conquered while staying within budget, subject to reduction. Trying to solve mundane, time-consuming tech-support questions can take up too much time.

It is critical for the senior executives to trust the CIO. This will encourage open views in mediating conflicts. Job priorities are flexible and subject to change, based on unforeseen factors uncovered through research and/or integration. All of this takes place while keeping the customer of the project informed of progress in a timely manner. When deciding on a request, the CIO must quickly evaluate the potential cost, benefit derived, and usefulness obtained. Then the CIO must determine if the new project aligns with business strategy. Such evaluations must be made honestly, disregarding pressures one way or the other from subordinates, and especially from superiors. Having a good working relationship with end users and senior management will go a long way toward helping the CIO avoid those pressures.

Once the commitment is made, it is the CIO's responsibility to deliver. If new priorities interfere with the previously committed deliverables, IT leaders must notify the customers, seek solutions, and reprioritize if necessary. Usually, IT project managers are aware of potential issues that may cause project delay, and it is important to share information with business users and senior management as soon as an issue arises. Recognize what cannot be changed and work with it until circumstances force current procedures to be analyzed. Determine where change is feasible and—through communication, persuasion or conflict—determine the most painless way to reach your goals, all the while keeping people informed of your progress.

IT serves two internal customers. One is the executive management (the true customer) and the other is the end users. These two customers' needs are not necessarily aligned. The senior management is more concerned with how IT can be a competitive advantage and help to achieve business goals at the lowest cost. The end users may only worry about why the network is slow today, who can help after hours, and so on. Each is important in its own way. IT has to satisfy both customers. It is critical to establish realistic expectations. For example, if IT is not funded to have a 24/7 help desk, it is unrealistic for the end users to expect 24/7 support. IT must inform end users of such constraints; if support is required on a consistent basis, IT must ask for funding. Without establishing a clear expectation, IT is often being blamed as unresponsive.

It is management's responsibility to ensure the team is delivering according to project plan. Try to assume that you have the best of the best working in various functions. Everyone must be informed of both short-term and long-term goals, using teamwork to reach them. People should be assigned to roles most suited for their abilities and should be informed of available support. People should not be pressured by unachievable goals.

Conclusion

In this section, we have tried to describe what it means for an IT shop to team up with its customers, and we have relied heavily on our own personal experience in this area. Working together with our customers we can create a win-win environment for all.

Learning from Our Mistakes: How to Avoid Pitfalls

Judy Armstrong

Introduction

There are a few things that every person wants to avoid, ignore, side-step, or push off onto someone else. Mistakes are on the top of the list. None of us wants to make a mistake, and when we do, we would as soon ignore them as admit to them.

This is in itself a mistake. You all have heard and have probably said that if you are not making mistakes, you are not working hard enough or being creative enough. This is true. No matter how good we are at what we do, mistakes are inevitable and are a sign that you are willing to take risks. The key is learning—I'll say it again, *learning*—from those mistakes. The second key is not to make the same mistake the same way again. Sometimes events create a similar situation, but your reaction (better still, your action) must contain the learning from the past event.

I know this all sounds obvious, but I can tell you from experience that, in general, people *do not* learn from mistake but, rather, look for reasons to excuse the results. As a CIO, you are the leader of your organization. If you show a willingness to admit and learn and support the same from your team, then your team will be willing to take the extra step, knowing that well-thought-out, if somewhat risky, steps can and will be rewarded.

As a CIO you most likely have an enhanced skill set. If you are in training to become a CIO, you need an enhanced skill set. This includes spending part of you career in areas that are not your expertise. To truly function well as a CIO, you need to have enough understanding of all the areas you manage to know fact from fiction.

To achieve this, you are absolutely going to make some errors in decisions and actions. This is your opportunity to learn and remember so that you can pass along "jewels of wisdom" to each and every member of your team when you have the top job. Many of the challenges that you will face are not technical. As a matter of fact, the most difficult to embrace and the most painful are not technical- but people-oriented. You will be presented with personalities that are diametrically opposite to yours; you will get trapped in lies and subterfuge, you will believe you know the right direction to take based on fact, only to find out that fact is not the key component to that particular decision. All of these and more will be presented to you on your path forward.

The purpose of this chapter, actually the whole book, is to help you learn from our mistakes. I will share some of my own painful experiences and hope that they will help you to better learn from your mistakes and not to look at them as something that needs to be avoided, but rather, as something that can be turned into a win, at least for yourself. Let's start with some of the easier things—the ones that don't involve personalities. Again, you may look at these and say *of course I know this,* but I continue to be amazed at the number of companies that do not employee these obvious measures to help ensure success and avoid chaos. First, let's take a look at operations.

Operations

Never Ignore Release Control

Every organization, no matter how small, needs to have a defined *release control.* This resides in operations, because operations takes the hit if something goes wrong, and the chances are, it will. What happens when there is little or no release control?

Everyone suffers when releases are not bundled, reviewed, and approved before being released. Projects step on each other, each day presents opportunities for misadventure, and your team is always on alert and focused on the short-term activities, which results in less-than-optimal productivity for your staff, as well as for the rest of the company.

This can be a simple process to institute. It most certainly will be more complex as your systems and processes become more interwoven, but if you have started with the basics, it will grow in a more controlled and defined environment. Expectations will be set, and there will be less push back to the tighter controls that needs to be in place.

Three controls should be in place:

1. *Create a change control board responsible for defining and managing the change process.* This board needs to include at least one person from all major departments in your organization: PMO (if you have it), applications (all major applications), DBA, network, servers, desktop, and help desk. This group needs to meet weekly and be made aware

of what will be in the next scheduled release, and changes to the agreed schedule or content, and any emergency changes made since the last release.

2. *Define the release schedule and stick to it.* I suggest starting with a weekly release schedule.

3. *Define, clearly, what constitutes an emergency release.* If something is obviously broken, or is preventing ordering, manufacturing or shipping product with no work around, then this is an emergency and should be fixed and implemented off schedule. A clear, simple approval process must be in place and followed. A predefined designation hierarchy must in place, in case an approver is not available.

Always Automate Version Control

No matter how small your organization, there needs to be an automated mechanism for controlling changes to software and maintaining versions control. This responsibility belongs to *applications*. It is not the responsibility of the team who moves code to production to know if the current release contains the right version. There are simple and inexpensive solutions that require very little to maintain and less effort to use than trying to manually control the revisions. With manual controls, it is next to impossible to roll back if necessary.

An added benefit is to have three environments for development, testing, and production. This allows for making the mistakes that are inevitable, without impacting the business, and it keeps many of the mistakes localized.

Clearly Understand Your Security Needs

The answer to how to design the best security system is not in this chapter. There are several good books on how to implement security for your company. At least one of the authors in this book is an expert in this area. However, this area is beyond the scope of this book; it is mentioned here as a warning, given that if you overlook understanding your company's security needs you will end up in a pit for sure.

You can over secure as well as under secure. The key here is to secure the right things well and not to worry about everything. All data are not equal. IT has the responsibility to secure the network and the servers. Conducting an annual security audit is a sensible practice and will help you avoid a nasty pitfall.

Another key is to put access rights to data into the hands of the people who own the data. That is not IT. Have a process where IT only grants access once given permission by the owners.

The closer you can get to single sign-on, the more conscientious users will be about managing their passwords. Regardless of how much people complain, make them change their passwords every ninety days.

There can be too much control. When it comes to securing your company's intellectual collateral, however, there is never too much control. You need to know what is collateral and what isn't. If you over control nonessential information, people may treat all information as nonessential.

As you start thinking about security issues, these concerns and others will naturally emerge. If you shortchange these items, you could be heading for an easily avoidable disaster.

Applications

System Lifecycle Methodology—Call It What You Will, but Organize and Manage Your Requests

I will venture to say that if you have a well-defined *system lifecycle methodology* that people can understand and follow, you will be a long way down the road to avoiding many of the prominent pitfalls in applications.

The *number-one* rule here is that IT does not own business requests. The minute IT takes ownership for business decisions, you are on the single most dangerous path to failure. IT as a business may make requests, and that is the appropriate time for IT to own the outcome. Every CIO has a horror story that he or she can share related to willingly (or not) taking ownership for a non-IT business project's success. We are project managers, not business managers. We always want to partner with the intent that business decisions are made by the business. A large-scale non-IT project must be led by a business program or project manager with supporting project management roles from IT and outside vendors.

Keep it simple, but cover these ten bases:

1. Always require a help desk ticket for any request.
2. Require a written request from users describing the *end result* they want to achieve. This should never be written by IT.
3. Define the various paths that a request can follow. Not all requests have to have the same rigor applied to them:
   - Bug
   - Simple requests
     - Single system, single user
     - Single system, multiple users
   - Complex requests
     - Multiple Systems, same organization
     - Multiple Systems, Cross Functional
   - Major projects
4. Collect, categorize, and prioritize all requests that are not *bugs*. I suggest that a steering committee be formed to prioritize complex requests and major projects. All other requests should be grouped into scheduled releases and can be prioritized between IT and the owning organization.
5. Require functional specifications for complex changes and major projects. The need to be reviewed by business owner, applications, and operations with sign-off required. This will avoid several pitfalls within and outside of IT.

6. Require a test plan. The test plan developers and the business owners will use testing to validate the success of the project.

7. Require technical specifications if the project is going offshore or is complex enough to require a separate document from the functional specification. This document needs to be reviewed by the developers and the analysts and signed off by the stakeholder(s).

8. Require test plan sign-off.

9. Follow the prescribed release schedule process.

10. Require post project review for any major project or any request that did not work after it went into production—learn from those mistakes!

Just remember that our job in IT is to provide service. At times, IT may know more than the business owner—great! Just make sure that IT assists the company's leaders in making the decision by sharing the knowledge within IT. In the end, the business determines the success or failure of a request; therefore, the decision on what the outcome should be is theirs. Our job is not to be right. It is to be knowledgeable and solution oriented, with the understanding that there is more than one way to solve a problem.

Now the road gets a little rougher. At a minimum, you need that system lifecycle methodology, but even better is to have some semblance of an architecture and roadmap. It would be great if your company could commit to looking at architecture from a holistic perspective, but if it can't, then pick and choose what you can and begin to build your future.

It is a mistake to believe the IT can determine what needs to be done. If you want to be a successful IT leader, you need to involve the business on a more strategic level. The business needs to have "skin in the game" or you will most likely be perceived as *not* delivering what is needed. So, in order to help us help ourselves, we need an architecture roadmap or framework of where we are and where we need to be. This, like many of the actions I am suggesting, does not have to be complex—just comprehensive.

Architecture or Roadmap

The *architecture* or *roadmap* provides a strategic planning framework that relates and aligns information technology with the business functions that it supports.

There are four major components to a complete roadmap. However, each company must determine how much of this is necessary or relevant, based on the ability of the company to absorb, adopt, and implement the strategies and technologies:

1. Business architecture
2. Information architecture
3. Portfolio (application) architecture
4. Technical architecture

Business Architecture

Business architecture defines the business of the company. Generally, it provides the following:

- It contains a business model that defines the business functions of the company independent of the organizations that perform those functions.
- It contains the current and future state models of business functions and who performs those functions.
- It defines the enterprise business goals and objectives.

Information Architecture

Information architecture describes the enterprise's information flows/value chains:

- It is based on the business functions defined in the business architecture and the business model.
- It identifies the key data elements of the defined business functions.
- It extends data flow beyond organizational boundaries to external sources and targets.

Portfolio Architecture

The portfolio architecture is the collection of information systems (applications and dependent technologies, purchased or developed) supporting the business functions defined in the business architecture and the business model. This includes the following:

- Current inventory of applications and components
- Planned applications and components needed to fulfill unsatisfied and EIA requirements
- Migration plans for moving the existing portfolio toward the planned portfolio

Technical Architecture

The technical architecture is a consistent set of information technology standards, and models with the following characteristics:

- They reflect and support the previously defined architectures.
- They guide the design and development of an organization's information systems and technology infrastructure across the various architectures.
- They include eight technical areas:
  1. Applications
  2. Database
  3. Enterprise systems management
  4. Information
  5. Integration

6. Network and telecommunications
7. Platform
8. Security

There are several models or frameworks that can be adopted, such as the Zachman Framework. However, they can also be very complex. The idea is to document what the current state is (as-is), what future state (to-be) is desired, what positive measurable impact the changes will make, and how the architecture strategy will be executed (publish the roadmap, define the impact on the organizations, define gaps in staff and technology, prepare recommendations for governance process).

Although the architecture helps to understand where you are and where you are going and the foundation upon which the company will operate, it will be necessary to make sure that you get there in a way that is measurable and can be tracked from a financial, priority and compliance perspective. To do this, you need a governance process.

Governance

The process is straightforward; the execution of the process is what is difficult. It requires commitment from the highest level of management, and a lot of due diligence (and marketing) before presenting a recommendation:

1. *Prepare the IT strategic plan based on the desired to-be model.* Make sure you are aligned with the business priorities.
2. *Create a high-level value proposition for each initiative.* The value proposition contains the business problem being addressed, the value in tangible and nontangible benefits, what impact it will have people, finances, and the organization, and how the success of the initiative can and will be measured.
3. *Make sure recommendations are aligned with the architecture roadmap.* There should be a group of people established to review all initiatives against the architecture.
4. *Present prioritizations, approval, and funding requests to the executive body that oversees strategic investments.* This group of overseers can be called many things. Most often, it is called the IT steering committee..
5. *Create detail plans using a system lifecycle methodology, which includes various reviews during the analysis, development, testing, and implementation process.* At critical junctures, the architecture review team needs to make sure that standards and guidelines are being followed and architecture directions are being adhered to.
6. *Put in place a portfolio management and project management process.* This does not have to be complex or expensive. Make sure you have access to and know the status of *any* request made to IT. Have a defined way to categorize requests (bug, small, medium, large, etc.). Know the value of any request to the company and whether it fits into the architecture. Track progress on requests in process both from a time and financial perspective. This includes people's time. If you do not know where people are spending

their time you will not be able to do a thorough job of planning and delivering. This can be accomplished with a simple spreadsheet and does not require a time management system.

7. *Communicate often and about those things that matter to the business.* A status report should be created on a monthly basis and published. Generally, when everyone knows progress is being published and posted openly, in the company, they will be more diligent about their deliveries.

If you keep this straightforward and simple, you can institute these processes even in the smallest company. The failure comes in trying to over engineer the process. Also, involve your staff and other business people in developing the mechanisms that you will use. This way, they have helped to build the environment and tools.

Now we come to the more difficult pitfalls, because they have to do with people—helping people, listening to people, training people, organizing people. So much of this is company culture, and therefore it is difficult to foresee. However, here are a few ideas that you can keep in mind.

Helping People

Help Desk Support—Yes, You Need It

People always need help. Some more than others, but there is a minimum amount of help that everyone needs sooner or later. This means that you need some kind of help desk support.

There are so many ways that a help desk can be supplied that I will not spend any time telling you how to do it. At minimum, you can outsource it. What I can tell you is that the worst help desk approach is to leave a message on voicemail. People need to believe that someone out there cares that they have a problem. So, at minimum, put together a simple Web site that allows people to report a problem and get a ticket number. (We feel better when we have something to track.) Or, if you outsource the process, make sure that the people who are doing the work have a site or someone that answers the phone.

The next thing to remember is that all requests deserve a response, even if the response is negative. People need to know that something will or will not be done, and approximately when they can expect some action. They want to know that when it is complete, they will be notified that you believe the problem is addressed. (At the point where the action is deemed complete, the customer should also have to acknowledge that it is fixed . . . or it is just your opinion.)

If you are a global company, it is not good enough to have a help desk at headquarters or people on call at headquarters. If this is as far as you take your customer service, you could end up with a company full of resentful people. This is a very good opportunity for outsourcing the help desk, unless you have staff in all your major locations. Local support is extremely important. It is always easier to explain a problem when you can use your own language and local customs.

Additionally, many people now work from home as a normal part of their workday, and most of them are not technical experts. If this is the case in your company, then it is absolutely necessary to have standards around network access, and minimum requirements for home network configurations. Standard equipment should be given to employees, with very clear instructions on how to get support for the installation and maintenance of the equipment. Think of the telecommuter's home like you would a remote sales office (which it often is).

Listening To People—Yes, You Need To

You will learn more about how IT is perceived and how you are really supporting the organization by asking questions and truly listening to the answers. The number-one pitfall that we all struggle with is to listen without defenses. Our natural inclination is to protect and defend our territory, our people, and our decisions. Does this mean that everything people will say to you is true? No! It means that people form their own perceptions of others.

I am not a big fan of surveys, as they are too anonymous and there is never enough data to really correct a perception or problem. However, they can be a starting place if they are reviewed as a beginning and not an end result.

I think it is best to work from the outside in when asking people what is working well and what could be improved. This gives you a measurement, which can be used to determine your staff's view of the very same questions. This will let you see immediately whether both sides view a problem as *being* a problem—a good place to start—and where they differ. Those areas where they differ can then be investigated for root causes and recommendations for changing the perception or fixing the problem. Often, human resources can help at this stage, or you can contract out to get a more unbiased opinion.

What I recommend you do *not* do is conduct a survey and then do nothing. You are better off guessing at what to fix then conducting a survey, which holds out a promise for change, and then ignoring the results. This is especially true with your internal staff. Their perception of you as a leader will be irreparably damaged if you ignore their concerns.

Remember that when all is said and done, information technology is a service organization. Although IT is definitely a critical operation, it is the functions that design, make, and sell the product that pay for our services. They care about what their customers think about the products and services they sell. So, we can take a lesson from their book and do the same for them, our customers.

There is a deeper listening and interaction that also needs to take place, and is an abyss if it is ignored. You need to interact with your customers or you will fall into that abyss. Ask questions of and listen to the responses from your business owners. You may not always have the whole picture, so, while you may think you know the answer or direction that a particular business owner should take, it behooves you to understand what the leaders of the company think and want before you start to sell your solution. It is imperative that you treat your relationship with all company leaders as a partnership, but one that is not always 50/50. If corporate executives have a solution that works with the architecture, supports their goals and those of the business, and is approved by the customer then it is a good solution—don't fight it. Save your energy for the times when it doesn't fit.

Training People—Yes, You Need to Do This, Too

All too often, when the time comes to cut the budget, and it always does, the first thing that goes is training. What many people do not understand—and what makes it a pitfall—is the longer-term increase effects this has on the budget. One of the reasons people leave an organization is that they become stagnant, or believe they are. When we cut out all training and seminars, it leaves people with the impression that the company thinks people are less important than the technology they support (or try to support, as it starts to get away from them). If we do not train people on upgrades and new technologies, the costs spent on learning, mistakes, and re-learning will far outweigh the budget cuts—never mind the cost of missed project deadlines.

Look at creative ways to leverage training, such as sending one or two people and having them write a white paper or doing internal brown-bag sessions on what they learned. Build training into every project's cost, not as separate line items but as part of the analysis or development costs.

Organizing People

This is my last pitfall subject. There is no right answer here, just a few things to think about when you are considering how best to organize or reorganize IT.

IT is most often organized as either centralized or decentralized, and within that it is organized by business function (finance, manufacturing, infrastructure), technology (Oracle, Agile), and/or skills (DBAs, business analysts, developers, etc.).

The pitfall is in not understanding your company culture enough to organize most effectively for the company you are in. We often tend to fall back on what has worked for us in the past, and that is not always the best for the current place and time.

If you are a global company, and some or all of your business functions are dispersed, then it may make sense to be decentralized. If your company is undisciplined and does not have any support, or a process for managing a portfolio, prioritizing projects, and budgeting based on value, then this will be a challenge to manage. The pitfall is the many rogue IT expenditures that you eventually end up supporting, with no easy way to integrate them. If you can, try to get your purchasing policy to state that any IT related expenses, that are used by more than one person, be approved by IT for architecture fit. The best case for centralization is control, which, with Sarbanes-Oxley, is more justifiable, than it may have been in the past. It may be more cost effective, but it requires a lot more marketing and selling of solutions to be successful.

I think one of the best models is to combine these by having the business functions decentralized and the infrastructure functions centralized. I believe that certain pieces of IT should always be centrally managed. The key areas are the network, security (especially since we are now controlled by Sarbanes-Oxley), e-mail systems, and telecommunications.

The reality is that no one can tell you how to organize. It is highly dependent on the way your company operates. If the departments are loosely coupled or operate as separate business units within the parent company with P&L responsibility, then it is highly unlikely that a centralized IT department will be successful.

Just remember that to organize against the company culture will be an upstream battle, and one that you will most likely lose. Get buy-in if you are planning on reorganizing. Don't do it in a vacuum. Yes, it is your organization, but your success is based on the perception that you support the business well. So, make sure the company can live with your model before you institute it.

I am sure there are a hundred more areas where pitfalls are lurking. This chapter has tried to make you aware of a few and, with that, hopefully you will keep your eyes and ears open and look for those that are waiting to snag you and your staff. Foresight is forewarning, and it is worth taking the extra time to look at your decisions from multiple perspectives.

One final thought on pitfalls has to do with decision making. In my mind, the biggest pitfall of all is in not making a decision and letting things happen. I believe it is better to make a decision and be wrong—because at least you had a basis for your decision and can most likely defend it—than it is to fail because the decision was made for you. Be thoughtful, ask questions, listen to the answers, understand the value, then make that decision and live with it. Don't second-guess your decisions; it is a waste of time. Spend those mental cycles on making your decision a success.

3.3
Defining Line of Sight from Strategy to Execution

Sunny Azadeh

Introduction

The company I had been with had recently gone through a major restructuring as a result of a leveraged buy-out, a down market, and bad company strategy. My boss, who was the CIO, had left, and the new CEO and COO wanted to see the IT budget drop from 7 percent of revenue to 2 percent. It is worth mentioning that there was a major investment in IT during the preparation for Y2K, and we were in year two of the five-year depreciation schedule, during which time the company revenue had dropped by 75 percent.

This was my first introduction to the CIO role, where there was pressure from all aspects of the business, market growth was declining in the United States and there was a major shift to Asia, our company was going through bankruptcy and heavy restructuring, company strategy was to expand to Asia and heavily leveraging outsourced partnerships, company employees were worried about their role in the new company, and I was getting calls from the CEO and COO at all hours of the day about their vision of IT being outsourced to save cost.

I had a problem to solve, which at first glance looked impossible. How could I extend services to Asia, extend services around the globe to many outsourced partners, maintain my services to existing locations, and prepare for major cost reduction, while leveraging the investment that the company had in the IT? How could I become a variable percentage of revenue while company revenue is declining? How could I manage change if I had to roll out a new technology, and most of all, what would I do about my team?

This chapter is about the vision of IT as enabling organization, developing strategies in line with business needs, putting together the plan and the team to execute the strategy, and communicating to the business and the global team.

Ingredients for Successful Strategy and Execution

If I had to simplify the type of companies and where they see IT strategies, I would categorize them as follows:

- *Early adopters.* The company believes in IT as enabling organization and understands that having a winning strategy is inclusive of information technology.
- *Late bloomers.* The company has grown successfully in revenue model and has reached a point where further growth in the company is not possible without a change in the information technology structure.
- *Procrastinators.* IT pockets are growing in many departments and many point solutions are delivered with no long-term value. Although the company can see there is a problem, it is not able to see how investing in the right IT strategy will streamline many of the operational deficiencies and help reduce risk for the company, even if the company was struggling with growth.

I have been fortunate to have had first-hand experience all three, and over time have developed what I call ingredients for successful strategy. While there is no one answer in developing the right strategy for your company, there are many questions in common that will lead you through the way. My focus here is more around the key questions and some of the common answers.

Vision

Vision is all about the value of IT. How as an IT leader you can lead your company and your team to success? What do want IT to be when it is at its best?

The vision is derived from series of activities: interviews with your business partners and internal customers, assessing current state of your assets and liabilities, review of your company strategy, trends in technology, value of IT in your organization and most importantly, your passion around your craft and the people that inspire you, and that you believe in. My passion is around my customers being external and internal—helping my company succeed and contributing to the growth of my people. Ask yourself, what is your passion?

If you develop a scorecard for these attributes and simply applied a measure of 1 to 10, is a perfect 10 needed in all areas to achieve success? Most importantly, what does success look like for you and your environment? It is one of the easier questions that, as CIOs, we sometimes do not ask the right people.

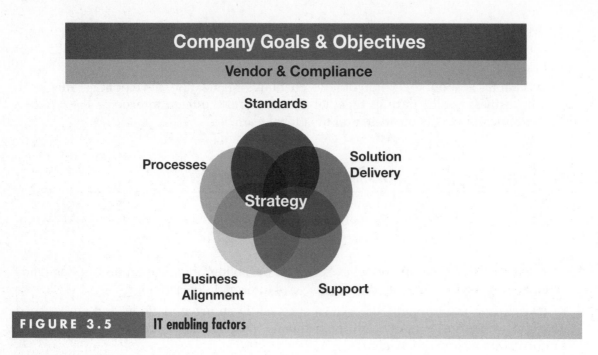

FIGURE 3.5 | IT enabling factors

Strategy

I have developed over the years a rule that I call the *rule of three*. Given that as humans we can only remember plus or minus seven things, and corporate memory is short term, this rule has allowed me to develop a framework for strategy around the four pillars as described next. What three major services can I provide within the next three years that affects the three areas of the company around revenue/cost, people and processes? The question of technology will be derived once the three other items are put in place. The next rule of three I incorporate is, what are the three major *unknowns* that could impact this strategy?

Here are the four pillars of strategy:

1. *Company strategy.* In a changing global market with heavy emphasis on merger and acquisitions, uncertainties in the business and rapid change in technology, most company strategies are short term and address three to five years. The trend we have seen in 2004 to now allow consolidation through M&A and outsourcing—in my opinion—will continue for a decade. A good IT strategy will address the unknown while focusing on known components of the business. Going back to rule of three, what can IT deliver in three years, which gets you closer to the vision and is in line with company goals and objectives?

2. *List of services.* IT is a service organization. Assessing the state of current services, what services will be required within the next three years. What other service providers are in your industry? This is a key component of the IT strategy. What are the top three services you provide for your company? Where can you get the best value? How do you expand or shrink these services for the unknown?

3. *Industry influences.* A successful strategy must include outside influences. What does the market look like for our services providers such as ERP, Telecom, Back Office, secu-

rity? What government or country or vertical industry regulations do we foresee influencing our global market? Major players in this market, such as Microsoft, Oracle, SAP, AT&T, Singtel, and so on will affect your three-year plan. Do you remember the change in Windows OS and the impact it had on your budget and plans?

4. *Technology trends.* We are living in an exciting time where many of the buzzwords a decade ago are becoming reality, Software-as-a-Service (SaaS), grid computing, virtualization, provisioning, wireless and voice-over Internet protocol (VOIP), and service-oriented architecture (SOA) are all reality. What technology trends will influence the list of services from IT, your industry, and your company strategy? How does this fit within the vision? Here is the most important question: Is there a competitive advantage for your company to be part of the early adapters in this area?

Team

The CEO, CFO, or the COO hired you to put together a strategy, either because your predecessor had failed or it is a blank slate and you are putting it all together. For the most part, it is probably the former rather than the latter.

You have spent a lot of time building what you consider a successful strategy. You are passionate about it; you think it is right, ties to the vision, and delivers value. Are you ready to sell your vision? Not if you have not looked at the team you need to execute. Going back to rule of three, when you start assessing the skill sets you need to develop the dream team, you will find out that you have to do at least one of the following:

- *Cultivate.* They do not exist, and you must hire or develop people with the needed skill sets within your organization.
- *Harvest.* There are hidden stars within the organization who share the passion and can see the vision. They have the skill sets to grow and, in some parts, are ready for change.
- *Infuse.* These are people within your company but not within your group. In this case, you have to infuse the knowledge within your group and build the informal internal teams or have a solid plan around staff augmentation with key partners or both.

We will talk about establishing line of sight at the end of this chapter, so hold that thought while we focus on building the team you need to be successful.

Having worked in extreme levels of organizations in form of maturity and tenure in years, I would recommend building on the foundation of people you have and infusing knowledge through staff augmentation strategy, new talent in the organization or a new leader to shift the thought process. With all staff, you need to create a win/win situation by focusing on their careers and skill sets and the value they will receive from being part of the team. In terms of skill sets and career path, financial rewards could be an outcome but cannot be the only driver for teamwork.

In my first CIO role, the company was downsizing in all areas while IT delivered 110 projects within the first year, working on a variety of activities: major ERP upgrade, cost reduction by 30 percent, overhaul of our external Web site, expansion of CRM capabilities to our partners, consolidation of data centers, and closing manufacturing sites while opening new design centers in Asia. The team worked hard not because it had a monetary incentive to do so, because it saw the vision, understood the value, and saw what it could do for their career paths and skill sets.

There can be no strategy without execution, and no execution without a team.

Execution

Many times I have seen failed strategies due to poor execution—more often in business than in IT. This may partly be due to IT being viewed as cost center in a local economy. I believe, however, that with the global expansion of companies and the global economy, U.S. companies have started to see the value of IT strategies. It is a great problem to have as IT leaders. Without failure, there is no success, and without execution, strategies will only be a vision and a dream.

Building an execution plan around a strategy should be addressed in what can be delivered in three years based on business needs first and is in line with company strategy, given the following parameters around the execution:

- *Incremental results in measurable time by quarter.* Many of us have managed or been in environments where project delivery extends beyond six months. I have seen ERP or CRM projects going in nine- to twelve-month phases where the objectives have changed, business has changed, or the team dynamics have changed.
- *Quarterly assessment of where you are against the plan for the current quarter, next two quarters, and the next eighteen months.* Are you working on the right projects, or do you need to reprioritize? What is the impact on the company goals and objectives?
- *Accountability tools.* Establish accountability and metrics for the objectives and measure your team accordingly.

Line of Sight

We have come to the end of this chapter, and so far we have talked about many aspects of line of sight—including, for example, enabling visions, successful strategies, winning teams, and great execution. The most important aspect of all is communication, communication, and communication.

I remember when I went on my first business trip as the CIO to our center of excellence, where we wanted to offshore many activities in Asia. I presented my strategy to the largest organization of our company, and the first reaction from the general manager was, "I have been here for over twenty years, and this is the first time I have seen a strategy presented for IT, where we are asked to participate on roadmap and execution." Much to my surprise, it was also the first time they had seen the alignment between company objectives, what our site does remotely, and how IT will enable them to achieve their goals. Apparently, the many visitors previously were more interested in what they wanted done, versus sharing what could be accomplished together.

Communication is a key success factor within the business. We all march better if we know where we are going and the path we need to take—for the most part, the IT strategy will require change in behavior within the organizations. The key factor is to establish a line of sight and become a salesperson for the vision, strategy, and execution for your team.

What works in your company in forms of communication? Some organizations are very formal through governance boards, steering committees, and large corporate structures. Others more informal in communication and execute on key decisions based on a conversation from key influencers. Identify which form works better for your company and structure.

Service organizations and functions are driven by many customers: the executive staff, the business, the IT team, and individual IT members. All four are critical to a successful execution.

Just as we started the strategy on four pillars, we could simplify the communication as the *four pillars of communication.* What you will need to communicate to each organization or individual is a different part of the same message from the 5,000-foot-level vision, down to, "What is in it for me?"

Executive Staff

Once the executive staff signs off on the IT strategy, you need to review the strategy with it on at least quarterly basis and communicate around the following aspects:

- Your perspective of where the business is going, and whether there is a change in strategy
- The next two quarter's projects, and what you accomplished last quarter in respect to achieving the strategy
- Where you need help or can see opportunities

Business

The business needs to know on a much lower level what you are doing for its group in achieving its goals and objectives, which may be fluctuating in time. In general, the operational committees are formed to address specific department or services needs and what you need to communicate to them and get feedback on the following:

- IT strategy focused on their services and validation
- Backlog review and prioritization for the next two quarters
- Change management and process improvement opportunities

IT Team

IT teams across the globe do not live the day-to-day activities of the corporate. They may deviate from the focus identified for accomplishing a global objective, specifically if they have been used to functioning in a self-sustaining environment. You need to communicate and get feedback on the following:

- IT strategy and what you know has changed in business assumption
- Collaboration around what needs to be done within the next six months
- What the teams need to succeed

Individual IT Members

This dialogue is sometimes the most time-consuming one; however, the investment has paid off for me, especially when developing the three-year plan.

The one factor that broken organizations have in common is that the individual IT members resist change, some due to not understanding a vision and how they can win, others because they are perceived as heroes who will step in and save the day.

Resistance to change is a common factor in many areas of IT, but to develop successful teams, you will need to get all your team players on board. You will need to communicate the following to your individual members:

- IT strategy and their role within the strategy
- What is in it for them, and how it lines up with where they are going
- What changes need to occur to make it a success

You have the vision, strategy, plan, and people lined up; how do you effect change in perception and behavior? By communicating and over communicating the vision and the roadmap to the vision on continuous basis.

Conclusion

It will be difficult for IT to be viewed as a partner in the business unless we develop and identify a method by which we can communicate the potential of what can be versus what is.

The passion, vision, strategies, execution, and the leadership styles we bring to our organization and companies are what make a successful CIO. We know there is a light at the end of the tunnel, and it is not a train—even though at times it appears as such. What is needed is to follow a simple principle of physics:

In order to see an object, you must have a direct line to the object. When you do, light will travel from that object to your eye along the line of sight.

Four Types of CIOs

Jennifer Diamond

A Tale of Two Misses

On a mythical street in Silicon Valley, at Megacorp 4Q, Inc., a very
excited meeting is taking place in the executive boardroom. Concep-
tualizing how to transfer 80 percent of the company's vast manufacturing operations to the new plant in China, the company's top management is reviewing a first shot at execution strategy.

"I think if we use a six-month phase conversion, we'll test capacity and all the other environmental conditions without a lot of risk,
Joe," says Brian, head of operations, to the CEO.

Evan, sales EVP, chimes in: "And in the meantime, the publicity
campaigns we're designing are hitting both the "better U.S. jobs"
angle and the "we build locally" message for Asia Pacific sales."

"Our lobbying arm has been working the Hill so we can leverage some of the upcoming diplomatic initiatives and get in on the
ground floor. There's a report on our approach in your packets."
Chief Counsel Andrea taps her copy of the three-inch black binder in
front of all the meeting attendees.

Joe turns to Mike, the CIO. "So where are we with IT to get 'er
done, huh, Mike? The IT plan in here looks kind of slim, and there's
not much in the way of timelines." Mike clears his throat. "Well,
that's the point, really. I can't tell you when we'll be investing until
you tell me what the revenue plans look like."

Joe stares. "What?" He looks around at the other bewildered faces. "Wh-what does revenue have to do with it?"

Mike shakes his head gently. "That's what I've been trying to say in the past few meetings on this. It's all well and good to get all gung-ho, but we have to remember that we're a big company with a big backbone to maintain." He points to a slim red binder in front of him, next to the big black one. "This is our IT project portfolio that was approved by the board, okay?" They nod.

"Now, if we were to divert the resources this manufacturing project needs from the approved portfolio, nothing else could get done!"

Joe speaks slowly. "Mike, we're talking about a completely new strategic initiative. What does initial planning on this project have to do with diverting resources from our existing portfolio, and why are you trying to incorporate revenues into the conversation?"

Mike blows out an exasperated breath. "Well, how else do you expect me to hold IT to 3 percent of revenue if I don't?"

Two blocks down the street, in a tiny leased space in one of hundreds of office parks with rotating name plates, three guys in shirtsleeves and loosened ties are huddled at a single workstation, pounding away at a spreadsheet.

"We've got the five-year R&D plan in there, rough estimates from year three on out, Bob."

"Great, Sudhir. Now we can lay in the joint agreements to see how that R&D is funded. Those guys at Harper are really going to be impressed with the initiative we're taking to get the business plan tightened down before the next funding meeting. Howard, where are we with the IT and facilities plan? You're the CIO, dude. What's the story?"

Howard leans back in his chair with a big smile. "Guys, I've got a surprise for you, something I've been working on for the past month." The other two sit back and look at him, grins forming in response to his obvious pride.

"Sudhir, you know how you were worried about how we were going to transfer designs and data back and forth to off shore labs and customers?" Sudhir nods. "And Bob, you know how you were worried that when we started having more and more partners and alliances, we wouldn't have the infrastructure to support them?"

"Yeah, Howard. We don't want to be those guys in the UPS commercial who freak out when their product starts selling."

"Exactly!" Howard stands up and reaches into his faded and beaten-up courier bag, withdrawing a fat, glossy folder with a flourish. "Voila! We are now outsourced! Data, tech support, application support, hosting, networks, the whole deal! We even have the help desk set up in the Philippines!"

Bob stands shakily, gripping the back of the chair. "We're contracted *now?* Howard, we don't even have second round funding. We're still negotiating the development contracts." His voice begins to rise. "The prototypes are still in my parent's garage!"

Howard smiles confidently and pats Bob's shoulder. "I know, I know, but aside from the really reasonable flat facility fees for the 24/7 data center, the rest of it is on a per-use basis."

Bob and Sudhir stare at him, slack-jawed, as he holds his arms out with a knowing grin. "Remember, guys, we have to think strategically!"

Where CIOs Go Wrong

Both Howard and Mike seem to be out of step with their customers, to put it mildly. And as exaggerations, we can laugh at the absurdity of their situations. But the fact remains that there has been no shortage of discussion on alignment between IT execs and the rest of the company. Somehow, CIOs by any title have gotten the reputation of being more vulnerable to not understanding the latest corporate strategy than other company leaders. And to be fair, that part may not be true. We all know that any company leader can be out of step: the HR VP who insists on obsolete qualifications in the face of major industry change, the CEO trying too hard to do the sales guy's job and ignoring the rest of the company, the CFO who's overemphasizing outside investments when some good, old-fashioned cost cutting is really what's called for.

But the CIO gets the rap for being the technologist out of place in the strategic planning session. Why is that? Part of it is just the fact that IT is still an unknown, and yet is so fundamental to business operation. Corporate leaders can cross many functional areas, but rarely do they include IT experience. It's fear of the technical aspects of IT, and if, as an business executive, I'm trying to run a business and I can't understand what you manage as a critical function for the business, I'll be darned sure I understand *you* as a fellow executive. More to the point, *you* have to understand *me.*

Part of it is that the nature of the CIO job is changing faster than any other corporate position. Let's face it. The head of R&D does the same thing now as he did a long time ago—thinks up new things and gets them to the manufacturing floor. Finance? Well, we know how fast that changes. It takes new laws to make big changes in accounting! But CIOs deal with the fact that the job scope doesn't even hold still, never mind trying to coming up with a baseline job description. What gets managed changes on a daily basis. The reason for this is that technology, the rate of investment required to use it, and the way to administer it, evolves and revolves faster and faster in relation to itself and those who use it. Your company's customers and suppliers drive what you use to run your business harder than the internal requirements do, and the offerings available to you barely keep pace.

And then there are the business unit leaders, from the chairman of the board on down, who read the twenty-word article in *CEO* magazine and are now experts in the truly current IT trends that they are now fully convinced absolutely must top the company's IT portfolio—standards (and vaporware issues) be damned. A CIO has to stay ahead of that curve just to be able to have the conversation.

But beyond that, and this is even harder, the role of the CIO within the company doesn't stay the same either, and just as you must know what your company's architecture needs to be, you also need to know how you, as the IT leader of your company, fit into the management architecture of your company.

Why Should There Be Different Types of CIOs?

Well, we just answered that, didn't we? Companies are in different states, needing different types of IT services, and it takes a different kind of account manager, in a sense, to serve the customer. So what is it about the customer that we need to know? How about the basics? What are the phases of corporate life cycles, and what kinds of business goals are involved? We had two examples, actually three, in the anecdotes at the start of this chapter.

4Q, Inc. is a big company with an existing operation that is looking to make a significant change in its operation to change or add capacity in the future. The little guy down the street is at a build-with-nothing phase, looking for very low investment.

There are a million ways to look at corporate life cycles, but for our purposes, we'll keep it simple and look at four phases, with their overarching goals for the company:

1. *Spark it:* Building/adding short-term capacity with low investment
2. *Grow it:* Creating sustainable capacity for ongoing business operation and growth
3. *Hold it:* Controlling costs in the face of steady capacity use and risk avoidance
4. *Trim it:* Retreating or diverting to alternate modes of operation

So 4Q, Inc. was going from hold to grow, making a significant change to the company's operations by moving their plant. The little guys, operating out of Bob's mom's garage and a rented office, were trying to spark their company with investment rounds. When we tie this back to IT strategy, you can see how the investment associated with growing and holding are very different from how much needs to be done with how little to spark or trim.

Howard and Mike are both good CIOs, sort of. They're both thinking long term, trying to apply good management technique. Mike is adhering to a portfolio, engaging management in defining IT priorities, and being a responsible corporate citizen. Howard is reaching to the marketplace to find solution alternatives to meet widely varying business needs. So what went wrong?

They applied right strategies at the wrong time. They weren't the right CIO for that phase in the company's life cycle.

Who Is a Good CIO?

Does this mean that a CIO is only good for one type of company at one time—some magic fit between company, life cycle phase, and CIO? Are there really different people who belong in a specific place and time?

We know that in the extreme, there are some people who do much better in highly entrepreneurial environments than in highly established ones. We know that there are folks who live for high volatility, and those who are the Rock of Gibraltar in a steady-state world. But aside from those extremes, we are learning, thinking, and adapting human beings. We just need to know *how* to adapt.

Leadership Characteristics

Let's begin with the ingredients. Before we decide what type of great CIO belongs where, let's identify what makes an IT leader great. We know, in this ever-volatile miasma of problems looking for solutions looking for problems, that there are key characteristics that must be present to for a CIO to survive. What are the hats that a CIO juggles every day?

- *Officer:* Be a full business participant.
- *Visionary:* Look to the horizon!
- *Technologist:* Know the field and the market.
- *Educator:* Teach, teach them all!
- *Controller:* Process and method makes it all tick and tie.
- *Executioner:* Get it done or get it gone.
- *Firefighter:* First responders save the day.

Let's look at them one at a time.

Officer

First and foremost, the great CIO is a member of the company's staff. Another way to look at it is that the customer always comes first. For the CIO, the immediate customer is the company, all of it, with its competing resource needs, strategic, tactical, and sustaining operations, its organizational and regional landscape, and its shareholder requirements. A CIO cannot succeed if he or she is not acutely aware that the job is within the context of the company.

Participating in the business means knowing the business. Products, markets, competition—the CIO has to be up on all sections of the *Wall Street Journal*, not just the Technology section. Relationships and alignment fall into this category, participating as a fellow business leader, a contributing team member, dedicated to company mission statement. Technology is the function; business success is the purpose.

Visionary

The great CIO knows that today's business or technology problems are today's. Tomorrow's will come, and there will be some the day after, too. Keeping an eye to the horizon makes sure that one of tomorrow's problems was not that you didn't see it coming. Having an idea of the long term, a plan for the nearer term, and a structure for what we have now is what makes a visionary a functioning member of corporate society. Without the breadcrumbs to take us from here to there, the vision is not particularly helpful. The highly functioning visionary knows that a vision no one else sees is just a delusion.

For the IT leader, the vision is the master plan that proves how business strategy will be served by an offering from IT that differs from what is available today, but that can be achieved. From incorporating new architecture to achieving service and performance metrics, targeting the future is what a visionary does.

Technologist

A technologist is not to be confused with the architect—or the support desk, for that matter. The technologist characteristic of a great CIO means knowing the field and the marketplace. What's hot and what's not is a knowledge set required for any business function, and IT is no exception. Only fashion changes as fast as the IT landscape.

So the technologist component to the great IT leader is a finessed one. Knowing enough to make a good decision without immersing too deeply is what makes a general and not a foot soldier. The CIO must keep view over the entire battlefield of technology to provide best business value.

Educator

Sell it. The CIO's job is to sell all the time. From selling the cost of a proposed solution against the business unit's expected benefits to selling the board on the five-year plan to selling the IT staff on the value of continued certification, you can call it education or you can call it sales, but at the end of the day, it's communicating.

A great IT leader knows that it's better to sell than tell. Telling informs. Teaching sustains. Selling creates advocates. Those who excel as leader-educators use all three, telling through ongoing disclosure and openness, teaching by example, and selling with a personal touch. We all still have instincts, no matter how hard we try to break them, that say knowledge is power. It's true, but only when you share it. It's why this book is in your hands.

Controller

But someone also has to mind the store. The controller institutes method and process, guidance and structure. It's not *just* about money, but does include it. The great CIO knows that to run an organization responsibly, there are requirements for systematic ways of doing the everyday, and governance is the job that makes that happen.

As onerous as many CIOs find this part of the job, it's also the main area of failing that sends CIOs down under the CFO on the organizational chart, the icon to business control in every company. A CIO with this area of weakness will quickly find him or herself supported more than wanted by someone who may be perceived as doing it better. A great CIO knows that respect as an effective controller of IT is a priceless commodity.

Executioner

At the same time, someone's got to "get 'er done"! Yes, IT operates in the business context, in the marketplace of offerings, under budgetary constraints, and in the scope that can be sold, but at the end of the day, it has to happen! Successful IT leaders organize to achieve, acting as effective and efficient business managers.

Managing to metrics, making tough decisions, and maintaining ownership of IT contribution are part of being the executioner. IT as a backbone of business operation demands leaders with backbones of their own, and great CIOs provide it.

Firefighter

Everyone knows what a crisis means. Nine times out of ten, the door a business interruption comes through is IT's. Risks to business have technology at their heart these days, and it's the CIO who stands at the ready. That's the point. A great CIO knows that it's not responding to the fire that makes the hero. It's being ready to respond and saving the day.

Firefighting means being prepared, with all the protection, planning and prevention the situation calls for. Successful IT leaders walk the tightrope of effective risk management, balancing prevention with acceptable risk, matching probabilities with investments. Then, when the time comes, the great CIO breaks the team into action, saving the day once again.

Managing the Mix: The Four Types

The way to match the right CIO with the right corporate situation is to manage the mix of these characteristics to be the right all-around leader of the day. Before we walk through those recipes, let's acknowledge one thing: This is not unique to IT. This isn't only about CIOs. We know that intuitively. That list, officer, technologist, visionary, educator, controller, executioner, and firefighter, applies to any business function where a leader needs to reach to the business as a team player while applying his or her own expertise to the best advantage. So why are we focusing on IT?

Go back to the beginning. IT leaders deal with more volatility, and came up through the ranks of technology. Their closest brothers and sisters are in engineering, where the focus is on the "what" first, and only later on the "how" and "for how much." It's a tougher road.

So let's think back to Howard and Mike. Starting with Mike, the path for him to take could have been confusing. He was focusing on executing his projects and managing his resources within the approval process and budget. He's doing well. He's even thinking about his customers and trying to be a responsible company officer in terms of managing to revenue. So what's wrong?

The company needs him to emphasize different characteristics. They need a more engaged officer, applying his vision and abilities as a communicator to participate in this strategic discussion. Just roughing this out on a five-point scale, shown in Figure 3.6, you can see below that there are key misses in what the company needs in the room, and what Mike brought today.

For Howard, the disconnect is even more drastic. His partners at Bob, Howard, and Sudhir, Inc., needed him to think very much inside the box of getting work done without spending any money until they were funded—very low investment, very immediate capacity.

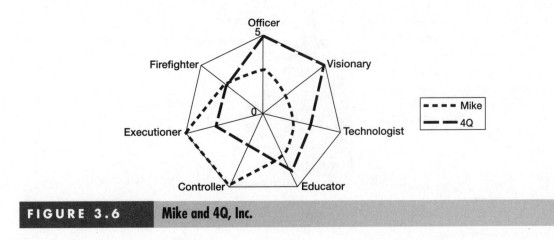

| **FIGURE 3.6** | **Mike and 4Q, Inc.** |

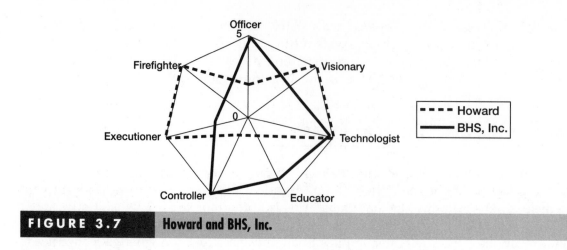

| FIGURE 3.7 | Howard and BHS, Inc. |

Instead, he was looking for long-term capacity, and had not even tried to sell the idea before he committed them to the contract (see Figure 3.7).

So are there rules for how to figure what needs to go where? No, but there are profiles, just as we profiled the life cycle phases of a company. Let's go back to those phases to figure out what recipe they need. There are four CIO types, or profiles, one for each corporate phase we defined earlier. We'll define each one in a single sentence first, and then explore what they mean. We'll map them against the seven characteristics, with two primary characteristics for each one. Just as a reminder, all of the characteristics need to be present to some degree to be a successful CIO, so every characteristic starts from baseline excellence and grows from there.

The Starter

The *spark-it* CIO, or *starter*, works tightly with other company leaders to spend every penny wisely, while looking hard to the future and selling the idea of investment when the business is ready. This is shown in Figure 3.8.

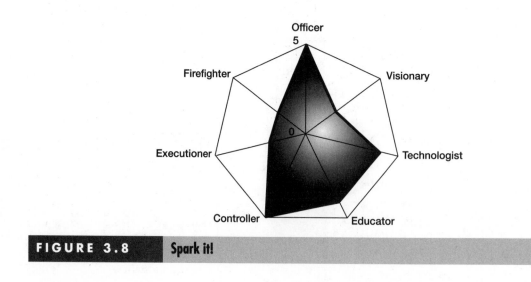

| FIGURE 3.8 | Spark it! |

- Top two characteristics: officer, controller
- Next priorities: technologist, educator
- Baseline excellence: visionary, executioner, firefighter

Howard missed the mark here by underselling and overspending, really not understanding where the business was. A more general interpretation says that the starter does the following:

- Closely aligns with business timetables
- Carefully uses today's IT dollars
- Establishes close controls over IT process and method right from the start
- Communicates widely and often on the strategic value of IT
- Keeps an eye for the future and what the market place will offer the company, when it's ready.

The Strategist

The *grow-it* CIO, or *strategist*, collaborates with other business leaders to explore and implement expansion initiatives while driving common understanding of the current and future value of IT to create business achievement. This is shown in Figure 3.9.

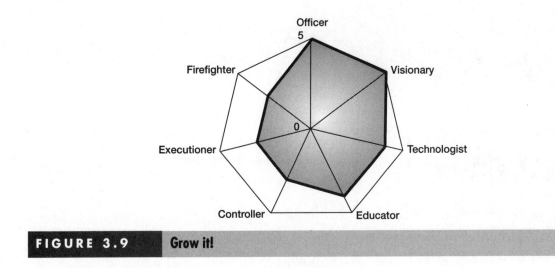

| FIGURE 3.9 | Grow it! |

- Top two characteristics: officer, visionary
- Next priorities: technologist, educator
- Baseline excellence: controller, executioner, firefighter

Mike missed the mark here by not understanding how much the business needed him to look beyond his current plans and to think like a business leader. A more general interpretation says that the strategist does the following:

- Knows enough about the business to think beyond just IT to how IT can expand the business
- Keeps in mind a longer-term vision of IT excellence in business context
- Knows technology deeply enough to keep an integrated architecture and architecture plan ready for adaptation to business change
- Can communicate both current state and vision clearly to stakeholders of all levels
- Maintains an effective and efficient sustaining IT operation that is change-ready and risk-managing.

The Sustainer

The *hold-it* CIO, or *sustainer,* manages risk and maintains a tightly run ship to provide cost and resource-efficient, stable and controlled IT environments supporting company operations. The characteristics are shown in Figure 3.10 and described as follows:

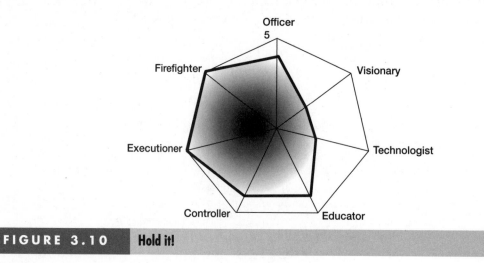

| FIGURE 3.10 | Hold it! |

- Top two characteristics: executioner, firefighter
- Next priorities: controller, educator
- Baseline excellence: officer, visionary, technologist

This is who Mike was, a solid risk manager and provider of reliable IT services. A more general interpretation says that the sustainer:

- Drives performance and achievement of targeted metrics
- Emphasizes process and controls to enforce compliance
- Drives continuous improvement toward increased efficiencies
- Encourages and rewards incremental achievement
- Maintains an effective and efficient sustaining IT operation that supports business efficiency and risk management

The Surgeon

The *trim-it* CIO, or *surgeon,* as an active member of a heavily tasked management team, reduces IT investment while increasing IT performance, scalability, and flexibility. These attributes are shown in Figure 3.11 and described as follows:

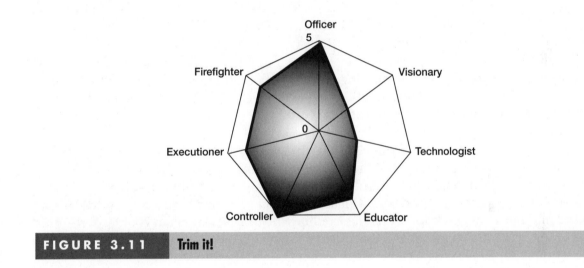

FIGURE 3.11   **Trim it!**

- Top two characteristics: officer, controller
- Next priorities: firefighter, executioner, educator
- Baseline excellence: visionary, technologist

On the face of it, you could say that this is the CIO no one wants to be. Looking deeper though, the surgeon has a home at very successful businesses just as easily as those on the downward road. Think of a company that grows and changes by mergers and acquisitions, maybe many times a year. Each time, there are redundancies, duplications and excess capacity that have to be trimmed, standards reinvoked, and processes and controls redeployed to lay the groundwork for the next phase of business evolution. More generally put, the surgeon:

- Deeply internalizes business objectives for all company functions
- Coordinates closely to define and fulfill business IT needs as efficiently as possible
- Establishes clearly understood baseline risk, process, performance, and efficiency requirements
- Identifies both strategic and tactical means to implement efficiencies

What the Four Types Are Not

Now that we know what the four types are—starter, strategist, sustainer, and surgeon—our job is done! All we have to do is pick the right one and be that, right? No, of course not. The four types of CIOs are profiles, archetypes of how the leadership ingredients can come together to be a situation-appropriate CIO. As four, they represent millions of situation-appropriate combinations, each tailored to the moment when you identify what the business needs most from you and you reach within yourself to provide it.

The four types are also not meant to replace any other sense of your own management identity you deploy. Leadership ingredients have nothing to do with culture. Being responsive and defining your recipe will work just as well at Starbucks as it will at H-P as it will at Pfizer. Enhancing your skills as a true firefighter has nothing to do with the type of company.

The four types also have nothing to do with management style. We tend to think of visionaries as "out-there" types with an absent-minded professor approach to their staff, being late to every meeting, and controllers as bean counters with visors and antacids. But the stereotyping does not work here. Collaborative and mentor-type CIOs can be just as focused and effective executioners as their militaristic or Machiavellian counterparts. This is not about *how* you manage. It is about *what* you manage.

Putting the Four Types to Work

So how to make sure we're not the Mike or the Howard in the room? How do we start? Well, what are you managing? We have talked about what different companies in different phases of life need from their CIO's. We talked about what characteristics make up a great CIO, and then we talked about the four representative types of CIOs that can be tailored to match what the business requires.

So how does all of that relate to you right now? By looking at the company's objectives for this year, and then at the objectives assigned to IT, you can tell pretty quickly if you're in a start, grow, hold or trim mode. Odds are really good that you've got more than one segment of the business operating in different modes. That gives you a sense of what the priorities are for those areas.

The one thing to remember right at the start is that only in a purely hold-it phase of life, one that very few companies are in, is it okay to not be a good corporate officer first. Start with the business, and you can't go wrong.

Then, once you have defined what priorities belong where, such as regional growth and global security compliance or a planned acquisition, you can define which of the best parts of yourself to bring forward. What are your focus points by initiative? Already, you're using your controller self to lay it out.

By thinking through what is really needed from IT, you will be able to better define what CIO leadership characteristics are needed most. Just like we did with the four types, we want to ask, what is the sentence that describes the job today? What two characteristics (and only two) are primary today? What comes next? Is there anything slipping below baseline excellence?

Let's try out an example. The company's strategic plan is heavily focused on gross margin improvement this year. Even so, slight revenue increases are forecast because the company is scheduled to open marketing and sales offices throughout the European Union in the second half of the year.

In looking through the IT portfolio, you know that there are some major system replacement initiatives this year that need doing, and some major hardware overhauls that have been put off and really can't wait.

So, what does this mean for who you are? Well, let's ask a few questions:

- How far is the business horizon?
- What is the nature of the business problem?
- How much risk is involved?
- How stable is the IT environment?

From the looks of it, the business horizon is just this year, partly because so much depends on the gross margin issue. That means the vision isn't all that long. Visionary isn't primary this time. And the nature of the business problem is effectiveness, when it comes to the factory, and connectivity, for those sales offices. It is not overwhelmingly long reaching there, either, so technologist isn't necessarily primary, either.

Because we know we've got major stuff going on, we do have officer as a primary, but it sounds like getting it done is a focus, and that sounds like the executioner. Then, with infrastructure to fix and some projects to get underway, we have firefighter and controller in play. We still will be looking ahead, so technologist might be quick on their heels. Maybe our sentence is the following:

As CIO, I need to partner closely with the business to execute business-critical initiatives and manage investment while updating and maintaining stable and reliable IT services and systems.

Figure 3.12 shows what our map might look like.

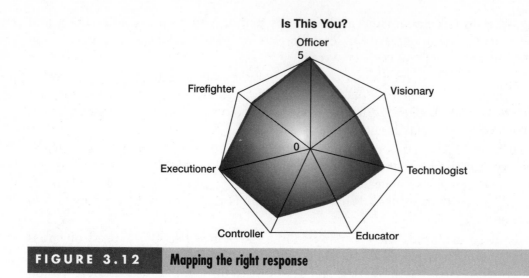

Is This You?

| FIGURE 3.12 | Mapping the right response |

Once you have an idea of where you are and what you're focused on, you can do a lot of things with it:

- *Confirm it!* Take opportunities to meet with your fellow executives and your CEO and confirm your understanding. Don't wait to be the Mike in the room.
- *Pass it on!* You've defined standard baseline areas. Delegate them! This is a perfect time to grow your people by trusting them with some of the areas that have a little forgiveness right now.
- *Pump it up!* Take the hot buttons or gaps and embrace them! Is it being a better controller? Go take a class on budgeting, or better yet, read the chapter on budgeting in this book! Need a better understanding of a technology component that may become the solution of all solutions soon? Call in a few vendors to educate yourself.

By understanding the job, you can prepare yourself with a more targeted approach to be a better CIO and leader, and stay aligned with what the business needs from you and your organization.

Summary and Conclusion

This chapter introduced you to the idea of matching your CIO type to your company. Companies have four basic lifecycle phases, sometimes within a business segment and sometimes for the company as a whole that we learned to summarize as: *spark it, grow it, hold it,* and *trim it.*

We learned that we can think of what a great CIO is in terms of seven summary characteristics:

Officer: Be a full business participant.
Visionary: Look to the horizon!

Technologist: Know the field and the market.

Educators: Teach them all!

Controller: Process and method makes it all tick and tie.

Executioner: Get it done or get it gone.

Firefighter: First responders save the day.

From there, we defined the mapping of those characteristics in certain recipes. They made a good match of CIO to life-cycle phase, and there are four archetypes to remember as examples:

- The *starter* works tightly with other company leaders to spend every penny wisely while looking hard to the future and selling the idea of investment when the business is ready.
- The *strategist* collaborates with other business leaders to explore and implement expansion initiatives while driving common understanding of the current and future value of IT to create business achievement.
- The *sustainer* manages risk and maintains a tightly run ship to provide cost and resource-efficient, stable and controlled IT environments supporting company operations.
- The *surgeon* as an active member of a heavily-tasked management team, reduces IT investment while increasing IT performance, scalability and flexibility.

We also talked about how following these characteristics doesn't change who you are as a manager, and is not dependent on the culture of the company you are supporting. What it does do is allow you to diagnose your environment and make sure that you have a more actionable understanding of what your company needs from you. From there, all you have to do is make sure you've got what it takes to be the right person in the room.

3.5
IT Governance

Richard Diamond and Jennifer Diamond

Asking a room of IT experts to define *governance* is like asking a room of doctors to define *medicine*. The word *governance* is the new peanut butter. Spread it all over everything and hope for the best.

But we all know that only lasts until the first real crisis. The first audit when the true cracks in the process become obvious, the first disaster that demands recovery, response plan or no response plan, or the first hard decision about the budget that will make or break the quarter—that's when the definition of *governance* strains and rips if it isn't grounded in reality.

So what is governance? Let's break it down into what IT is governing. There are four categories of IT governance:

1. *Investment governance:* How we oversee the way company resources are used to generate IT services.
2. *Execution governance:* How we manage getting things done, usually on an initiative basis.
3. *Operational governance:* How we administer the foundation of IT services, for continuity, effectiveness, and efficiency.
4. *Organization governance:* How we lead the human effort of IT, developing, qualifying, segregating, and coordinating as appropriate.

Given these categories of what IT governs, we can see how just the word *governance* can be confusing. The most critical confusion, however, is the confusion that IT customers, from executives to line end users, have about *how* IT governs itself. This is confusion that gives IT bad reputations and breaks the careers of earnest and well-intentioned CIOs who didn't spot the moment when the glazed looks at the steering committee meetings faded and were replaced with furrowed brows.

So what do we do about that confusion? First, admit we share it! We get it; we need to govern spending, projects, ops, and people. But what makes governance work? It's not just managing, and it's not just reporting. What is it?

The IT Governance Framework

The governance framework starts with rules that are then supported by relationships. Verifying governance content as being the right thing at the right time comes next, leading right into how you communicate it and let everyone know, in all the ways that are meaningful to them, what requirements for compliance are. Making sure that those requirements are met includes both testing compliance and demonstrating it, rounding out the framework. This is shown in Figure 3.13.

Put another way, we decide how we want to govern our actions. We confirm those decisions with our customers and suppliers, and that gives us the stake in the ground, how we define success. From there, we verify periodically that those decisions are still solid as are our interactions with those groups. We also check to make sure that we're abiding by those decisions, and as a result, are maintaining a predictable level of quality in our work.

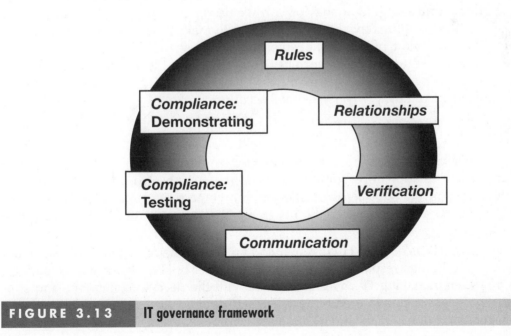

FIGURE 3.13   **IT governance framework**

IT Rules

Let's take a deeper look for IT. If we start at rules, what are we talking about? Rules are our guidelines. They have a lot of different sources, types, and varying depth. For IT, rules are our policies, our procedures, and our standards. They can come from our company's objectives, IT best practices, from this year's auditors, or from industry requirements that, because of our company's goals, we choose to adopt and adapt to our own operations. As a group, the rules we define capture what we are deciding to take on as achievable objectives for our organization in a meaningful future. In real terms, it's what we believe we can achieve on a repeatable basis this year.

The rules themselves can be in different forms. Methods, such as how we handle project management or business continuity, are one type. Policies—statements of general direction that come from senior management—are another. Procedures and process flows—defining what steps are performed by whom and when—are another. We have all seen many versions of every one of them.

What we may have missed, though, was why we had those specific rules done *just that way*. Well, once we define what we want to say, we can use the three Cs to define how spelled-out the rule needs to be:

- *Complexity:* How detailed does guidance need to be because of how complex a process is?
- *Control:* Is there a system of scrutiny that ensures that we're all on the same page?
- *Consistency:* Is there a good business reason, either risk or efficiency or the like, that requires that this process be executed the same way every time—maybe even across different locations or situations?

These questions guide just how much detail we need to get into to define rules. Can an overarching policy suffice to guide behavior? Do we need a standardized checklist everyone follows? At the end of the day, the rules are there to make an activity or process more predictable. Based on what policy management has published, a person filling out an equipment requisition knows to check current IT standards for the specific type of equipment to buy, or another person knows that it's not okay to send 40 MB holiday photos out to friends and family from the company's e-mail account.

Relationships

That leads to the next step in the framework. How do employees know that this applies to them? That's where relationships come in. During the course of defining the rules, IT checks with customers and suppliers to make sure that these rules make sense. Who owns the area being talked about? What credibility is needed to make sure that the rules are taken seriously?

As an example, HR is both an IT customer and an IT supplier. HR senior management is a key provider of human resources to IT, and is a key user of IT services and technology. How does IT, when managing IT governance, deal with the need to collaborate and support HR credibility as well as IT credibility when setting the rules? It takes working with all the management teams to make it real, and then leading by example.

If we say that violating a section of the security policy is grounds for dismissal, well, there needs to be process steps and agreed-on guidelines between business unit management, HR, and IT that say how everyone goes about finding and proving an offense that leads to termination. It's through relationships and joint credibility that governance is real.

And the audiences for guidance aren't just there to be punished. Governance has a very important sales requirement in the relationship side of the equation. Two pertinent questions need to be answered in an effective governance system:

1. *WIFM:* What's in it for me?
2. *WDIC:* Why do I care?

Every participant in the governance process needs to be able to answer these questions, and hopefully with a smile! Hey, good security means protected company assets, which means company success, which means I get my bonus!

IT governance rules, in particular, have a lot to do with services and offerings. Beyond the offering of secured business data and operating environments, most of what IT does has to do with providing continued and continuously innovating technical solutions to business needs. That means that there are agreements about governing in good faith that IT and business users share. IT and IT customers share the following:

- An obligation to communicate
- An obligation to receive communication
- An obligation to comply with agreements, including rules

Sounds simple, but start with the first obligation, an obligation to communicate. This means that both IT and IT customers are obligated to openly confirm requirements of IT products, services, and function as part of the company. IT is not solely responsible for identifying the objectives and opportunities for IT offerings, nor is IT solely responsible for identifying every conceivable control point where IT can provide additional support or oversight to protect company resources and integrity. IT is a party to an agreement with IT customers to collaboratively confirm the scope of IT reach.

Then, once we get to that point, all parties have to listen, too. Yes, it would be great if our financial systems could verify with certainty the identity of every single person making a transaction, and store that information for seven years. Unfortunately, the current state of the budget and the useful life of our system does not allow for installation of biometric security layers this year, and perhaps, if it is defined truly to be a priority, the corporate controller could lead the discussion at the next IT steering committee meeting to talk about deferring the manufacturing system upgrade one more year. In other words, we have to agree to receive communication and respond to it reasonably. And once we come to agreements, such as IT agreeing that it is time for the company to have a 24/7 help desk to operate on a maximum one-hour response time for trouble tickets, then we have to comply with those agreements.

Sincerity is part of these relationships, and while this all sounds pretty obvious, reaching shared agreements, abiding by them, and taking on the same language on the same topics across the entire management team is one of the most powerful characteristics of a governance system, whether for IT or broader across the organization. When the same policy direction or company definition for success comes from the VP of sales and the VP of manufacturing, employees understand that management isn't just paying lip service, and that a true new day of governance is dawning. It's amazing what that can do.

Verification

Here's a huge surprise. You're probably not going to have every single rule for every area right the first time. No matter how good your relationships are, and how hard you work to come to agreements that make sense today and include a little stretch, you are going to have to verify those rules.

The first process you verify in a new IT governance environment is the governance environment itself. IT policies are first, the highest-level agreements among management that set the tone and theme for everything that follows. Verifying them means shopping them, just like IT executives now know to do with the budget. Test market IT policies with audit committees, steering committees, and fellow executives, and verify that these rules make sense. And once there's agreement, set the plan right then and there for when you'll check back again to make sure they stand the test of time. That's the definition of a verification process.

And as you go through and identify the other rule types, depending on what the three Cs help you to define as needed, you work those relationships, and verify that these are the right governance benchmarks to set. Verifying comes here, before you do the full-court-press to release the rules to everyone, but it also happens over and over, when you continually and periodically check on them:

- Are the rules still relevant to the business, aligned with business objectives?
- Do the rules effectively address all areas of IT governance, investment, operation, execution, and organization?
- Are the rules still providing the appropriate levels of control?
- Are the rules still addressing the right levels of detail?
- Are the rules still reflecting the current state of organization and relationships in the company at this time?

You can see that answering these questions more than once is important, and is a key part of making sure that your governance content makes sense, today and every day.

Communication

We just made sure that our rules made sense and earlier we covered how relationships enforce *what* gets communicated and *to whom*, but what about *how?* Communication in business is actually sales. We are always selling, whether we're selling the value of an IT service or the value of a new control.

Any advertising executive will tell you that a successful campaign addresses multiple channels. Just as the local dealership who promotes the President's Day sale on radio, in

TABLE 3.1		Communicating the Rules		
Audience	**What They Need to Know**	**Primary Communication Method**	**Secondary Communication Method**	**Tertiary Communication Method**
Company executives	Role of IT in organization	Executive meetings	Monthly status presentations	IT Portal—IT mission
IT users	IT service offerings	IT portal—user guidelines	IT help desk	IT newsletters, e-mail updates
All company employees	New IT security measures	IT publicity campaign	IT portal—Company policy	IT help desk
All business unit leaders	IT project prioritization methods	Monthly portfolio review sessions	IT portal—portfolio queue and guidelines	Executive meetings

the Sunday paper, on local cable, and with a long balloon arch visible for five freeway exits, so too does responsible management use an array of channels to communicate governance intentions and commitments. The IT exec thinks through each audience member, what they need to know, and the best way to reach them. Table 3.1 is a short example that could go on to include all the rules that apply to all governance categories.

From Table 3.1, you can see that slapping the new security policy up on the portal and shooting out a quick e-mail isn't good enough. Depending on your beliefs about honey over vinegar, you may see the value in positive reinforcement as well as negative. Keeping that security policy example, a lot of companies have gone to an attestation model, suggested by auditors, to get formal acknowledgment from every reader. But does that really lead to compliance? Do people know the policy any better?

What if, in addition to your audit-ready roster of acknowledgments, you did something fun? Could this be dinner out for the best-submitted short story depicting a scenario in which correctly following the new security policy in a time of crisis saved the company? Sounds out there, doesn't it? But the goal is not to be taken seriously. The goal is compliance, and you communicate any way you can to get there. As proof, think of the most stupid and annoying jingle you can remember. Something you catch yourself humming, or actually using in conversation. Annoying, isn't it? But you remember it, which is the point of effective communication of governance and compliance-related content.

A Note about Change Management

The sacred texts of management say that *change management* is the most important process when instituting a new way of doing things. For most things, that makes a lot of sense. For governance, though, it's a bit of a set-up.

Governance as a process, when done properly, includes its own initiation steps. When you define rules for the first time, you're doing it for a business reason, these days related to audits and shareholders as an impetus, if you didn't have other reasons before. Going through the steps of identifying and working through relationships, verifying content with those relationship participants, and communicating thoroughly are exactly what change management would have you do to inform and gain buy-in.

So what's the problem? Well, change management implies a change from here to there, in effect, only once. Once this change is managed, we will have completed our task of change management. No matter how often we try to convince ourselves that change management is perpetual, we know that we think of it in linear terms, with a beginning and an end. In IT, we "finish" changes all the time, and after migrating them to production we call it a day.

For governance, the finite nature of change is explicitly *not true*. The graphic for this framework is a circle intentionally. A governance cycle that only goes by once is a failure. There are decisions to make, people to inform, results to generate, and proof to be gathered, over and over again. That's how the world needs to be, both here *and* there. But as managers and leaders, if we need to hold on to change management as a concept while we begin to perform steps involving more outreach than we're used to, more consensus gaining than we're used to, and maybe more clarity and repetition than we're used to, that's fine, but recognize it as the crutch it is. A time will have to come, rather quickly, for governance to be in place to a successful degree, when those things are how you work, all the time and every day, not a transitional set of activities that won't be needed later.

Compliance

Getting back to the framework that will be a way of life, shown in Figure 3.13, once you have verified that you have the right rules and that you have communicated thoroughly, often, and perpetually, how do you check for actual compliance? As a first step, we need to know what we are checking. To manage any business function, we all know the PPT model, people, process, and technology. It's tried and true, so let's try it here:

- *People:* Does everyone understand what needs doing? Do company employees understand why we agreed on these rules and what happens when they comply and what happens when they don't? Are we providing what they need to meaningfully participate appropriately?

- *Process:* Are the processes operating within the guidelines we agreed upon? Are we achieving the control points and process objectives we expected? Are events triggering the right responses? In effect, are we living up to our agreements with these rules?

- *Technology:* Are the tools we have chosen operating as we needed them to? Are we protected against failure and taking best advantage of the investment we made?

How are we checking? There are two aspects to this: *demonstrating* compliance and *testing* compliance.

Demonstrating compliance is replicating a process in a controlled environment to capture statistical data. Engineers do it all the time to prove quality. Finance and IT do it all the time now, with the help of auditors. Not really an ongoing part of IT processes, this is the one-off, even if every quarter, activity that is aside from what IT does all day to prove compliance with governance commitments.

Testing is a different thing. IT performs testing all the time, as a part of running a solid shop. From a quick review of server logs every hour to the warning alerts that come from a network intrusion to the quarterly management review of application access granted to users and administrators, testing is a part of doing business. Logically, then, if this is part of our ongoing governance system, and is in effect yet another IT offering, testing must be performed with methods that are as cost-effective and high-yield as the rest of our services. We can make sure of it with a few questions about what we're using:

- *Automated testing:* Are we effectively using automated tools to provide the highest coverage of compliance testing for the appropriate levels of investment? Are we using them in such a way to collect the lowest tolerance and highest integrity data we can?
- *Manual testing:* Are we taking the time to objectively review our processes that have requirements beyond systems and need human validation? Do we clearly prepare for that task with guidelines on what needs to be checked, and how?
- *Manual testing with automated tools:* Are we verifying the overlap of man and machine, checking the tools we use to verify that there are no gaps where a system error could go undetected?

Answering these questions provides a level of comfort in determining what should go in front of the steering committee, makes it easy to respond to a help desk request with the right answers the first time, and makes IT governance part of good business.

The relationship between demonstrating and testing is an interesting one. We know that compliance itself is a fixed thing—it has to be done, no way around it. And you have to prove it, right? The less testing you institute, the more demonstrating you're going to have to do to fill in the gap later. If you can't produce the change control log from last year showing the workflow through development, QA and production with roll-back instructions and the rest, you will be expected to demonstrate several times how you handle a change to business applications before you have credibility when you say it's under control. Keeping testing and demonstrating in the right proportion makes management attestation just another part of compliance, not an annual task that starts with a sinking feeling in the pit of your stomach and ends in nightmares that slowly fade—until next year.

Where Is the Benefit?

Wait a minute. That sinking feeling thing brings up another point. Now that we have an understanding that IT governance is a comprehensive system that addresses all areas of IT functions and includes defining intentions to the right level of detail, confirming them with customers and suppliers through relationship management, and then checking to make sure we're doing it right, don't we need to step back for a minute and ask a really basic question? Why are we doing this? This is not a flip question. *Something that takes so much time and cost of its own deserves a serious answer.*

Firstly, we know darned well that there are *regulatory requirements* all over the place that apply to our organizations in a dizzyingly varying set of ways, depending on whether we're public, global, in health care, or financial industries, and that's on top of the basics relating to taxes, employees, customers, and the rest of Business 101. IT governance systems give IT leaders a mechanism to respond, incorporate, and most importantly, prove compliance with new requirements as they arise. Without an existing system to work within, you can guarantee increased risks as conflicting requirements are imposed and you struggle to find the right context to comply.

Then there are *stakeholder requirements.* Let's face it: IT is expensive. It yields the ability to be in business, to be sure, but it costs a lot, and its benefits take a lot of proving. IT governance provides the forum to explain what IT does with the money the company entrusts to it. When you can define the need for business cases for all investments over a dollar threshold as an IT policy safeguarding appropriate use of company funds, you have quoted an agreement you made on a rule that you verified and are complying with. Governance makes shareholders happy, and gives a business foundation for discussions with IT stakeholders. Keeps things civilized.

And then there's *market differentiation.* Wouldn't your company's customers prefer to deal with a vendor who has a good relationship with regulators and has a sound approach to controlling its business? It's becoming more common for customers to include corporate oversight and management practices in vendor selection criteria. From automakers publishing their own internal quality metrics to SAS70 requirements for non-public vendors of public companies, governance is part of the product.

And then there's the best reason of all to put in an IT governance program: *It pays for itself.* If you begin with a contract review of all vendors to make sure they comply with new vendor qualification standards the result will most likely be a 15 percent reduction in annual maintenance costs. Move on to restructuring current projects and associated budgets to match approved business cases in the new portfolio review procedure. Add in the shortened time to on-board new employees. Once you have translated transient tribal knowledge into managed methods, it will be easier to get things approved and you will also experience reduced cycle times. This will allow you to provide increased service offerings that you can provide to your customers. You will also find that the better use of your budget and the overall improvement in IT's company profile is worth every minute. Remember WIFM? For the CIO, that's an easy question to answer. Governance allows the CIO to institutionalize decisions, criteria, and processes, eliminating the "reinventing the wheel" hours and leaving them for much better and effective time use, both for the company and for his or her own career!

How Do You Know It Works?

Once you get into this, how do you know that it's working? Valid question, since we're talking about verification and compliance. One way is pretty easy. Are you passing your audits? Are the auditors a little shell-shocked because you are no longer letting them drag you around by the nose and doing data dumps on a dime as they ask for them and are instead giving them your own audit reports from the past few quarters? Isn't that part of the fun? Aren't you glad you managed your balance between testing and demonstration?

But better than that, are the following statements true for you?

- We know why we do what we do.
- We know when we're doing it well.

- We know how to respond to problems.
- We know what's critical to our success.

Can you get more specific?

- We know this year's business and IT priorities and the projects that will get us there.
- We know how to make decisions on how to respond to new circumstances or opportunities as they arise.
- Our production environments operate efficiently and effectively in a controlled and safeguarded manner while supporting agile business function.

Okay, that last one might be a bit thick, but you get the idea. Can you say this stuff with a straight face? Then you're there.

If not, will you know when you *are* there? Have you set achievable targets to get there that are directional to where you want to go? Have you gotten agreement from your customers that it's what they want and from your suppliers that they can help? Have you figured out how to check yourself on the way, looking at your projects, your ops, your spending, and your people?

Then congratulations. You've embraced governance.

3.6
Compliance

John Mass, Dean Lane, and Gary Kelly

Background

The Sarbanes-Oxley Act of 2002 (SOX) resulted in executive initiatives to implement controls and ensure compliance. The precepts and ideas around compliance are now omnipresent in every aspect of corporate policy. Some areas of policy have improved for employees—policies are better documented, and some companies have implemented whistle-blowing hot lines. Although SOX was likely the motivation for such improvements, the need for corporate policy reform existed long before new regulations pertaining to financial responsibility and integrity were enacted.

With all the documented control surfacing from internal and external audits, corporations are faced with the question, "When does it become necessary to consider a task as a controlled activity?" Managers and auditors seek to answer this question by looking at a control in terms of what should be considered material and significant, given the objective of the organization. In some cases, organizations have uncovered thousands of necessary controls for financial responsibility alone. Defining what is material and significant uncovers controls that are important to an organization achieving its primary objectives and critical business goals.

Introduction

Compliance is a focus of every corporation today, and now spans beyond financial processes and applications.

Improved efficiencies remain at the forefront of corporate executive and management goals. The requirement for compliance has increased overhead associated with attaining a compliant state. It is therefore imperative to put systems in place that monitor and ensure the effective implementation of required controls. Corporate earnings are at risk; various fines, inefficient audits, disorganized communication, and wasted employee time all contribute to diminishing a corporation's profitability.

To obtain and maintain compliance, discipline is required of both management (top-down monitoring) and employees (bottom-up action); coordinated approaches prove most successful. Following is an analysis of the difficulties that employees and managers alike face in monitoring complex systems.

Increasing Complexity of Systems and Control Activities

Governing the requirements of a system that controls activities for compliance is complex, regardless of the environment requiring compliance. Documenting the efforts to meet audit requirements will be reviewed.

Regulatory statutes and industry standards have added complexity to the corporate environment, with literally thousands of regulations and policies to track and audit. Tracking all of the control regulations, policies, and best practices necessary to stay current with audit requirements is an ardent task, and it requires reliable systems.

When regulatory agencies set standards by which organizations must abide, they also set the minimum requirements for achieving compliance. Failure to comply with defined rules and guidelines can result in penalties and sanctions, negative press, and in some cases, criminal prosecution.

The list of regulations and industry standards, which are regularly updated, increases annually. These standards exist simultaneously in most public companies, and also in large private companies. Here is a short list of standards that may commonly appear in public organizations:

- SOX
- FAR
- MIL SPEC
- HIPAA
- FDA

- CFR
- ISO
- CMM
- CAPAs

Example: A global provider of equipment and services in the medical industry is regulated by HIPAA and SOX, two primary controls. In addition, it might be necessary to strictly control the standards for the technical certification of equipment in the field, service contracts, and technician and engineering certifications.

When conducting an audit, it is common for regulatory agencies to conduct a follow-up review to address breaches and other material deficiencies found in the preliminary audit. Recent studies have found that many companies struggle to obtain compliance during follow-up reviews.

Table 3.2 shows feedback based on the findings of various regulatory agencies.

Corporations seeking compliance must also adhere to internal policies and best practices.

Corporate governance has received so much attention that it is now seen as pivotal in producing a competitive product, and is considered a requirement for successfully managing cost and quality. Compliance monitoring systems that report the status of *percentage compliant* are an absolute necessity to anticipate risk and take any necessary corrective actions.

The efforts of corporations to comply with SOX regulations have produced hundreds of thousands of documented controls over the past two years. Such documented controls have been produced through a concerted effort by management and independent audit.

Not only have controls been documented, but they are now also well-formed. Managers have learned how to construct controls that are aligned with corporate objectives, while considering the risks associated with those objectives. The end result is a group of defined activities that minimize those risks while still achieving compliance.

Lack of Tools for Employees

Business drivers over the past two years have forced corporations to create complex systems that demand a considerable amount of maintenance. Important, everyday tasks are

TABLE 3.2	Typical Findings of Regulatory Agencies
Current State	**Necessary Environment in the Future**
Compliance systems are one-offs and therefore not consolidated	Unified compliance systems and eventually integrated
Must conduct audits by validating numerous stand-alone systems. This increases cost of maintenance	Validation and maintenance of consolidated infrastructure
Because created as one-offs many items go on hold, delayed investigations, and lengthy reviews	Compliance systems will be a hybrid of batch and real-time investigation
Inability to identify process improvements	Trend data delivered on demand and detailed drill downs will assist in the ability to proactively manage issues and risk. Enterprisewide visibility of compliance activities

often overlooked as a result of employees tracking more complex systems of controls. An employee must be familiar with all controls, the function that must be performed, and when it should be executed. Common issues employees face include:

- Keeping current with compliancy requirements
- Recognizing when to execute actions necessary for obtaining compliancy
- Prioritizing controls based on their importance to the organization
- Understanding the tests for compliancy, and how to record the results

Daily workloads are filled with controls that require action from employees, in order to fulfill management requirements. These volumes of controls require hours of training to perform, schedule follow-up, review, document, archive and audit. Actions to be performed have a range of equipment calibration and maintenance, certification training, process execution, financial accountability, and product quality assurance.

Having numerous control activities to schedule, with no supporting monitoring system that has escalation built into it, often results in a lack of visibility, slippage and increased risk to the company. Remaining in a compliant state does not take into account employee workload or allowance for a backlog. While training is essential to keeping new control activities current, old activities may suffer and be pushed down in the queue.

Loss of visibility frequently occurs and controls go unattended. Equipment may not be calibrated in a timely manner, certification reviews may be late or missed, and lagging security audits leave the organization exposed for breeches. The most recent control that is receiving attention may not be the highest priority, or the greatest risk to the organization.

For an organization to succeed, employees must have access to tools that possess traceability of controls.

Lack of Tools for Management

Managers must direct employees, and verify the results of their reportees' daily tasks. Managers have limited options when it comes to overseeing the status of systems that require the organization of many control activities. Most systems manufacturers have developed idiosyncratic methods of managing compliance from their perspective. With limited options and resources to bridge these differing systems, managers have become accustomed to using spreadsheets, emails, and makeshift devices for tracking a vast numbers of controls. Spreadsheets provide little help in integrating the actions required for compliance, managing employees and their tasks, and assessing current risk levels. Common issues managers face include:

- Tracking the productivity of employees responsible for control activity execution
- Identifying the current status of key business process controls activity at all times
- Training employees on the business processes and systems that require compliance

- Verifying that schedules are kept and activities are consistently performed
- Verifying that documentation standards for completed controls are met

Surprisingly, paper systems are the norm for following most compliancy requirements. Managers often use paper systems over automated forms because of the vast number of one-off needs. Systems and data are kept in silos where they are typically organized by department, making it difficult for executives to access necessary information.

Executives instead need summaries of each silo, presented in a usable format, and providing a comprehensive view of their organization.

Policies are often managed reactively; only when processes fail are their effectiveness evaluated. Such ad-hoc policy management allows for oversight of the most important systems. There is little opportunity for creating systems that are predictive and preventative. This results in management losing necessary agility.

Compliance Monitoring

A number of software solution providers are responding to the need for comprehensive compliance in their solutions, but they fall short in providing a holistic approach to organizations. The solutions may address one business process (ERP, security, etc.) and provide excellent compliance reporting and audit trails, but neglect to consider various other applications and regulations that organizations face today.

Regardless of the system, the requirement for a compliance solution remains the same:
- It must manage the standards and controls over business units and processes.
- It must create and preserve an audit trail that is secure, easily accessible, and verifiable.
- Notifications must be deployed so the enterprise is proactive and preventive in its actions.
- The portal must be easily accessed, with an executive dashboard that has drill-down capability.
- A single system supports compliance efforts with the greatest speed and at the lowest cost.

To address compliance requirements, the systematized solution must have the following objective: Provide management and auditors a full accounting for the actions taken and results achieved by the organization in maintaining the systems that are required to comply with regulatory laws and statutes, governing codes and ethics, and best practices of the enterprise.

The systematized solution must allow for the creation of controls across business units, areas, and business processes. The controls within the system are documented by objective and risk, giving employees all the information necessary to complete their work. Risk factors offer the ability to manage status and dashboard views so that information is relevant to the organizational priorities.

The systematized solution documents the activity from control creation to test result documentation, and provides management with fully audited results. The system audit function must be close-ended, resulting in an audit trail that is secure and verifiable. The solution must provide scheduling and alert notifications for employees to effectively manage their control activities. When those actions do not occur, the system should notify a designated superior to take action. Escalation is a key feature of a proactive and preventative organization.

Management must have current information and reports on the status of a controlled system. This should be addressed through a Web portal. The dashboard view gives management access to information in real time, using both color and numeric feedback. The color-coding and count is reflective of the completion status, and the number associated with the color describes the number of controls in that specific area or group. From the executive dashboard views, management can easily focus on the controls and can access detail information. *Hotlinks* take the viewer to specific controls by functional area and business process. Access to views can be customized, giving managers the flexibility to view the status of systems based on individual needs.

What the System Must Deliver

The best solutions are systems that are complete and self-contained. Systems must be logical, while addressing each component of the area in which compliance is sought. A single compliance application is necessary to be the "system of record" (for compliance) and must maintain all compliance data in one place. Another feature that the solution should deliver is the ability to operate completely outside of the organizational IT environment, thereby providing security and isolation for compliance data. Third-party hosting is preferable so that the provider becomes your honest broker for information that is isolated to prevent manipulation. Automation and computerization will reduce errors, time requirements, and costs.

Look for solutions that deliver the following:

1. Automation
   a. Online forms
   b. E-mail integration
   c. Scheduling and alerts
   d. Internet-based browser access
   e. Online storage and access to results and evidence
   f. Extensible data fields for control information
2. End-to-end visibility and work-flow reporting
   a. Clearly understandable status views
   b. Dashboard visibility with drill down
   c. Responsibility and ownership tracing
   d. Escalation paths

    e. Accommodations for the business unit structure

    f. Unlimited storage of controls and tests

    g. Risk-based monitoring

3. Metrics

    a. Establish goals

    b. Measure progress

    c. Measure processes

    d. Measure improvements

    e. Provide "red-flag" notifications

    f. Provisions for backup and disaster recovery

    g. Problem escalation procedures

Conclusion

To remain compliant, a system must utilize available technology and a regulated process, and it must employ people who can validate that appropriate actions are taken. This is best accomplished through top-down monitoring and bottom-up actions.

Communication in Information Technology

Sam Gill and Dean Lane

Communication is one of those activities that everyone recognizes but few can define satisfactorily. Communication is talking to one another. It is television, it is e-mail, it is spreading information, it is our hair style, it is a project status update, and it is literary criticism: The list is endless. This definition by example seems satisfactory on the surface, but we will discover that many variables influence communications, and even more affect effective communications.

When information technologists communicate with their business counterparts, the probability of communication failures rises. Keeping the discussion at a business level is complicated enough, but when the conversation moves to integrating information technology into the business processes, it quickly becomes quite complex. One of the complicating factors is the lack of a shared understanding and shared nomenclature, on both sides. The business personnel usually don't have the in-depth understanding of all aspects of technology that an IT person possesses. Similarly, the IT person may be unschooled in the business processes being discussed. Understanding all aspects of IT communications is a must if greater productivity is to be realized, when utilizing technology.

Elements of Communication

Four fundamental elements must be present if communication is to occur. Importantly, the mere presence of these elements does not guarantee that communication has occurred. Context is an element of communication, as well. Communication could occur without having a contextual backdrop, but it is easy to see that context is quite important. For example, when communicating information technology funding needs to a line of business, it is an imperative that IT personnel understand the budgeting and prioritization of IT initiatives, as well as who are the key executives and stakeholders. This is important because it provides the context within which communications must occur.

Message

A message is an idea, concept, or some other form of notification that is transmitted by the communication process. Many believe that *intention* is a crucial factor in deciding what constitutes a message. The sender's intention may be stated or unstated, conscious or unconscious, but must be retrievable by analysis. The message is what the sender puts into it by whatever means.

Transmitter

The sender, or transmitter of the message, is defined as someone or something that originates and sends the message. Knowing who originates a message contributes to the context of the message and may be a factor in taking the appropriate action, if any. For example, the transmitter may have some shared understanding of what the content is about and therefore might create the message differently.

Receiver

The recipient or receiver is someone or something that gets the message. With the receiver, the emphasis shifts to the message and how text is *read*, or the medium and how it is *interpreted*. Once the receiver has received the message, one might assume that communication has occurred. To be certain that communication really did occur requires that other elements (action or feedback) be present.

Medium

The medium is the means or vehicle by which the message is sent. There are many media (facial expressions, e-mail, telephone, pictures, gestures, etc.). The medium is important when considering what message is being sent. It is well known that communicating in person is the strongest form of communicating and provides the best opportunity for the receiver to understand the message. That said, it is not always practical to use this medium.

How Do We Know That Communication Has Occurred?

If you were to walk into a room where I was seated in a chair, and you asked me to stand against the north wall, would communication have occurred? Well, we have all of the elements: you are the *sender;* the *message* is to stand against the wall; I am the *receiver;* and the *medium* is the spoken word. But what if I do not stand and move to the north wall? Did I not hear you? Did I not understand you? Am I ignoring your request?

Feedback

Feedback is the transmission of the receiver's reaction back to the sender. If I reply to your request with the statement, "Could you say that again, please?" then something did occur, but the communication was incomplete. Likewise, if I repeat the request and say that I don't understand what you are asking of me; then again the communication is not completed. If you receive no feedback from me, then you might surmise many things, but it would be clear that something went wrong in the communication process. Finally, should I say, "No, I am not moving to the north wall," then we know from the feedback that the communication completed, but I have elected not to carry out the request.

Action

Actions are a form of feedback. However, they have the same characteristics of uncertainty. Using the same example, if I stand up from my chair and leave the room, you are again left to consider whether I received the message and the communication was complete. By contrast, if I stand and go to the north wall, even though there is no spoken reply, it is safe to assume that I heard the message and carried out the request.

What has been briefly outlined, thus far, are the elements of communication. For the remainder of this chapter, we will explore the mechanics for creating a plan to ensure that communications occurs. The process of communicating in an IT organization is critical because creating or modifying business processes and supporting IT need to be based on a thorough communication and understanding of requirements. This is complicated by the semantics associated with information technology. Without multidirectional communication and understanding, the redesign of business processes and IT might be hazardous.

Project or Work Communication

There are many different communications that can occur daily in the business environment. Most are work related, while some are of a social nature. The planning and models presented are geared for work communications and will be couched in the context of a project. The concepts are still the same and the goal is to communicate more effectively with business sponsors, stakeholders, and end users about IT products, services, and projects. The ultimate goal is to improve user adoption after technology has been deployed.

Multidirectional Communications

IT has a responsibility to its internal customers to communicate clearly and with great transparency. There are several different vectors of communication. There is upward communication, to one's supervisor, executives, and in some cases stakeholders. Downward communication is primarily to direct reports, such as a project team and others in the IT department, although it should be noted that end users must also receive communications. Cross communication may be viewed as those interested parties, who are on the same organizational level and are involved in a project or have a need to know.

The function of communicating is one of the most important tasks that an IT professional undertakes. Some IT personnel do not handle this function well. Those that do, quickly rise within the organization.

To communicate to the business about IT products or services in a more business-friendly way and to improve user adoption after the technology has been deployed, a formal, structured IT marketing and communication planning process must be established.

Creating a Communications Plan

The planning process begins with the creation of the overall communication plan, which should be integral to all communications; projects, meetings, announcements, etc.. This should include the objective, strategy, and approach for communication on each particular project, meeting announcement, and so on.

One of the first components in creating the communication plan is the construction of a stakeholder map. That document will identify all individuals or groups who have a stake in the outcome of the IT communiqué that is being prepared. The IT stakeholder map also outlines the potential roles of the stakeholders and the total estimated time required for their participation in whatever activity is being communicated. Clear ownership is necessary in the same way ownership is critical for all other project tasks tracked in a project plan.

Standard Practices

We often hear about *best practices*. However, I prefer the term *standard practices* because different environments and cultures may require adjusting a process or practice so that it is acceptable to firm. To develop a strong communication plan, one should begin with standard practices. These standard practices are obvious when you list them and are usually derived from years of experience and other knowledge that may have been transferred to your firm by consultants with communication and change management expertise. Let's look at five standards practices in detail.

Communication Goal

Presenting the goal is a standard practice with two dimensions. In every presentation that I give, the first slide after the agenda is "The Goal of the Presentation." It is important to tell the audience what you would like to accomplish. It is also a good idea to pause after this and conduct a mini-discussion around the goal of the presentation. It is important that everyone is on the same page.

The second dimension of the communication goal is at the macro-level. This part of the goal applies to all communication. The following three items should become intrinsic in all communications. First, the communication must be timely. We all know that information loses its value over time. Second, the communication must be succinct. There is nothing worse than communication that rambles on ad nauseam. Finally, the message must be targeted at the right audience and adjusted to their level of understanding.

Effective Communications

Regardless of the medium used to deliver communications, the delivery must be effective. I don't necessarily mean humorous or powerful, but effective. For example, a call will be effective if, just prior to ending the conference call, you reiterate the action items and who they are assigned to. However, it you were to follow up on the same call with a summary of the meeting (minutes), it would be even more effective.

E-mail can be a very effective tool if used to enhance communications, internally and across long distances. E-mail allows an additional means of communication with other people. No attempt should be made to replace existing communications practices, and you should ensure communications by e-mail are as clear as if another method of communication (letter, fax, etc.) were being utilized. This tool, when utilized effectively, can pull people together from other locations, and even other continents. However, you must be wary of overdependence on e-mail, or sending too many e-mails.

Global Perspective

With the evolution of technology and globalization of the business community, many firms continue to implement solutions for a global audience. This means taking the time to consider global impacts and regional differences. To do this requires obtaining and implementing a global perspective early in the communications planning. Even if time zones and cultural differences on a global scale are not directly impacted, there could be an indirect effect. And if communications need to expand at a later stage, the local cultures and nuances will have already been taken into account.

Clarity

One of the primary purposes of the communication planning process is to ensure clarity. That is the purpose for creating a communications matrix that identifies for every message its owner and recipients. Without a clear definition of owners and recipients, communication planning often becomes an afterthought that may prove to be inadequate and ineffective for the task at hand. Problems can be avoided by communicating messages with clarity.

Match the Message to the Audience

When the stakeholders are known, then an effective message can be prepared for each specific group. These messages will be based on how a specific group is impacted, its knowledge is of the situation, and the each group's expected reaction. Messages requiring preparation may include such diverse stakeholders as executive committee members who are responsible for the financial impact of the plan and the business unit and IT staff who charged with execution of the project. One can see the importance of structuring a communications campaign for each constituency based on its projected concerns. Collaborating with the person or group most likely to influence a given constituency's opinion is recommended. Following are messages that are appropriate for the particular audience.

Executive Committee—Build Momentum for Change

One way of sustaining initial executive committee support for IT is by communicating the potential cost savings available during a time of great economic difficulty or one of expansion. There is a widely held belief that information technology generally costs too much and promises benefits that are not realized. This belief is a lightning rod and should be avoided. The CIO owns the relationship to the executive committee and should engage it on plans to rationalize systems, reduce cost, and increase value.

Line of Business Directors—Foster Business Ownership

It is in the line of business organizations that rogue IT departments are found. This phenomenon occurs because the director believes that he/she is not being provided adequate service from the corporate or "formal" IT department. The message for this group is that its line of business costs can be reduced while simultaneously improving its IT service. This can be accomplished by migrating business unit managers from owners of their own IT capabilities into clients of a centrally provided service. Although not all choose to participate, those that do become clients can demand higher service levels rather than manage performance.

IT Steering Committee—Selecting and Obtaining a Supportive Committee

Input should be solicited from line of business managers on the committee as to whether the right team has been pulled together. By seeking input from the committee and having it participate in the selection process of its own members, IT is seeking to put in place the right decision makers and to have the committee invested in the outcome.

IT Management—The Right Managers

To demonstrate a new or improved service culture of IT, the selected team must be composed of managers who exhibit approachability, listen and respond thoughtfully, are accountable, and have a results orientation. Clearly communicating this process of evaluation brings a future-focus to the IT management and staff.

IT Staff—Minimize Risk, Promote Continuity

To preempt rumors that can undermine employee confidence, regular updates via a Web site, e-mail messages, in-person team meetings, pan-IT town halls, and a CIO road show must be undertaken. In addition, the needs of individual employees should be taken into consideration for future activities and decisions. For example, to avoid disrupting previously planned holidays, pursuit of education, and the like, managers should commit to schedule decisions in advance, allowing affected employees to either work free of the stress created by uncertainty or at least plan their individual schedules accordingly.

Vendors—Reinforce Central Procurement

Trusted vendors should be required to work with IT in a manner that provides rewards or penalties based on committing to and accomplishing the one-year IT strategy. This strategy must incorporate all of the communications facets discussed thus far and be communicated during an in-house presentation for vendors. Questions from vendors, suggestions, and other input should be incorporated (when possible) into the IT strategy so that the commitment is shared. Regular updates on progress and changes to the plan should be provided to the vendors.

A Communication Template

There are many ways of creating, organizing, and executing a communications plan. Although organization of the plan is important, it must also be easy to use. The value is not in the plan itself, but in the execution of the plan—that is, in the deliberate and organized communicating of the message(s).

Table 3.3 is a representative communications template. This particular template was created for an offshoring project. This template can be customized to the specific needs of a project to accommodate different departments and stakeholders, as well as varying communication goals. The template for projects occurring within a single department may be less complex than for projects requiring cross-functional global teams. However, the need to communicate does not diminish. The communications template for various types and sizes of projects should be adjusted to ensure effective communication to those directly involved in the project as well as stakeholders.

An IT communication template should be jointly developed by the IT communications function (if one exists) and the core project team. In smaller organizations, this responsibility may need to be assumed by the project team alone. The template delineates the communication goals for key project stakeholders, the most appropriate format and channel for those communications, the optimal communication frequency, and an owner for communication delivery.

Integrating Information

Information technology departments that are just beginning to formalize their communications plans and that start operating with an organized approach may find that with just rudimentary planning they can achieve stable and consistent communications. This is a

TABLE 3.3	Offshoring Project Communication Template/Schedule

Instructions: Based on the needs of the Offshoring project, select the suggested deliverables required for effective, open communication with all impacted audiences. "Does not include all deliverables required for all projects."

Communication Deliverables	Message/Goal	Audience	Method	Timing	Owner	Distribution Date	Status
Project Team							
Project Plan Distribution	Communicate project plan	Project team		VP staff meeting	Project manager		
Project Status Update	Announce selection of offshore partner	Global support organization	E-mail	When required	Project manager		
Project Status Update	Notify volume channel managers of training date, time, location, and other prep details.	Volume channel managers	E-mail	Three to four weeks prior to training	Project manager		
Project Status Briefing	Update on project status, timelines, milestones, & impacts	Volume channel managers	E-mail, web	As required	Project manager		
CIO Staff Meetings	Project status, business decisions, and issues resolution	VP staff	Meeting	Weekly	VP		
Distribution of Talking Points	Party line on offshoring, why, and the benefits	VP staff	Memo	One time	VP		
Project Management Meeting	Project status, interdependencies, decision making, and issues resolution	Project team	Meeting	Weekly	Project manager		
Project Status Update	Announce completion of knowledge transfer	Global support organization	E-mail	When required	Project manager		
Executive Team							
Executive Briefing	Executive presentation signal intent to sign contract (go/no go)	Executive team	Presentation or e-mail	Just before contract	VP		
Executive Sponsor Formal Briefing	Project status	Executive team	Meeting	Quarterly meetings	VP		
CFO Staff Meetings	Issues and resolution and project status	CFO staff	Meeting	As required	VP		
Distribution of Talking Points	Information on why offshore, and benefits	Executive team	Memo	One time	VP		

good first step and should be acknowledged. In short order, the plan should be reviewed to ensure that the communication is not creating silos, based on business applications, organizational structure, or other criteria that may limit effectiveness.

Many organizations often demand more integrated systems be implemented so the company can fully realize the power of information across the company. IT assumes the role of facilitator and point of contact for cross-functional technology solutions. This axiom should be applied to communication and the communication plan. To accomplish this, IT

TABLE 3.3	Offshoring Project Communication Template/Schedule *continued*						
Communication Deliverables	**Message/Goal**	**Audience**	**Method**	**Timing**	**Owner**	**Distribution Date**	**Status**
Offshore Partner							
Request for Proposal	Communicate requirements to third party service providers	Offshore vendors	E-mail	One time	Project manager		
Offshore Partner Meeting	Issues, timeline, accomplishments, key decisions, activities, and milestones	Project team	Conference Call	Weekly, after engaging a TPSP	Project manager		
Offshore Partner Update	Make offshore partner meeting minutes available	Project team	E-mail	Weekly	Project manager		
Follow Up with IT Managers							
Follow-up Survey	Project review of how service provider is doing	Volume channel managers	E-mail	After knowledge transfer	Project manager		Project review
Survey Briefing	Survey: highlights & identified action items for the project team	Volume channel managers	E-mail	One to two weeks after survey	Project manager		
Postmortem Meeting	Conduct follow-up meeting once regular process being followed	Volume channel managers	Meeting	One to two weeks after going live	Project manager		

and business organizations must work in an integrated fashion. When addressing the need for integrated information, robust systems must be deployed that cross departmental boundaries. When addressing the need for integrated communications, a robust communication plan must be created, shared, and executed.

At the integration level of maturity, IT organizations will move out of a limited and even a silo-based view of departmental information. This will result in relevant departmental information being shared with and consumed by other departments. Improved communications will also improve the quality of business decisions, because the input upon which decisions are made will have been enhanced.

Summary

Information technology department members need to communicate constantly and consistently with many stakeholders, as well as among themselves. In a virtual organization where others (outside the company, such as vendors or customers) are involved in the business process, very clear lines of communication with them must be set up and enforced. Within an organization, there may be dozens of groups to be interfaced, including upper management and various support and service groups. In some instances, interfaces with other equipment manufacturers or software developers whose equipment and/or software are being used on your project may be required. The project's communication plan should first identify where a liaison is required and should then address the following considerations:

1. *Who on the project has overall responsibility for the communication plan?* Depending on the project size and nature, the designated person may be different from the project manager. When this person has been established as the owner of the communication plan, this person must then designate prime responsibility for each type of contact. People who have prime responsibility for each type of contact are sometime given different titles, such as business relationship manager or IT liaison. Names, titles, and pairings of those teamed to communicate should be designated.

2. *Who can commit to changes in key areas, policies or agree to architectural or technological design changes? Who can agree to a schedule change?* These questions are usually addressed as part of change management, but deserve emphasis here. Information technology management must decide who can speak for projects and in various operational areas. Additionally, it must make certain that the decisions are communicated to the customer and project personnel. Often, the communication process may begin before decisions are made in order to inform, hear a different perspective, or gain support. Good information technology policies and practices make clear to internal customers that they are free to talk with their designated representatives at any time. This might be to exchange ideas, suggest changes, or receive additional information. However, these same internal customers should also understand that only specific individuals can commit to making a change. This is so because the designated individuals have the overview necessary to assess change impact. All the stakeholders, including the customer, *must* understand this from the beginning.

3. *Just as the customer must understand who speaks for Information Technology, or an Information Technology project, how should IT personnel understand who speaks for the customer?* This should be done as early in the process as is possible. Meeting and maintaining contact with key customer people is vital to success of any endeavor. Whether these stakeholders are concerned with facilities, acceptance of completed IT work, or technical decisions, they should be engaged, and that engagement should be maintained. Finding out who commits the customer in signing off specifications, agreeing to design changes, and so on, is important. Equally important is who from the customer side influences that decision maker. A good strategy is to insist on an effective working relationship. Don't allow poor communication to cause delays in decision making that will affect initiatives and their schedules. Whenever possible, state clearly, in writing, the customer's responsibility in communicating on all matters: system design, programming, testing, supplying test data and support services, and so on.

4. *What should be the communications internal to the information technology department?* With the advancements in technology assisted communications, good communications within the IT department should be facilitated and expected. Many IT decisions rely on various pieces of information from a diversity of IT groups. All of the principles used to communicate to internal customers and stakeholders should be applied to ensure good communications within IT.

5. *What are the requirements for exchanging technical information, aside from normal status reporting with other groups?* Establish during project planning efforts a readily undated directory, indicating types of information exchanges necessary and who the contact in each group is. As an example, often, those outside the IT department believe that understanding the technology will assist them in better understanding the business side of an initiative or project. An entire discussion could ensue on just this one point. Rather than waste valuable time, it would be more prudent to simply communicate the information being requested, thus ensuring that an inordinate amount of time is not being spent on providing technical information that will be of no value to the business user.

Communication in the business environment is critical to the success of any undertaking. Good communications cannot ensure good results, but bad communications will most certainly fuel poor results.

SECTION 4
Learning and Growth

Career Path to the Position of CIO

Tim Hanrahan

CIO Geneology

Although the title did not surface until the 1990s, the chief information officer (CIO) role has been in existence since the introduction of computers in the 1960s. The roots of the CIO sprouted from management and operational roles in data processing, which were predominantly found in the large mainframe environments of the insurance, government, and scientific research industries. Back then, as well as today, no single job description applied throughout industries and companies.

In the 1980s, only the visionaries recognized the value in the *data ore*. Today, however, businesses in all industries have become converts. The value of the data ore has skyrocketed. Adoption of mining the data ore and refining it into operational and strategic information was gaining momentum prior to the Internet. Today, operational information is table stakes, and strategic information and the infrastructure to get and maintain it are as critical as the financial side of running a business.

This increasing importance of information has not only moved the data center from the basement to the lobby, but has elevated the *director of data processing* to CIO, with a prominent seat at the executive table.

The CIO Today

A current CIO position description will vary, based on industry and company size. There are four major components to the position: technology management, relationship management, financial management, and personnel management:

- Technology management is strongly influenced by the industry and corporate environment at hand, but common denominators will include distributed footprint (global or national), networks (WAN and LAN), security, communications (voice, data), computer infrastructure (ERP, databases, back office servers, storage), user computing, and corporate user support. Project management, a critical skill, is a joint component of technology and personnel management.

- Relationship management is often an unwritten requirement, frequently implied, overlooked, or assumed in the position description. Establishing, developing, and maintaining relationships from inside the sphere is critical to being a successful CIO. These interactions must be effective in all directions, upward to the CEO and BOD, laterally to the CFO, COO, and other corporate officers and operational VPs, and downward to the corporate clients, internal customers, and employees. An equally important skill is to quickly learn the business at hand. This includes the company's products, customers, business drivers, and processes to effectively run and control the business. Another sphere of relationships outside the company is also critical to the CIO's success. Relationships with vendors, industry executives, fellow professionals, and potential employees must always be maintained and nurtured.

- Financial management skills are a key component of the CIO's job today. Information technology and services are expensive, ever changing, and often compose a sizable chunk of corporate operating expenses. Although most CIOs do not have the luxury of being a profit center, and generating revenue, it is nevertheless important to run the information technology (IT) organization like a business. Developing an intuitive sense of value, return on investment (ROI), and true need of requested services, along with a disciplined monitoring of spending, will favorably impact a CIO's tenure and status within an organization.

- Personnel management skills are also often shaded, or considered secondary. The IT organization's success is based on the strength and effectiveness of its staff. Recruiting, developing, motivating and retaining high-performance and highly skilled employees is a prized attribute of a CIO. In addition to maintaining a skilled staff, the CIO must have the organizational development skills to create an efficient and effective management structure to ensure proper command and control.

As stated earlier, based on industry and company size, the title of the information executive (IE) and its responsibilities will vary. At a company where information technology is the core business, like Google or Yahoo!, the IE may be titled chief operating officer (COO). At a company whose core business is developing information technology or software, like

Synopsys or Oracle, the IE may be titled chief technology officer (CTO). Often, CEOs may not feel that their company size or function warrants a position or title of CIO, and choose to employ the title of VP or director of information technology. No matter the job title, a company IE, has tremendous impact potential, responsibility, and purpose.

Let us turn now to some of the new qualifications of CIOs. In recent years, due to increasing regulations, CIOs have had to be experienced in regulatory compliance issues, including but not limited to Sarbannes-Oxley, HIPAA, customer, and employee privacy. Although these statutes are U.S.-centric, global operations will have specific regulations and compliance implications by country.

Security is also a major focus today, somewhat prompted by regulations, but also driven by the sheer volume and rapid increase in electronic intellectual property (IP), and the proliferation of methods and avenues of information dissemination.

The flavor of outsourcing appears to be somewhat cyclical in nature, however, like the tides, it is a fact of life in the IT industry. Experience in analyzing opportunities, sourcing and selecting appropriate vendors, and managing ongoing corporate operations in an outsourced environment is a highly desired skill.

A recent industry trend related to traditional outsourcing is service-related delivery (SRD) or Software-as-a-Service (SaaS), and Storage-as-a-Service (StaaS). Although the primary skills needed for these environments are related to vendor management, the volume of offsite services may require delving into the architectural design of a hybrid operation.

Let us turn now to the question of where new CIOs come from and their backgrounds. A survey of current and former Silicon Valley CIOs turned up three primary career sources: 80 percent of the CIOs come from within the IT organization, with an equal distribution from an application development background and a computer operations background. The remaining 20 percent come from a business background, nearly all from engineering or R&D.

Educational backgrounds were surprisingly varied, with only 30 percent graduating with an IT-related degree. The majority, over 90 percent, did graduate with technical specialties in IT, mathematics, or engineering. Less that 50 percent of the polled group had advanced degrees.

Average tenure and work experience of the polled group exceeded 16 years in industry before moving into the CIO position. Average time as a CIO at one company exceeded 3 years.

Keys to CIO Success

What are the keys to CIO success? From the polled group, there were three primary areas cited as critical to the successful performance in the position:

1. *Understanding of the business.* The interviewees unanimously cited this factor. As mentioned earlier, gone are the days where the IT department is in the basement, or treated as a simple utility. Technology is a tool of differentiation, both strategically and operationally. Understanding the business drivers, how to leverage the technology, and the

use of information to positively impact the business solidly places the CIO at the executive table.

2. *Project management.* Ranking highly with the interviewees, and described using various terms was the ability to deliver on promises. The variety of techniques used, from "underpromising and overdelivering" to "managing and communicating expectations," was overshadowed by the personal and organizational commitments to reliable delivery.

3. *Customer and client relationships.* Being successful at the first two keys to success will make this third key easier to accomplish. Maintaining positive relationships with your corporate and external clients through understanding the business and delivering results will help produce the ever-illusive business alignment. Because the IT customer is the company itself, the direction to maintaining these relationships is often counter-intuitive. That is, specific customer requests might be denied, in favor of a more sweeping corporate initiative or a higher payback project. Making the tough decisions will be accepted as long as there is transparency and effective communication. Beyond the top three, there was a fanning out of other suggested keys to success. Among the other cited areas were: staff development and retention, strategic planning, vendor management, and budget/financial management.

Summary

In summary, the CIO role has either already reached, or is rapidly approaching, its sustainable zenith. CIOs have been elevated from basement data centers and invited to be a full participants at the executive table. The tremendous leverage of IT as a corporate weapon is the frequent subject in many boardrooms today. In numerous cases, the CIO is now the career stepping stone to the corner office—CEO.

I would like to thank the Silicon Valley CIOs who took the time to participate and share their views and backgrounds used in this chapter.

CIO as Anthropologist

George C. Lin and Jeffrey J. Ward

A new CIO often walks into his or her position as an agent of change. It is a rare company that seeks a new CIO because things are going well. But it is also rare to find a company that is entirely ready for the changes a new CIO wants to make. The new CIO must be an *applied anthropologist* of sorts, exploring an undiscovered culture in the hope of introducing changes that may make a critical difference in the company's success or even survival. As newcomers to an organizational culture, CIOs often find that their success depends on *how* they introduce change more than the specific changes they make. This idea runs counter to most of the conventional wisdom regarding the CIO's role.

Many CIOs approach the role as experts who have been hired to fix problems in technology and process; their mandate is to change these to conform to *best practices,* as defined by the IT industry. But new CIOs often find that they struggle to realize their goals because they encounter barriers within the company that are not rational. There are two approaches that a new CIO can use. The first and more conventional approach is to assume the mantle of the expert who is mandated to drive change within the organization. After all, throughout the interview process that got the new CIO his or her job, every member of the executive staff complained about the current situation in IT and stressed the need for a new direction. What was left unsaid, of course, was that these executives expected those changes to be entirely transparent to them and to have no major impact on the workings of their own departments. Now the new CIO is faced with barriers to implementing best practices and introducing new efficiencies into processes, work structure, and technology. Many CIOs dismiss these barriers as political or attribute the resistance to ignorance or inflexibility on the part of their users. As change agents, their job is to push the organization in the right direction. The more enlightened CIOs recognize that they will have to lobby for their vision and sell the key executives on the value of new efficiencies.

The anthropological approach, however, starts from a different perspective. The anthropological CIO reminds him- or herself that the ultimate goal is to introduce the most *effective*, not necessarily the most *efficient*, process and technology. *Effectiveness* is based as much on acceptability within a company's culture as it is on best practices; the most efficient processes and technologies are ineffective if the community refuses to adopt them, undermines their implementation, or mounts an outright insurgency. The anthropological CIO starts by recognizing that organizational communities are like any other community, with members who share some strongly held conceptions that define the identity of the community and who also compete and conflict with one another. Introducing change means learning about these *soft* aspects of the organization and navigating a course that flows *with* rather than *against* the cultural currents that travel through it. And because organizations are *multicultural* (consisting of many subcultures, each with its own set of values, loyalties, and territories), the anthropological CIO recognizes that going with the flow will also mean dodging a lot of rocks and whirlpools in the cultural stream.

In this chapter a CIO and an anthropologist (turned business consultant) collaborate to describe successful applications of these principles in real-life situations. Our experience is gained through working with dozens of companies, either directly or as a result of company mergers and consulting engagements. We offer some unconventional advice for IT executives who have been handed a mandate for change but recognize that there may be a huge gap separating best practices from achievable realities. This advice combines the collective experience of anthropologists working both within corporations and out in the field with the experience of CIOs who have successfully navigated corporate culture to make significant positive changes within their organizations.

Corporate Culture

The concept of *corporate culture* was first popularized by Deal and Kennedy (1978). Their work emphasized the encompassing and somewhat uniform culture that ties a company together. They argued that successful corporations are characterized by a clear and strongly held culture. Later research by anthropologists working within organizations suggested that notions of a single corporate culture are naïve; corporations actually consist of many interlocking subcultures with fuzzy boundaries, all of which jostle against one another to achieve not only the overall goals of the organization but also the more parochial goals of individual departments or groups within it. Big or small, the various cultures within a company determine its *feel*, its politics, and its capacity to absorb change and accept new structures, processes, and technologies.

In the common vernacular, culture is about art, literature, manners, and society. But anthropologists have long recognized that the root of culture is *knowledge;* it is the set of things that we have learned that help us to understand our world and guide our behavior (McCurdy, Spradley, and Shandy 2004; Spradley 1979). It determines how we think about ourselves as individuals and as a group, how we interpret new experiences or ideas, and how we adjust to changes in social structure and the rituals that reinforce it. This knowledge can be explored by asking open-ended questions and listening carefully both to the substance, language, and phrasing of the answers. When a CIO acts as an anthropologist, he or she takes time to interview other executives and key employees with an open mind before drawing conclusions about the organization's needs. The anthropological CIO asks open-ended questions such as, "Tell me about the challenges of your job" rather than beginning with restrictive questions, such as, "What applications do you think need to be replaced?"

In the following sections we demonstrate how this approach can be used in four key areas in which new CIOs must succeed: setting a strategic plan, governing the IT spend, improving customer satisfaction, and influencing the wider company culture regardless of its specific relevance to IT.

Creating an Effective IT Plan

Creating and communicating an effective IT plan is often one of the first important tasks that a CIO must complete when starting with a new company. An IT plan usually consists of a proposed architecture and standards for the company's business systems and infrastructure, a roadmap that details major system initiatives and enhancements, and related financials that support the roadmap. The IT plan may also include higher-level information such as discussions about the IT vision/mission, an IT governance framework, the CIO's strategies for the IT organization and operations, and so on. Needless to say, the IT plan is an important document for both internal IT consumption and for communication to the rest of the company.

All too often, IT plans are colorless. They may be nothing more than a compendium of best practices that reflect common wisdoms of the IT industry. If IT is about *me too*, then such IT plans are perfectly fine. But if IT is about creating competitive advantages and strategic values in support of company goals then an effective IT plan must reflect the unique aspects of that company: its marketplace challenges, its relationships with vendors and customers and competitors, its industry alliances, the peculiarities of its management structure (including internal politics), and the ways in which its employees communicate, plan, and execute. If an IT plan does not reflect these unique features (explicitly or implicitly), it may look good on paper but it will not be effective when the time comes for its execution. The plan must resonate well with the people and the cultural forces at play in a corporation. If an IT plan reflects a company's uniqueness, such a plan will at least create more buy-in and the execution of it will certainly be easier.

What factors determine a company's unique signature? There are many, but culture is certainly an important factor. Successful CIOs create IT plans that blend in cultural elements. For example, an aggressive sales-oriented and numbers-driven company's IT plan should look very different from a company that prides itself on product innovations and customer service. The IT plan of the former company may be skewed toward creating front-office applications and road-warrior tools. The roadmap may have frequent milestones that depict deliverables by quarter. The overall presentation may be more numbers and ROI oriented. In contrast, the IT plan of the latter company may be skewed toward supporting quicker time-to-market and improved customer interactions. There may be more extensive discussions on proposed solutions and the pros and cons of competing options. Readers of such a plan may also be interested in understanding internal IT service offerings and service-level objectives. What is the best way to blend corporate culture into an IT plan? It is deceivingly simple. Normally, when CIOs create an IT plan, they (or their business analysts) interview key stakeholders to understand their requirements. Then they work with IT teams to come up with a plan that can satisfy those business requirements.

Our suggestion is to go one further step and involve the wider business in the creation of the IT plan. Have key stakeholders nominate their power users, who will then participate in the actual creation of the IT plan. These power users can participate in focus sessions, act as consultants to IT, and perform a reviewer role. The goal is to have a deeper and a more meaningful engagement with the business so that additional subtleties (in addition to the normal business requirements) can be captured and be considered during the plan creation efforts.

Pacifying the Corporation: Tailoring IT Governance

In the eighteenth, nineteenth, and early twentieth centuries, the major colonial powers (Great Britain, France, Spain, Portugal, Germany, and Italy) invaded and subjugated territories on almost every continent. One of the problems that they encountered was persistent, low-level warfare among the competing tribes, villages, or ethnic groups in these territories. The elimination of such warfare was called *pacification*, and it was met with mixed success. In Africa, most pacification was undertaken at the point of a gun; competing tribes were compelled to live side by side in peace, because the alternative was to face the technically superior forces of the colonizer. In the long term, this approach failed because the withdrawal of colonial powers removed the only barrier to the resumption of hostilities. But the new tribal warfare was no longer a low-level conflict; the introduction of modern weapons of warfare enabled a much more deadly set of intertribal or ethnic conflicts. Wars and revolutions in Angola, Ethiopia/Eritrea, Rwanda, Nigeria, Sudan, the Congo, and other African nations all began due to the colonial presence. In the Pacific, however, one island was pacified in a very unusual (and unintended) way that proved to be uniquely stable.

The Trobriand Islands of New Guinea were one of the first cultures to be studied by a newly minted area of social science called *anthropology* and one of its founders, Bronislaw Malinowsky. When the British colonized the Trobriands, there was ongoing tit-for-tat warfare among the various villages that resulted in a small but steady rate of homicide. This inter-village rivalry was disruptive to the management of the colony but critical to the stability of the village structure. The introduction of the game of cricket provided an unintended substitute for warfare.

Americans usually think of cricket as a lengthy and slow-moving game, but the Trobriand version was more colorful. The participants dressed in full war regalia, including feathers and body painting, and entered the field while performing traditional war dances. Dancing broke out at many points during the games when significant scores were made. But the outcome was never in doubt: the home team always won. The medium of cricket allowed villages to continue to express rivalry in a less violent manner, and the home-team-wins rule ensured that the tit-for-tat balance of the previous warfare was maintained. Unwittingly, the British colonizers had introduced an effective substitute for violence.

In the corporation, low-level warfare is often waged around the way that limited IT dollars are allocated. This warfare can be conducted in various ways, many of which are unproductive. Sometimes various constituencies (villages, if you will) lobby IT directly, using bribes, threats, or personal relationships to get the time and attention of the IT organization. Sometimes the constituencies conduct open warfare in rancorous executive staff meetings or engage in tugs-of-war at lower levels of the organization. These chaotic forms of disagreement can result in unnecessary conflict, wasted time and effort, and a zigzag course for the IT organization. It can even contribute to conflict within IT as various lobbies within the company enlist the support of their favorite IT employees. The corporate version of Trobriand cricket is a carefully conceived IT governance process. There are a few definitions of IT governance. Some are broad and elaborate. We tend to be more practical so we prefer the narrower and simpler definition by Weill and Ross (2004): "specifying the decision rights and accountability framework to encourage desirable behavior in the use of IT." IT governance defines the ownership of decisions, the actual process of setting priorities and making decisions, and the accountability of outcomes.

IT governance is one of the three pillars that we often look for in an effective IT shop: governance, an organization that is based on people, and operational excellence. Arguably, IT governance is the most important of the three pillars. The right governance framework helps a CIO run IT like a business, aligns IT projects to business needs, and regulates supply and demand. But is there one best governance framework that CIOs can simply copy and adopt? As we contrast best practices with effective solutions, we think the answer is no.

If IT governance is the framework for making IT decisions, then it must take into consideration a company's existing culture—the way that employees tend to work and interact and the context in which decisions are made. Is the culture formal and rigid, or is it open and relaxed? How is the company organized? Are decisions made autocratically (by a small group of decision makers) or democratically (delegated to a larger group of managers)? It is not the role of the CIO to pass judgment about this culture, just as anthropologists are not in the field to judge the cultures they study. Instead of complaining about the company culture, a successful CIO designs an IT governance framework that is effective for the given environment.

Some may argue that what we are proposing waters down the role of the CIO as a change agent or that we are giving in to the establishment. But if a CIO establishes policy or process that conflicts with the collective wisdom of the community that he or she tries to engage, common sense tells us that this CIO won't be a change agent there for very long. We had an opportunity to design and implement an IT governance framework at a mid-cap company. Best practices suggested that a governance council of second-level, operationally focused executives would be the best solution. But it turned out that the framework for this company was far more elaborate than the ones that we had deployed at much larger companies. Why? Because the executive staff was very hands-on compared to other corporations. It preferred to be included in every operational decision. Delegation did not seem to be an effective approach because the executive staff was notorious for vetoing lower-level decisions on an *ad hoc* basis, often late in a project. As a result, mid-level executives with operational responsibilities (and the best understanding of IT needs) were unwilling to commit to IT priorities or plans, fearing that their decisions would be overturned.

We designed the governance framework to fit this culture. It consisted of two layers: the executive team and its lieutenants. The lieutenants met regularly as a cross-functional team to set IT priorities (based on project proposals and business cases) and to make project go/no-go recommendations. The executive team was the second-level governing body with final approval authority; this formalized its veto authority and turned a potential roadblock into a recognized step in the governance process. Frequent status updates between the two management layers ensured continued project support from the executive team and avoided executive vetoes too far down the road of a project when the costs of reversing course can be very high.

In a company where operational decisions are routinely delegated, this framework might have seemed inefficient. But at this particular company, the framework proved to be extremely effective. We moved far more IT projects (in terms of both number and relevance to the business) through the governance process and delivered them successfully than any other period in this company's history. Even more important was the number of projects that did *not* make it through the early stages of governance—they were weeded out before any substantial investment by the business. (This was a significant change from the previous history of projects that failed halfway through implementation due to lack of ongoing support.)

Improving Customer Satisfaction

Old-fashioned CIOs worry about efficiency. Modern CIOs worry about customer satisfaction. Anthropological CIOs recognize that customer satisfaction depends on culture—customer service efforts that work for one company (or, for that matter, one department within a company) may not work elsewhere.

An effective assessment of customer satisfaction must be based on an understanding of the culture (and subcultures) within a company. One way of gathering such an understanding is the open-ended questions in any customer satisfaction survey. We have found that the classical numerical data (based on, for example, questions that are answered by ratings) are useful for presentations to executive staff members, but the open-ended questions that allow employees to write comments are much more useful in truly understanding the issues that affect them. Although it requires more effort to read through written responses, they are a rich source of information that cannot be captured in purely numerical results. In fact, these comments have helped us refine the quantitative questions.

But we don't recommend taking a customer satisfaction survey if you are not going to respond to its results. Once a survey is taken, a clock begins ticking until the announcement of survey results and a plan of action to correct low ratings or problems identified in comments. If there is too long of a lag between the survey and this announcement, employees lose interest and will not respond to subsequent surveys, figuring that the results are being ignored.

In both the survey and in the announcement of results, it is important to use culturally appropriate terminology. Such terminology both increases the likelihood that employees will clearly understand the survey questions and results and the positive effect of the survey itself. For example, in one company our customer satisfaction survey used terms like *company* and *department* because the culture was very business-oriented; in another company these terms were replaced with *community* and *group* because the prevailing culture there tended to emphasize interpersonal relationships. While this difference may seem small, in the end the care that we took to recognize subtle cultural elements was critical in successfully measuring and then improving the relationship between IT and the rest of the company.

The success of an employee may be as much about his or her fit within the context of a company as about purely technical skills. Similarly, improvements in IT's customer satisfaction are as much about soft skills and the ability of IT management to navigate a company's cultural currents as about technical efficiency. The anthropological CIO takes notice of cultural subtleties within his or her environment and uses that understanding to both assess the effectiveness of the IT organization and launch efforts designed to improve that effectiveness.

Influencing the Wider Culture

The job of a CIO must extend beyond the confines of the IT organization. Effective CIOs are not just supercharged IT managers but also members of a company's most senior and strategically oriented executive team. In the latter role, the CIO is responsible for assessing and influencing the company's wider culture to improve its strategic advantages in the marketplace.

A CIO who understands underlying cultural currents within a company and properly leverages them can become a powerful influence in making wider changes. The IT organization touches every part of a company and is in a unique position to inspire positive change throughout the organization. This is not merely a matter of going with the flow; it involves understanding and actively managing that flow. The flow then becomes a force in support of the CIO's change agenda. The following example illustrates the application of this principle.

Our mid-cap company had a problem. For several years in a row, employee satisfaction surveys showed that employees believed a lack of effective cross-functional communication and collaboration was the most serious issue hindering the company. This had serious consequences for IT. When there is no cross-functional communication, there are information and business process silos that impede end-to-end solutions. The end result is that the information systems supporting these silos are also fragmented and difficult to maintain, enhance, upgrade, and integrate. Moreover, this problem impeded the company's ability to effectively deploy its solutions to customers and communicate its mission to the marketplace.

By understanding the underlying cultural currents, we were able to ride this cultural stream to bring positive change to the entire corporation. We asked ourselves: What are the most effective means of introducing cross-departmental communication within this particular context? We decided that the various departments and business units needed (1) to feel connected to one another on a personal basis, (2) forums for effective collaboration in establishing end-to-end business processes, and (3) clear and visible milestones that demonstrated the positive results of collaborative thinking.

To meet the first need, we began to publish IT newsletters that emphasized interdepartmental collaboration efforts. Although the professionally designed newsletter was made available online, we used the low-tech method of publishing it on paper. We knew that a purely electronic newsletter would probably be skimmed rather than read. A paper copy could be taken to lunch, on the bus or commuter train, or even to the bathroom. It could be set aside on someone's desk and then picked up later. Its presence at the lunchroom, coffee station, or mailroom was a constant reminder of its existence and an invitation to browse its contents while waiting for the microwave, coffee maker, or copy machine to finish its job.

In support of the second need, we provided forums, structure, and tools for stakeholders to engage in productive cross-functional conflict resolution and problem-solving discussions about IT systems and business processes. This involved a careful selection of forum participants based on the company culture and social organization. We selected the most collaborative and big picture executives from the various departments and gathered them in a carefully structured setting. The success of this effort set an example. Other executives liked what they saw, and these efforts turned into company-wide business process reengineering efforts that ultimately led to the streamlining and the automation of major business processes end-to-end.

At this point, careful project management allowed us to manage the resulting projects as collaborative efforts rather than IT projects. Each project was able to demonstrate the tangible fruits of collaborative efforts. In the end, the entire company benefited from the changes made in the IT sphere because other departments began using cross-departmental forums and projects to ensure the success of their own objectives. The company even began to publish a company-wide newsletter modeled on the IT publication—it was an immediate hit with employees.

When a culturally sensitive CIO has the entire company behind him or her in support of change, the possibility of failure simply does not exist. And the CIO who is able to influence the effectiveness of the entire corporation is a significant asset.

Becoming an Anthropological CIO

The notion of an anthropological CIO may seem attractive in the abstract but hard to realize in the rock-hard world of business. However, the anthropological approach is really just a matter of attention. By attending to the way that colleagues, employees, and members of the corporate community speak and conceptualize themselves and the company, a CIO can explicitly seek to learn *corporate culture* as rapidly as possible (rather than spending years learning by hit or miss experience). And by using this knowledge as an integral part of planning—planning for projects, planning for changes to the organization, planning for the introduction of new business processes—and communication, the anthropological CIO can achieve a degree of positive influence in the corporation to which a technocratic CIO could never aspire.

References

Deal, Terrence E., and Allan A. Kennedy. 1982. *Corporate Cultures: The Rules and Rituals of Corporate Life*. New York: Perseus Books.

McCurdy, David W., James P. Spradley, and Dianna J. Shandy. 2004. *The Cultural Experience: Ethnography in Complex Society (Second Edition)*. New York: Waveland Press.

Spradley, James P. 1979. *The Ethnographic Interview*. New York: Holt, Rinehart, and Winston.

Weill, Peter, and Jeanne Ross. 2004. *IT Governance: How Top Performers Manage IT Decision Rights for Superior Results*. Boston: Harvard Business School Press.

4.3
Innovation

Jennifer Diamond, Sam Gill, and Dean Lane

Our achievements of today are but the sum total of our thoughts of yesterday. You are today where the thoughts of yesterday have brought you and you will be tomorrow where the thoughts of today take you.

—Blaise Pascal

Introduction

Simply stated, innovation is the introduction of a new idea. That is a truly simple definition, because it leaves out too much to be useful. Consider the following:

A successful CIO innovates constantly to improve business processes, create business advantage, or drive new business opportunities.

The enhancement to the second definition is that it defines success on the basis of results. Innovation has to have a purpose, a meaning, and a result with recognized and acknowledged value.

And to raise the stakes even further, the risks associated with introducing change, which is what innovation is, include lack of acceptance, missing the target to solve the business problem, or just going too far for the organization to accept. A successful CIO must understand where to innovate and what risks are involved. A successful CIO must also understand the risks associated with standing still; the twentieth and twenty-first centuries are littered with the remnants of companies who ignored the imperative to innovate.

Let's use Tiger Woods as an example. When thinking about Tiger as a business, what would be the one thing that you would be very hesitant to change? Well, the golfers in the audience probably got it right off. You wouldn't want to make uncalculated changes to Tiger's golf swing. The reasons are obvious, since his golf swing is the very thing that makes him a success or a failure on the golf course. This doesn't mean that Tiger Woods can make absolutely no change or innovation to his golf swing, but he must proceed with caution. By contrast, changes to Tiger's apparel, endorsements of product, and so on can have innovation applied to them with less scrutiny. If Tiger Woods found himself in a slump as he did during the 2005 season, he would *need* to make changes to his swing in order to get back on track. Using a similar analogy, Jack Nicklaus, one of the greatest golfers of all times, leveraged his success in golf to become one of the premier golf course designers in the world. Nicklaus is an example of using innovation that drives new business opportunities.

Innovation can be undertaken as a process—it is done all the time. That may sound foreign, since the common perception of innovation is often to mistake it for invention; the *Eureka!* that only comes every so often, with a stroke of genius. To innovate consistently means that there are roles, methods, and means by which it becomes a way of life, not a moment of breakthrough.

Solving Business Challenges

This goes back to the idea of purpose. Innovation for its own sake is at best research engineering, and that's when it is restricted to the lab and no one tries to actually implement anything. Successful innovation drives toward solving business challenges; finding ways to get there that weren't known or exercised before. The flip-side of innovation is being aware of the breadth of innovation required to get to a solution, which may be even less than originally envisioned. Choosing to *not* reinvent the wheel is judicious innovation. Knowing on what to focus innovation and how much effort to put into an innovation initiative is at the heart of the innovation process.

Creating Business Advantage

Innovation as a process must continuously seek opportunities to create business advantage either through incremental improvements or through seeking out new business products and services. Just because successful business innovation is always in the interest of the business does not mean that it need only be responsive or reactive. A successful IT innovation process should allow for unfettered creativity; proactive innovation allows the pursuit of new product and service strategies. A fully participating CIO knows that as part of his responsibility to the management team is to be the agent of change that drives innovation as a continuum from business improvement (incremental innovation) to the introduction of new products and services (revolutionary innovation). Another way to look at the breakdown of the innovation process is to answer the questions: How do we innovate, why do we innovate, and to what scope?

Consistent Innovation

Declaring innovation to be a process feels like writing a manual for being an artist. Or maybe it's taking that exhilarating *MacGyver* moment of duct tape and chewing gum and demystifying it with instructions. Some may make the claim that the more structure is applied, the more creativity will be stifled, until innovation is just impossible.

Even so, business needs predictability. Business processes are predictable when their steps are fully detailed and understood. To be predicable, innovation must be laid out as a sequence of actions and activities that include many detailed steps. The right innovation methodology will both nurture and enhance innovation while providing the predictability that businesses require. Even MacGyver had a method.

To figure out what the process is, innovation itself has to be broken down into its fundamental activities. One key aspect of innovation is to gain a sense of how to apply problem-solving skills to a situation, before the situation arises, when the situation is at hand, and after the situation is resolved. This means that there is a time dimension to innovation: *before*, *during*, and *after* phases.

Before Innovation Phase

From boxing, where being stable but light on the feet is essential, to firefighting where preparation is the only way to save lives, the importance of being ready is clear. Innovation is no different. In the context of IT management, the CIO and the IT team are inundated with new products, services, solutions, and techniques every hour of every day. Not all, if any, of those new things will apply to any specific problem or need. Some of the new technology heard about today may not be ready for realistic implementation for years. However, it is imperative for the CIO and the IT team to stay abreast of coming changes.

By maintaining curious receptivity to potential solutions, without trying to fit them to a current problem or a current need, CIOs are simply building their inventory of potential solutions and allowing them a general context, whether or not they are needed later. In meetings with vendors who bring an emerging technology to the table, CIOs can ask to be shown one or two use cases, not to understand every detail, but to simply have a sense of how such a thing might fit into a solution set. The innovation enabler becomes an arrow in the CIO's quiver to be utilized later. Smart CIOs ensure that this practice permeates their organization.

In the time frame preceding innovating, the IT executive can demonstrate responsiveness by actively pursuing activities that ferret out a company's needs. Intuitively, the business looks to IT as having a different sort of inventory—an inventory of what might become a need or a solution to a problem in the future. Throughout the IT function, this is the job of a part-nered service organization. By being responsive, the *before innovation phase* of the innovative process results in a constant state of renewed understanding that creates stability and readi-ness for change.

During Innovation Phase

Once the timing is right, and the spark is lit, the innovation process enters the *during inno-vation phase*. In this phase needs must be addressed and ingenuity, frugality and invention take over; they define the space and scope of innovation—the boundaries of exploration for the innovation process. Frugality, in the form of resource use, defines how to responsibly apply time and resources to arrive at a solution. Ingenuity defines how to utilize solid criti-cal thinking to analyze and define needs and identify an appropriate response. Invention defines the creativity that draws from the inventory of solutions, blending them, to create a unique elegant solution to the complex problem at hand. In the *during innovation* phase, the innovation process follows traditional change management steps that include needs confir-mation, design, development and bringing the solution live.

After Innovation Phase

Go live and *implementation* are not the same thing. No change is complete the minute it hap-pens and in the case of a business, full implementation may take up to a year after the solu-tion has been brought live. Adaptability and improvisation define the flexibility needed to adopt the new idea. Whether the change is a tiny increment to an existing method or a completely new approach to doing business, how it becomes reality rarely goes exactly according to plan. The *after innovation phase* of the innovation process includes the fine adjustments that are required to take the new solution across the finish line.

Seeing the innovation process in terms of before, during and after lets us see the simi-larity to well-understood change management processes with which we have long and well-documented experience. There is one caveat; the innovation process requires that the CIO demonstrate a state of readiness and awareness for potential needs and solutions that may face the business. Appropriately, readiness and awareness enhance the CIO role in leading change.

The Innovation Mandate

Human beings are creative. Successful managers have learned to listen to their employees and to pay attention to their ideas. While change management as a process has been defined and defined again, its application to innovation requires refinement. In business, the challenge for truly effective and successful innovation starts with solving business problems—even think tanks strive to define and solve a problem. OK, maybe they spend a little too much time defining the problem. Nevertheless, in the CIO's world, the immediate requirement for innovation is to support the business, and the usual suspects for goals are right up front:

- Improved revenues
- Access to new customers
- Improved customer delivery
- Improved use of resources, including time and money
- Offer a new product or service

This is where the CIO must provide the leadership for the IT team in the nuances of innovation. Once the broad strokes of innovation to solve business problems have been covered, the details of analyzing the problem to pick the best solution require a deeper look. This is the transition from asking, "Why innovate?" to asking, "How much should we innovate?" The characteristics of the problem that needs to be addressed: how widespread: how critical and how risk-laden, define the appropriate innovative solution to the situation.

Case 1: Fast-growing Retailer

Consider the problem of a fast-growing retail manufacturing company with products that have just reached the maturity curve plateau. This company must now change how it handles its operations and information or forgo the next increment of growth, and in the process, hurt its brand's reputation. This company had been successful to this point because top management had fundamentally focused on the reputation of the company as a family maker of excellent products. The crisis that now looms has been reached because of the company's resistance to make significant IT investments. However, with the opportunity of explosive international growth, through a new distribution relationship, the need for change is unavoidable.

This is not the time to get too inventive. The company is at a critical point, and more importantly, the problem is not a new one. There have been many other retail manufacturers who have reached this point and solved this problem, and the market is rife with possible solutions tailored to this exact need. So in this case, IT innovation should be constrained to helping with the selection of the best solution available on the market today, using ingenuity and frugality to guide incremental changes in the business. The IT goal is to take advantage of the best solutions readily available and supported by the market.

The business drivers in this case that guide these actions are:

- Critical and risk-heavy crisis point
- Change-averse organization
- Traditional business operation
- Option-rich marketplace

What if the business situation was different? If the decision point were not so critical, it might have been appropriate for the CIO to gradually expose company management to what the market had to offer without any pressure to implement anything. If the problem itself would have been less traditional, then the need for an ERP system, appropriate to an established industry, might have been replaced by a more customized solution. But as it was, this was a time for a traditional response to a traditional problem. Any other solution would have been less effective.

Looking at the situation a different way, it is obvious that implementing an ERP system is a departure from the way that we've always done it and in a fairly dramatic way, representing a *revolutionary innovation.* Innovation seems to be most recognizable as revolutionary, but it is only one of three main classifications of innovation: *incremental innovation, evolutionary innovation,* and *revolutionary innovation.*

Incremental innovation is defined as a class of innovation that pursues small yet constant changes to create a new state of being. Another very familiar phrase to describe this is continuous improvement. Establishing and constantly moving targets for performance is a state of incremental innovation. This class applies ingenuity and adaptability to reach the next level of achievement, always driving toward even more efficient use of resources. Cost cutting, cycle time reduction, and quality improvement are usually best implemented and create the longest lasting impact when they are done incrementally, systematically moving toward an improved state.

Evolutionary innovation is defined as a class of innovation that pursues longer strides along a logical path. Just as incremental change is heavily influenced by the current state, evolutionary innovation takes its cue from the way things are now, seeking to find ways to enhance them and in so doing, make progress. Out-of-the-box thinking can go a long way in driving toward the accomplishment of business goals. With evolutionary innovation new products and services are actively being pursued.

Case 2: Redefining the Product

A classic example of evolutionary innovation is Arm & Hammer Baking Soda. The Arm & Hammer Baking Soda product began as just that, a product for baking. The business goal in this case was to increase sales. A decision was made to market Arm & Hammer Baking Soda as an odor-eating product to be placed in refrigerators. This was an evolutionary change in sales requiring no modification to the product itself. The implementation of this sales strategy provided a huge business benefit in the form of new customers, increased revenues, and brand identification. It was so successful that Arm & Hammer went on to market its baking soda as a cleaning product and toothpaste. It even got the public to buy more baking soda to pour down the drain!

Revolutionary innovation is defined as a class of innovation that pursues abrupt change to divert from the logical path emanating from the current state. Some examples of this are deciding to outsource or in-source a function or restructuring operations to respond to business needs. Revolutionary innovation requires receptivity to new ideas and the inventory of options to solve a problem that requires a fundamental change. The word *innovation* is frequently associated with this type of change, but quantitatively, it is the rarest kind. In a well-minded CIO store, revolutionary innovation is instigated by outside sources addressing immediate challenges or opportunities that are beyond the capabilities of the IT team. This is usually the case because the internal IT team is focused on ongoing incremental and evolutionary innovation.

For CIOs, the most frequent cause of revolutionary innovation is acquisition. Whether the acquired or the acquisition, the odds of evolutionary paths of achieving business goals being perfectly aligned are extremely low. Someone will have to make an off-path change. The second most frequent cause of revolutionary innovation is a change in business executive strategy based on business conditions. The example of the retail manufacturing company needing to address a very significant market opportunity falls into this category. As another example, the responsive CIO knows that when the CEO decides that it is time for corporate headquarters to take over direct management of international operations that were formerly delegated to a partnered company, the IT path will have to shift to a fully global operation. This means that revolutionary innovation is on the horizon. It goes without saying that an unplanned contraction of the business calls for the ability to improvise and re-form an IT strategy that takes into account a more frugal model.

At this point in the discussion, the relationship between innovation and change management should be clear. The responsibility to maintain readiness for innovation, leading change at an appropriate level of departure from the current state, is also clear. We can now explore the overall scope of IT innovation.

Mapping the Key Components of Innovation

There is nothing more mystifying to new CIOs than the resistance encountered when trying to put forward what seems like the obvious answer to a business problem. After all, they are only doing what they perceive as their job to help create business advantage by proposing a change in how things are done. What could be wrong with that? The variable in successful innovation that causes the most problems is the scope permitted, or exacerbated, by the organization's dynamics. Culture, management style, organizational structure, leadership trends, whatever terms are used, all combine to contribute to what constitutes the innovation environment. This is the reality in which any IT manager operates and strives to innovate.

What will never be acceptable, however, is for a CIO to say, "I can't innovate in IT because I don't have the authority." That is abdication of the responsibility to work within an existing environment and deploy an innovation process that can make a difference.

To navigate successfully, any captain needs a map and sextant. We have to know where we are, where we want to go, what distance we need to travel, and what obstacles we must navigate around. Finally, we must be aware of what it takes to get there, as well as the opportunities, such as favorable winds, that can be counted on.

Similarly, a CIO must have a map and a sextant for the company and its goals. There will be times, however, when we find ourselves in uncharted waters, and that is when we can only rely on our experience and skills to extrapolate our knowledge to map out the best course. Our knowledge is based on the four main components of the innovation environment: jurisdiction, communication, ownership, and credibility.

Jurisdiction

Law enforcement defines what crimes and locations fall under what precinct, county, or agency's jurisdiction. Nobody in an organization wants to play the role of a cop, but the responsibility for various functions within a company's operations must be defined. And just as law enforcement, as an industry, has a management style unique to itself, specifically hierarchical and territorial, so does every company. Knowing what that structure and style is reveals how to map progress across the organization.

If we apply this concept to a CIO, then a successful outcome of the innovation process will depend on having a clear understanding of the company political decision-making structure and the ability to enforce change. Failure to recognize jurisdictional restriction will lead to innovation failure, even though the ideas were well thought out. To obtain a successful outcome for the innovation process it is imperative that the chain of command be respected!

Communication

To be successful in the introduction of the outcome of an innovative process, it may be necessary to air, test market, or pilot the proposed change. What determines whether new ideas require airing to test market and build awareness before a decision can be made? In the exchange of ideas, are decisions made by a majority, a leading minority or a total consensus? How does this determine the depth to which exploration and discussion are critical to make innovation acceptable? Think of this in terms of the time and effort needed to supply the journey, planning the length of time at various stops along the map.

From a CIO's perspective, what if the business environment operated like a farmer's co-op, with shared responsibility and consensus requirements as core values? The successful journey includes many stops along the way to discuss and explore the solution. In such a case, perhaps the CIO tried to implement the change without enough exposure of the idea to garner support for it. The lack of shared understanding led to rejection out of hand because the CIO did not recognize the need to include shopping the idea sufficiently as part of the process.

Ownership

Not to be confused with jurisdiction, ownership defines the depth of responsibility assigned for an area. On the map, jurisdiction identifies the waterway, but ownership identifies its depth. Knowing the depth chart, the captain can successfully navigate and avoid being trapped in the shallows, or misjudging a decision maker's authority. In some organizations, jurisdiction is very clearly defined, but the authority to enact decisions within them is very limited. In others, that decision-making authority, and the responsibility for the results that arise from it, can be significantly deeper. Of all the areas on the innovation environment map, ownership is probably the most challenging to navigate.

To illustrate, what if the CIO worked for a company that operated in a deeply entrepreneurial model, where total ownership of results was the sole responsibility of each business function, and only by overlapping targets did the executives collaborate at all? In this situation, it would be entirely possible that the only mistake a CIO can make in introducing an innovative idea is to open it for discussion rather than just implementing it. In this culture, owning the requirement and being solely responsible for its success would have a positive impact on everyone else.

Credibility

Consider the message, and consider the messenger. Credibility is a powerful engine through which navigating around the map is possible. The strength of credibility IT enjoys within the innovation environment helps determine the momentum of the trip. Of all of the components of the journey, credibility is the area a CIO can affect the most directly. No matter what events brought the current level of credibility to be, it is part of the landscape.

The CIO may have either inherited or created a situation in which the credibility of the IT Team is in question. The lack of confidence that line of business executives display could emanate from several causes:

- The IT team may not understand the situation well enough to propose a solution.
- The innovative solution being proposed may not potentially deliver the results.
- The IT team may have overestimated how easy implementing the solution would be.

These are not challenges to personal integrity of the CIO, which is beyond the scope of this discussion, but challenges the IT team's business acumen—its understanding and conclusions. Other ways this could be put might include:

- I don't trust that the IT team is familiar enough with my business function.
- I don't have any exposure to the IT team's operation or their record on previous innovative solution implementations.
- I don't understand the method through which the IT team will accomplish the innovative solution.

Based on these objections, the way to improve credibility, as teachers always said in school, is to show your work. The only way to improve credibility is through exposure. To strengthen credibility in proposed innovations from IT, a CIO might invite business leaders to vendor demonstrations simply to share what the marketplace is offering. Another possibility is to encourage the IT team to follow a standard format that includes rationale, payback and required investment when proposing solutions to business problems. This would tend to expose the thought process behind the recommendation. Backing up even further, the CIO might establish periodic brainstorming sessions simply meant to bring business and IT people together to share ideas and thought processes. Fundamentally, there is no excuse for allowing low credibility to remain as a barrier to successful innovation. A good captain tends his boat!

Summary

Innovation in IT has to migrate from simply coming up with new ideas to defining success as follows:

- A successful CIO implements an innovation process that consistently solves business problems and creates business advantage.
- To do this, IT teams must maintain a state of innovation readiness utilizing change management methods that incorporate all of the elements of innovative thinking.

- By managing innovation with a high level of business rigor, IT adheres to business goals and objectives, using them to determine the right depth of innovation, whether incremental, evolutionary, or revolutionary, depending on the characteristics of the situation. This focuses IT innovation on solving problems that result in the most elegant solutions to complex problems.

- Managing IT innovation scope means clearly understanding the innovation environment, encompassing all of the cultural and style aspects of business interaction. Successful CIOs map the key components of their innovation environments, including jurisdiction, communication, ownership, and credibility.

- Given a high level of environmental cognition, a successful CIO can innovate in both responsive and proactive situations, incorporating the realities of the environment into a consistent innovative process.

Softer Side of IT

Frank Hannig and Christine Rose

How would you like to work for yourself?

Now let's be honest. Many of you would say heck no, I'm too demanding . . . others would say sure, but with a big grin.

How about this one? How would you like to be married to yourself?

Now we are hitting home.

One more. Do you have employees or hostages?

Does you staff work for you because they have to? I'm not suggesting that being a good manager is all about a popularity contest but what sets a good leader apart from a great leader are some of the soft and often less evident skills.

Soft doesn't mean weak . . .

You know, this reference to soft skills can sound confusing – it sounds like *soft skills* are weak, unimportant, or something that you don't need to care about. We challenge that, and you should, too. The skills that we are going to talk about here are often more important than the other *hard* skills. Some of these go to the very core of what makes you who you are.

Before we talk about soft skills, it is important to differentiate between skills and talents. Why is that so important?

Talents can't be taught, and skills are learned behaviors. This is quite a difference that is important to understand so that you don't waste your time and the time of others. There are two primary ways you gain skills: being taught or having experiences. Taught skills are evident, we have all gone to school to learn how to do something. Experiential skills are learned on the job, they come from observing others and learning from their behaviors or from trying something out on your own. Some obvious examples of talents are artists or athletes. It is easy to see these examples of talent, and we often hear someone say, "He is a natural-born athlete." Or, "She has a real knack for performing on stage." Good leaders can help you make the best of your talents. They can often bring hidden talents to the surface. But what they can't do is put in talent that isn't there. We can easily see talents in those professions, so why don't we recognize that those of us who are not performers, but technology professionals, also have talents? We do! These talents are our ability to work a problem until we find a solution, being able to defuse a tense situation between two individuals, being able to develop a vision and plan for an organization.

These talents are a result of the way we are wired. We are all wired a certain way, and we typically don't change much from our basic orientation. If that is true, you may ask, "So does that mean that a great leader is not made, he/she is born?" Well, to some extent and to be blunt, yes. If you are not predisposed with some of the natural talents to be a leader, then it is going to be a tough road. For example, you can learn the skills of how to make a presentation and write business plans, but when figuring out how to deal with a tough personnel issue or to lead a team through a tough acquisition, you are going to be on your own. This is where your innate talents as a leader make the difference. However, you can be assured just by the fact that you are reading this book, and especially this chapter, that you have some of the talents to be a good or even great leader.

So what are the some of the skills that make a great leader? That is what we are going to cover here.

Skill 1: Ability to Assess Your Own Goals, Principles, Strengths, and Weaknesses

The first and most important skill is that of *self-introspection*. Wait – is this a management book or a book on philosophy? It's a little of both as it turns out; one goes with the other. If you expect to lead others, you first need to lead yourself. How can you expect others to follow you if they can't see you leading and managing yourself? You need to develop an ability to look into yourself and figure out what you are made of, how you are doing, and what are your basic operating principles. Without going through this process you can't be *a person of character*. Remember the questions that started this chapter? Now let's take a moment and drill down on some of these. Pull out a piece of paper and write the answers to these questions. (Don't worry, this is just for you.)

1. What do I enjoy the most about my work? What delights me? Do I feel that my work is important?

2. Do I walk the talk? Are my actions in line with what I believe? Do I present myself in the best light at all times?

3. What do I think are my strengths (talent, skills, and knowledge)? What am I best at? What are my core values?

4. What do I always put off to the last or avoid doing at all?

5. What are my personal goals (work, family, social; both short- and long-term)? Am I on target to achieving these goals?

6. What are my relationships like at work? Have I formed any new relationships in the last six months? Do I have a best friend at work?

7. What will my coworkers and staff say about me when I have left? What do I want them to say? Are these the same?

Hopefully you have learned something from going through the process of answering these questions. If you feel that you would benefit from further discussion and inflection on these, I encourage you to seek out your mentor (you have one of these, right?) or a good friend or peer. One of the best ways to find peers to interact with and discuss this with is through professional roundtables or other management organizations in your area. Monster .com names the following organizations as the top IT organizations for networking: Association for Computing Machinery, Association of Information Technology Professionals, Association of Shareware Professionals, BDPA, Computer Professionals for Social Responsibility, Independent Computer Consultants Association, Institute of Electrical and Electronics Engineers (IEEE) Computer Society, Network Professional Association, Society for Technical Communication, Software Development Forum, Washington Alliance of Technology Workers, and Women in Technology.

It is essential to know what you are good at and figure out what you are going to do with the things that you are not good at. We are not perfect. One of the key things to understand about a weakness is whether it is a talent or a skill weakness. If it is a talent weakness and you are in a role where this natural talent is essential, you have three choices:

1. Find a new role that better suits your natural talent.

2. Find a complementary partner who will balance out and cover for your missing talent.

3. Develop an approach or support system so that the talent is not an issue.

If it is a skill weakness, the solution is much simpler. You can do one of these three, or you also have the option to learn how to perform that skill. In this case, you need to seek out the education or an opportunity to learn it on the job.

Skill 2: Operate Based on Your Core Principles and Values

One of the best ways to *walk the talk* is to get your IT organization focused and aligned with these principles and values. This is done by developing a mission, vision, and guiding principles.

Mission

All of us work for companies and in groups that have a mission statement. A *mission statement* defines the purpose of the organization and defines why you exist. It will allow your staff to focus and ensure that the things they do align with the mission. It is probably one of the most important statements about your organization, and is worth an investment of your time and your staff's time to develop it and internalize it.

So how many of you can recite your current mission statement? Do you feel you have internalized it? How often, when deciding on which course of action to take, have you gone back to see how well aligned your decision would be with your mission?

The answer to these questions is, probably not very often. Conventional wisdom would tell you that all you need is a mission statement. This does not take it far enough. You need to internalize your mission and make it part of your core beliefs. The process is fairly straightforward:

1. You and your core team draft a *strawman* mission statement. This statement needs to be short, concise, and clearly able to focus the team. Example:

   The information technology department provides our customers with a significant advantage over the competition by delivering user focused information systems, technology, and services on a timely basis.

2. Pull your extended team together and work through the statement word by word to gain agreement and consensus. (Often it is helpful to have a facilitator who has done this before to guide you through this process.)

3. Once you are reasonably satisfied, the next key step is to define *each* of the words in the statement. For example: *timely basis.* What is the service-level agreement to get a ticket resolved? By doing this, each and every person will be able to better understand what is meant by the mission, and ambiguity will be removed. Here is an example for the mission statement:

   - *Provides*—to deliver on time, to deliver consistently, and to deliver the total solution
   - *Our customers*—our employees, departments, and business partners
   - *Significant advantage over the competition*—provide measurable advantages that contribute to improved company profits and greater market share
   - *Delivering*—to provide a complete solution that includes research, design, development, implementation, and support that exceeds customer's expectations
   - *User focused*—for and about the users, tailored solutions that empower them in the most efficient manner

- *Information systems*—integrated set of tools consisting of hardware, software, communications, and applications
- *Technology*—the foundation upon which systems and services are based and the underlying framework for the company
- *Services*—all solutions that meet our customer's needs including network, e-mail, servers, voice, video, and gateways to information
- *Timely basis*—meeting the customers' service-level agreement (SLA) or their agreed-on time

4. Provide reinforcement for the mission by posting it, providing each member of your team with a quick reference card, and so on. Ensure that all new hires go through a process to learn the mission, vision, and guiding principles. This will help them get focused and indoctrinated into the culture of the organization.

Vision

Vision is a vivid picture of where and what you want the organization to be – how you want to be seen. This is important, because it can help the staff better visualize where the organization is headed. Although the mission gives the purpose, the vision gives you the picture of what it looks like. In fact, if you can express the vision in a picture, it is even better.

Ask yourself and your team some of the following questions to develop the vision:

1. If you could picture your organization on the front of *BusinessWeek*, what would the BusinessWeek authors write about your group?
2. What are the three things that you want to be known for? Customer service that delights your users? Infrastructure that is rock solid, like a utility?

Here is an example:

- *Deliver infrastructure and services like a utility.*
- *Partner and align with the business to provide solutions that contribute significant business value.*
- *Measure and manage based on client experience and expectations (services and SLAs).*
- *Drive and develop processes enterprise-wide.*
- *Be agile and improve continuously in all we do.*

Guiding Principles

These are the core principles on which all decisions should be based. There should be a brief list of these; five or six key principles. For example:

The information technology department embraces a set of guiding principles that inform and guide the performance of all our staff members. These guiding principles include:
- *Our customers come first.*
- *We value the contributions of every individual.*

- *We seek and reward innovation.*
- *We will exhibit a high level of professionalism.*
- *We will operate as an effective team.*
- *We will strive for technical excellence.*

Skill 3: Techniques and Skills to Improve Communication

We are all familiar with employee or customer surveys, and I'm sure you have either commissioned one or participated in one in the past. Have you ever used a survey as a peer-to-peer tool to improve communication?

In many of today's complex IT departments, many groups depend on and work for each other. We often hear the mantra about providing great service to our customers, but what about great service to our peers? How about using a survey to measure and improve working relationships, service, and communication within your IT department? It can work quite well for you by following this process:

1. *Each group develops a list of ten questions that it would like to be evaluated on by the other groups.* For example, Do we have a high sense of urgency when handling other groups' requests, such as adding a network address? Each of the groups in the department should tailor the questions to the areas that are of most interest and importance to them.

2. *The groups will then exchange the surveys between the groups.* Now here is where the first important twist occurs. The groups will respond to the surveys as a group, not as individuals. We used a staff meeting to show the survey on the screen and then as a group, grade each of the ten questions from 1 to 5, with 5 being very satisfied and 1 being very dissatisfied. This stimulates dialogue, simplifies the process, and makes it a group rather than individual survey.

3. *The surveys are then exchanged, and each group meets with the others to review the results.* A further enhancement is to require a comment when the scores are at either the high or low end of the scale. This works to highlight problems as well give recognition for a job well done.

4. *The identity of each group was keep confidential from the management and also from the groups in total.* This keeps it from becoming a political document and more as a communication tool.

Figure 4.1 is a sample team-building survey.

After doing the survey quarterly for over a year, the results were unanimous that it was a good tool, had improved communication, and had addressed issues in a non-confrontational way that improved the overall workings of the organization.

Application Development Group

	Disagree Completely				Agree Completely

1. Is helpful and accessible for issues/requests
   Reason for my rating
   ❏ 1 ❏ 2 ❏ 3 ❏ 4 ❏ 5

2. Responds to requests/issues in a timely manner
   Reason for my rating
   ❏ 1 ❏ 2 ❏ 3 ❏ 4 ❏ 5

3. Courteous, professional, respectful
   Reason for my rating
   ❏ 1 ❏ 2 ❏ 3 ❏ 4 ❏ 5

4. Takes ownership of issues, problems, requests
   Reason for my rating
   ❏ 1 ❏ 2 ❏ 3 ❏ 4 ❏ 5

5. Communicates and listens well
   Reason for my rating
   ❏ 1 ❏ 2 ❏ 3 ❏ 4 ❏ 5

6. Is open minded and willing to share knowledge
   Reason for my rating
   ❏ 1 ❏ 2 ❏ 3 ❏ 4 ❏ 5

7. Possesses sufficient technical skills
   Reason for my rating
   ❏ 1 ❏ 2 ❏ 3 ❏ 4 ❏ 5

8. Provides quality and innovative solutions
   Reason for my rating
   ❏ 1 ❏ 2 ❏ 3 ❏ 4 ❏ 5

9. Demonstrates sufficient project management skills
   Reason for my rating
   ❏ 1 ❏ 2 ❏ 3 ❏ 4 ❏ 5

10. Works well in a team environment
    Reason for my rating
    ❏ 1 ❏ 2 ❏ 3 ❏ 4 ❏ 5

11. Gives advance notice of future service requirements
    Reason for my rating
    ❏ 1 ❏ 2 ❏ 3 ❏ 4 ❏ 5

12. Overall, I am satisfied with the service I receive
    Reason for my rating
    ❏ 1 ❏ 2 ❏ 3 ❏ 4 ❏ 5

13. How can the group improve?

Other comments (baseline/projects)

| FIGURE 4.1 | IT team building survey |

Another tool to use in improving communication involves the *golden rule:*

> *Treat others the way you would like to be treated.*

However, there is a new golden rule:

> *Treat others the way they want to be treated, not how you want to be treated.*

That stimulates some interesting thoughts. What is wrong with treating people the way I want to be treated? And how am I supposed to know how they want to be treated, especially if I have only had limited interaction with them?

One of the best ways to do this is by understanding their *social style.* This is the pattern of behavior or the way an individual is wired to respond to others. Typically, individuals are classified as being one of four different social styles:

1. Driver
2. Analytic
3. Amiable
4. Expressive

Each of these social styles has unique characteristics of how they like to be approached, presented to, and worked with. It is beyond the scope of this chapter to be able to educate you fully on this. In fact, many books and classes are taught just on this skill. Just Google *social styles* to see organizations that offer some training and assessment tools to help you determine your social style and those of people that you interact with.

For further development of your communication skills, refer to *CIO Wisdom,* Chapter 5, "Communications: Communication Excellence in IT Management."

Skill 4: Managing Effectively

IT is all about managing people effectively. IT is easy, technology is simple! How does that sound? Can you agree? Well, depending on your current role, you might disagree. If you are like my son, an electrical engineer at a major networking company, and are trying to get a thin film integrated circuit to process those bits, you might disagree. If you are a manager you might agree with me. Getting people to work together is much harder and more complex than bits and bytes. Why? We are all so complex, and the number of interactions and reactions to a given occurrence is almost infinite. So what is a manager to do?

In search for the answer to this, I uncovered a great book called *First, Break All the Rules* by Marcus Buckingham and Curt Coffman. Their book is based on twenty-five years of surveys by the Gallup Organization, and they were able to distill management down to four key things that the world's greatest managers do differently:

1. *Select a person.* Select for talent (not simply experience, intelligence, or determination).
2. *Set expectations.* Define the right outcomes (not the steps).

3. *Motivate the person.* Focus on strengths (not on weaknesses).
4. *Develop the person.* Help the person find the right fit (not the next rung on the ladder).

Let's talk a little more about these.

First Key: Select for Talent

Talents are the recurring patterns of thought, feeling, or behavior. These are very different than the skills or knowledge that you have. Each of us has many different talents. The key is to understand the talents that are needed to perform the job and then hire someone into that job who has the right match of talents.

Second Key: Define the Right Outcomes

One of the mistakes I made early on, and I'm sure repeated in my management career, was thinking that it was my job to *tell* people what to do. Instead, it is better to define the desired end result and then let each person develop the best way to get there. So while someone may have the talent to do the job, he or she might also need assistance with the skills on how to do it. This is different than telling people what to do.

Third Key: Focus on Strengths

The key thing in motivating someone is to focus on strengths, not weaknesses. This seems contrary to what most of us tend to think and the way we may have been treated in the past. The old school of thought, or old wisdom, was to review your strengths and weaknesses and then create a development plan that focused on compensating for your weakness. The *new wisdom* is to build on your strengths, cultivate your talents, and when you have a weakness, as we all do, manage around them. So as managers it is up to us to manage around a weakness by devising a support system, finding a complementary partner, or, if you are spending too much of your time managing around the weakness, then admit to a *casting* error.

Fourth Key: Find the Right Fit

The best way a manager can help someone develop is to find the right niche for that person – what that individual is naturally wired to do. This involves matching the talents, skills, and knowledge to the role. As IT people, let's talk about an example that is close to home. We all know what a programmer does, and have met and I'm sure worked with some great programmers in our careers. One of the talents that these individuals have is the ability to solve problems. Show them what you want done, and boy, a good one will get it done. However, if there is ambiguity in what needs to be done, many times this will cause frustration to a programmer and make it difficult to achieve the desired result. By contrast, business analysts often thrive in their talent to work with ambiguity and formulate an answer. They like to seek out unresolved and ambiguous business problems and figure out how to solve them. As a result, a great programmer will not always make a great business analyst.

For more in-depth information on this, I encourage you to read the full book. It also contains an interview guide and a survey that can be used to evaluate the health of your own organization.

Skill 5: Your Personal Presentation Matters

Have you ever sat across from someone at a business lunch and found yourself more distracted by the manner in which they ate their lunch than the conversation at hand? Have you ever walked away, not really remembering what was said but instead what you saw?

These types of distracting behavior are more prevalent than ever. With the pressure to get things done, often we forget some of the simplest things to make everyday business interactions more successful. Now I know what you are thinking – we all know how important good manners are, and it is only slobs that don't. But what about when you are doing business in a different country. Do you know the proper way to exchange business cards in Asia? Do you know how to establish a business relationship in Germany? Do you know the proper way to address someone in France?

These types of small behaviors can have a lasting effect on your business dealings. Technology professionals have a stereotypical reputation of being poorly dressed people with a pocket protector and horrible social skills. These are portrayed in movies such as *Revenge of the Nerds.* Slowly, this stereotype is changing, and now we are seen as cubicle dwellers in *Office Space,* but at least we are better dressed. As the world gets smaller, the need to send IT people out in the world becomes a certainty. We need to have the business etiquette skills, like our other business counterparts, to make a positive statement about ourselves. With such large business deals on the table, we only have one chance to make a first impression. It is also highly unfair to send out our IT staff without properly preparing them for what they may face.

Typical things to know:

- Business card protocol
- Presenting yourself in meetings
- Dinner table seating etiquette
- How to entertain international guests
- Gift giving
- Business dress
- How to introduce yourself
- Business culture
- Marketing material

Skill 6: Adapting to Change

We have seen and experienced a lot of change in the IT industry. Those of us with gray hair, or perhaps none at all, can remember when we wrote programs on paper and they were then punched onto cards. For those of us not quite so old, we can just look at the revolution that the Internet has created. Technology change is all around us, and those of us in IT pride ourselves on being the stewards and facilitators of that change. Although we all embrace this technology change, often we as individuals are not as embracing of changes in our work structure, organizations, and individual change. Why is that, and what can we do about it?

Some of us are naturally wired (we have the talent) to adapt to change. You already know if you are one of those individuals. For the rest of us, as well as those that want to be more adept at adapting to and leading change, our recommendation is that we develop the skill (yes, we said skill) to be able to accept and foster personal and work changes. So how can this be a skill? Earlier, we discussed what a skill is and how you acquire skills, either trained or experienced. Can you be trained to accept change? Or is it better to experience change so that you are more able to adapt and change with it? The answer is both. By learning and understanding about your environment and situation it always makes it easier to change. Start by getting a better understanding of the situation at hand by working through an analysis of the change.

The other component of this is that the more change you experience, the more adept you are at changing. So how do you experience more change? Only by establishing a goal, each year, to experience something new both in your personal life and at work can you make this happen. Use your personal plan to establish this goal.

In case we haven't convinced you enough, we wanted to give you another reason to develop the skills to change. Why is this so important? Well, the IT industry is beginning a major transformation as a result of the change in the work force. This change has the potential to be even more far-reaching than many of the technology changes we have experienced.

In 2007, the oldest baby boomers will be 61 years old, and many of them will begin retiring. The impact of having such highly skilled workers leaving the IT workforce will be significant. This is further complicated by the fact that the individuals who replace them will likely be much different in both talents and skills. In addition, according to the U.S. Department of Labor, there is expected to be a shortage of IT workers. Wow, sounds like a perfect storm and one that we must be prepared to address.

Skill 7: Revitalizing Yourself by Being Part of the Community

So how do you revitalize yourself? By giving back you will always get more than give. Although it is important to work on improving yourself and your career, if you take time to look back you will see that you probably did not get there alone. There were many people who have either helped you or have given you valuable advice on your career.

How about returning this gift? It is only appropriate to think about the people that are coming up the ladder behind you. You can give them a hand coming up or ignore them. Our firm belief in people is that most people are good inside, and they will lend a hand to those around them. We encourage you to get involved. You will get back more than you put in.

Many, if not most, of us have graduated college and have alumni organizations that could use us for career days or assistance with designing technology curriculum. If your college is not technology focused, seek other opportunities to talk to young people about a career in technology. If we do not foster the desire in young people, who will?

Christine Rose Personal Story

Bound and determined to be a part of the community, I found a speaking engagement available at Girls Inc. Girls Inc. is a national nonprofit youth organization dedicated to inspiring all girls to be strong, smart, and bold. Girls Inc. invited a few women from the technology, math, and science field to come talk to young girls about their jobs. Dressed in a suit and raring to go, I arrive at Holy Names School, where I was to present with all the enthusiasm and nerves of a job interview. We were asked to bring a few items for discussion, and the girls were suppose to guess what we did you a living. After a few moments I noticed the girls did not seem to relate to the items I brought, and I felt I was losing them. Just then, my pink RAZR phone started to vibrate in my pocket. On instinct, I pulled it out to quiet the annoying vibration and the girls eyes lit up. "You have a pink RAZR phone?" one of the girls squealed. Keep in mind this is when they were first released, and were quite the hot commodity, as I was later told. I said yes, and then used the phone to illustrate the different types of jobs and skills needed to put together and market such a product. The girls were very excited to learn that a cute pink RAZR phone needed software developers, assembly personnel, graphic designers, marketing staff, product managers, hardware designers, and so on to make the product a reality. Just using something that they could all relate to opened up their eyes to the technology world. This is the generation that we should be focusing on to enter the high-tech field.

The Ethical CIO

Roger Gray

Introduction

Perhaps it is best to start by asking the question, "Is there any difference between an ethical person and an ethical CIO?" Fundamentally, the answer is no, but some of the specific requirements applicable to CIOs perhaps don't apply to all people. Additionally, I assert that CIOs, in their capacity as leaders, have additional requirements and a higher standard to meet. Another relevant question applicable to CIOs and leaders in general is whether business ethics really are any different from ethics in general. This chapter discusses some of the ethical issues that CIOs face and provides a high-level ethics framework for consideration.

Compliance

First, let's address the issue of compliance and laws or regulatory requirements such as Sarbanes-Oxley. Compliance with the law should not be confused with ethics. It is not a given that regulatory or legal compliance is assurance that one is meeting ethical standards. Laws represent the government minimum standard, and adhering to the law means one is acting lawfully. Ethics, by contrast, is a branch of philosophy and generally arises out of habit or action with considerations for value, quality, right, and wrong. Whereas the law is generally intended to be black and white, ethics are not always so. The gray area in ethics arises out of differences of opinion about right and wrong, as well as social norms and cultural values. However, there are certain social and cultural values that the overwhelming majority of people would agree on. Right and wrong cannot be painted entirely gray. I like to think some things are black and white, but acknowledge that some things fall into a gray area.

Whether one must risk one's own life to save another is more a question of heroics than ethics. For example, if you see someone drowning and you yourself cannot swim, it is not unethical just because you don't just dive in to help. Some people perhaps apply a higher standard and say the ethical person would jump in. This is one of those gray areas that is driven by personal and cultural values. I think, however, that almost all would agree that not doing what you can to save the person, such as throwing a life-ring or calling for help, is an unethical decision. As a leader, it is best to err on the conservative side and avoid the gray area altogether, because one's actions in these matters speak much louder than one's words and maybe, just maybe, leaders do need to look a little more like heroes and less like people just complying with the government minimum standards. Leaders must strive to apply the highest ethical standards to themselves. When they do they can also hold peers, bosses and employees accountable. Watching the unethical behavior of others in silence is acceptance of unethical behavior. Leaders are in a much better position to set the highest standards whether by their own words and actions or by how they reject or accept the words and actions of others.

Ethical behavior and the best leadership requires going beyond the government minimum standard of complying with the law. However, ethical considerations should not let business decisions be muddied by making them ones where legitimate differences of opinion on business decisions are elevated to ethical decisions. For example, the issue of outsourcing and off-shoring is occasionally debated as an ethical issue. It certainly is a public policy issue; however, it is not clearly an ethical issue. Companies and organizations must consider a variety of factors when making decisions, such as outsourcing, including matters related to company profitability and public and customer responses to those decisions. In is neither necessary nor appropriate to let straightforward decisions that involve business trade-offs become ethics-based decisions.

Business Decisions versus Ethical Decisions

A company's primary purpose is to generate a profit or return for its shareholders. This is generally true, but it is not without constraints or other considerations. If it were completely unconstrained, all companies would be in the business of literally making money, or what is commonly known as counterfeiting. Clearly, making money is limited by certain constraints. Laws and regulation represent one set of constraints. Making money can be viewed either as a short-term objective or a longer-term and sustainable objective.

Sometimes I find arguments around business decisions being debated on an ethical basis, when in reality the debate is about a short-term versus long-term perspective and sustainability. For example, producing a product that is cheaper, but of lower quality or reliability, is a business decision trade-off. A router that has 99.99 percent reliability is more expensive than a router that has 99.9 percent reliability. Some would argue that knowingly producing a less-reliable product is unethical. This is misplaced. A company that makes routers that are only 99.9 percent reliable is not making an ethical decision. It is making a business decision and staking its business on a belief that there is a market where the price point and reliability requirements will create demand for its product.

Too often, company ethical policies and standards sound terminally politically correct, and people will use ethics as the basis for what are properly differences of opinion. I call it playing the ethics card. Escalation of all business decisions to an ethical basis is often misplaced. The decision about establishing the router reliability and cost targets is a business decision. Lying about it in advertising is, however, an ethical decision.

A good example of straightforward business decision inappropriately becoming an ethical decision is a classic situation of a CIO attempting to launch a new IT system. It is close to impossible to launch a complex new system that is perfect. There is enormous pressure for CIOs and IT departments to produce systems that work, but to also meet scope, schedule, and budget. Competing pressures and demands do not necessarily create ethical issues in and of themselves. For example, a decision to launch a system with known bugs is not an unethical decision if it is made and communicated openly. It should be a business decision where the trade-off of additional cost and time of development is considered against the cost of launching a system with known bugs and fixing them later. However, what can quickly turn it into an ethical issue is when a CIO knowingly and intentionally makes this decision for the wrong reasons. A CIO that goes to the executive committee or the users of such a system to discuss the trade-offs between budget and schedule and bugs is allowing a business decision to be made. The decision is transparent and it is exposed to the light of day. Equally important, the CIO should communicate the decision within his or her IT organization to help them understand that the decision was a business trade-off and not a decision about deception versus honesty.

The CIO, however, who unilaterally makes decisions with known material effects on other parties, is not necessarily making a business decision particularly if the motivations are wrong. That CIO is treading on matters of ethics. If the only underlying motivation is meeting budget or schedule, then a decision to launch an IT system with known bugs of a material nature is potentially unethical if the issues are hidden from plain sight. This is because the decision transfers the problem to someone else without his or her understanding or agreement. It is an unethical decision. Sometimes the issue of ethics might be more subtle. What happens if bugs don't appear to exist? Is it really because they don't exist or is it because the CIO creates an environment where known bugs are not allowed to surface because the environment punishes disclosure and candor? How leaders deal with issues of disclosure, dissent, and disagreement usually is an indication of their own values and ethics. To conclude that no problems exist because one has created an environment where problems are not allowed to exist is not a quality-control strategy; it is a slippery leadership strategy.

Setting Ethical Goals

Like leaders in general, CIOs must challenge their organizations and people to produce results. Stretch goals are typical ways to challenge people. It is a business decision to set forth challenging schedules and to drive an organization to produce results. If the last IT project took twelve months and cost $1 million, it is not unethical for a CIO to expect that a project of similar scope and complexity should perhaps take eleven months and cost less, too. Again, this is a business decision, and it is reasonable to expect people and organizations to get better at doing things. If they don't, competitors will. However, where ethical issues arise is when a CIO or any business leader creates goals that are so unrealistic or creates an environment of fear and intimidation that issues are not allowed to surface or that the organization is run into the ground. Again, this is a matter of focusing on producing long-term sustainable results as opposed to short-term unsustainable results. It's easy to produce the right result the wrong way once. It's harder to produce the right results the right way over and over. However, it's darn near impossible to produce the right results the wrong way in the longer term. Eventually, the wrong way catches up to you.

CIO Ethical Standards

CIOs, like other C-level executives, should adhere to their personal standard of ethics as well as their company expectations and requirements. Hopefully, most CIOs have personal standards that go well beyond the law and their company standards and expectations. If they do not, then they likely will run into issues with either the law or with their company culture. CIOs, however, perhaps should consider an additional set of standards or framework for their decision making and conduct. CIOs, like certain kinds of professionals such as doctors or lawyers, often have technical knowledge that goes far beyond that possessed by the people they deal with. Depending on the governance structure of the company, it may be that the CIO is not necessarily the final decision maker, but perhaps a business-unit senior VP is the decision maker. The CIO should look at the senior VP the same way a lawyer would see his or her client or a doctor would see a patient. If I am diagnosed with cancer, I don't want a doctor who just tells me what to do. It is my decision. I want a doctor who uses his or her vast knowledge to help me make the right decision from my context, and not his or her context. Just because my doctor's knowledge of medicine is vastly superior does not give the doctor the right to make my decisions.

I find some CIOs and IT professionals have a little problem with this concept. Perhaps it is technical arrogance. The attitude is almost one of seeing the client or business unit decision maker as naïve for not making the decision that I would make as an IT professional. Where the issue goes from one of being a relatively straightforward difference of opinion to an ethics issue is where technical knowledge is not shared—or worse, is intentionally withheld in order to influence the outcome in a way that the CIO prefers. For example, a lawyer advising a client to litigate a case rather than settling a case because the law firm might get more billable hours is clearly unethical. A recommendation to use the company ERP system rather than a specialized tool because it is easier for IT should be a business decision, but all parties should understand the trade-off.

When I was CIO at PG&E, we sometimes had departments or business units that wanted to implement various IT tools such as work-management systems. Often, a vendor had gone directly into business users, showing them all the benefits of their tool. Of course we already had a large, integrated ERP system with a work-management module. I could have simply said no to the system or the users could have argued that it was their decision. This debate is not one of ethics, but one of corporate governance. Even where I had clear authority to say no or the better technical knowledge to understand the IT implications, I did not believe in the dictator model. Having come from the business side myself, I would find a dictator CIO just as unattractive as a dictator doctor or lawyer. I want my doctor to give me his or her honest opinion and discuss my options with me as opposed to just telling me what I have to do. I'd argue that the best CIOs use their knowledge and influencing skills as their primary tools and not the corporate governance rules that say you are in charge.

A few people would encourage me to tell the business users that their work-management system would simply not work. However, we all have too much experience to know that there are very few cases like that. We all have made dozens if not hundreds of disparate applications work together. It may not have been ideal and it may have been more costly than a single integrated ERP, but to say it would not work was not the truth. Lying to create an intended outcome is not ethical. Using your technical knowledge and intentionally withholding it to produce an intended outcome that is not necessarily what someone else would want knowing all the facts and information is not necessarily lying, but it is not telling the truth, either. Telling the truth is a higher standard than not lying. I would argue that not lying is equivalent to complying with the law. Telling the truth is a measure of one's ethical behavior, values, and beliefs. Not lying is a pretty low standard when you think about it. Telling the truth is a tougher standard, and it is one that ethical CIOs and ethical people strive to meet. In the long run, not lying keeps you on the straight and narrow with respect to compliance and the law; however, telling the truth demonstrates your character as a leader.

The Ethics of Privacy and Confidential Information

CIOs, of course, lead IT professionals that, by the nature of their jobs, have responsibilities for sensitive data and IT systems. The issues around management of data and IT systems go well beyond simple access and access controls. IT professionals often have enormous access to both the IT systems and the data. Historically, this was not well understood. It is the responsibility of CIOs as a core job responsibility to protect company information. Unfortunately, IT professionals sometimes see their roles almost in mechanical terms, where they simply are providing tools and systems and question why ethical issues are even a concern to IT professionals. Doctors, lawyers, and HR professionals have specific ethics training due to the nature of their jobs. IT professionals may not make life-and-death decisions each day like doctors do, but ethics do enter into the picture. Protection of information and privacy is critical. CIOs must ensure that their staff power and access are always used ethically. Sarbanes-Oxley has brought to the forefront issues such as access and access controls. This has put issues such as who can access records and how they are accessed on the front burner.

Code of IT Behavior and Ethics

In the end, however, it is not Sarbanes-Oxley or any other regulatory requirement that will assure personal or corporate ethics. CIOs and other C-level leaders in companies and public and private organizations set the tone and expectations for ethics by their words and, more importantly, their personal actions. CIOs cannot simply reduce their roles to system mechanics that simply build and run IT systems. CIOs should be the advocates for the importance of data and IT systems controls, how data are used, and how data are treated with care. CIOs and IT staff should use their technical knowledge to educate and not manipulate users of information technology to make informed decisions. CIOs, like all other leaders will make daily business decision trade-offs. The transparency surrounding these decisions and clear communication about the trade-offs will assure that the business decisions are based on ethical values. No matter how difficult or unpopular a decision is, if is made with transparency, it is much more likely to be viewed as a business decision that is perhaps unpopular, as opposed to being unethical.

We haven't all received the same upbringing and education with respect to our understanding of ethical behavior. As a result, it is hard to know what to expect when an employee is faced for the first time with an ethical dilemma. Some companies recognize this problem and have introduced a company-wide code for business conduct and ethics. Where such a code does not exist or doesn't have specifics that apply to IT, it is necessary to have or supplement the company code with an IT code of conduct and ethics. There are many published codes on the Internet that can serve as a template for creating your own code of conduct and ethics. Typically, an IT code of conduct and ethics covers the following items:

- Administration of the IT code of conduct and ethics
  - Duty to come forward
  - Duty of supervisors and leaders to act
  - Making confidential or anonymous reports
  - Investigation of complaints and disciplinary action
- Accuracy of reports
- Conflicts of interest
  - Outside engagements
  - Investments
  - Related parties
  - Consultants and agents
  - Gifts and entertainment
  - IT opportunity
  - Other situations
- Relationship with people and entities external to the IT department
  - Customers
  - Vendors
  - Global IT community
- Protection of company assets
- Confidential information
- Copyrights and patents

Each new employee is introduced to this code, and in some organizations must sign that they have read and agree with it. In addition to having read the code, each IT employee should receive some training on an annual basis on ethics. The value of this training is to act as a refresher for employees on what is considered to be ethical behavior. We find that many companies rigorously pursue a code and annual training for discrimination and harassment, but very few companies pursue, to their later chagrin, the same diligence with respect to business conduct and ethics. All the codes and training in the world are not enough. Business leaders like CIOs set the real expectations by their own words and actions. They are the real code and training.

Conclusion

In this chapter, I have shown that ethical considerations usually involve going beyond legal considerations. Sometimes matters of ethics are a gray area because of social or cultural values and norms. I have expressed my personal bias for an open and transparent process that will serve two purposes. First, it assures that decisions that really are business decisions remain on that basis, and second, it assures that ethical values are always considered. I have also expressed the need for a code of business and ethical conduct with annual refresher training to keep employees, at the very least, on the right track. Finally, the most important message is that the CIO's own words and actions will set the tone for his or her organization's ethics performance.

SECTION 5
Historical Perspective

Identity and the Technology Manifesto

Sam Chughtai, Sam Gill, and Dean Lane

Introduction

When a fellow employee asks, "What it is you do in our company or organization?" You might answer, "I work for IT."

The response is all too familiar and predictable: "I have this problem with my laptop; maybe you can help me . . ."

When you respond, "I really don't do that," you receive a blank stare.

A follow up question almost always follows and you are asked, "What exactly do you do then?"

At which time you feel you have been called on to justify your existence: Why are you wasting company resources if you can't even fix a simple problem with a laptop?

The Identity Crisis Began a Long Time Ago

Before even the first computer was introduced into an organization, various card-processing devices were utilized to perform repetitive and mundane sorting and tabulating functions. This valuable service proved faster and cheaper than tabulation by hand. The *technicians* who were working on these strange, noisy contraptions were known as those people working in *recording*. Their job was to maintain the equipment and program the boards to accomplish the desired functionality. When the first computers arrived, there was no department to handle this new and unknown apparatus (the computer). There were only some technicians that could make the thing work. As time went on and the function grew, a *data processing department* was created.

The people who worked in *data processing* were very technical people. Their role was to program the computers to accomplish the business functionality. As the limited business functionality grew, the role of these computer gurus was expanded to include the analysis and design of computer systems to meet this increased business demand. Analysis and design meant that the data-processing function had to have some familiarity with the business process and how best to integrate the computer system into then-manual processes, to "automate" and to gain process efficiencies.

The role continued to grow. It later included the operation and maintenance of the computer systems, as well as responsibility for the day-to-day functions of managing the inputs and outputs for the various applications. With the advent of more sophisticated systems for processing data into information, the department name was changed to the *management information systems* (MIS) department. This name change reflected the increase in the responsibilities and span of the department. The department no longer operated on individual applications serving business process silos, but was now made responsible for cross-functional business processes. The charter in some cases included not only the analysis of the information system requirements but also the analysis of the business processes themselves that the computer systems were supposed to serve. This responsibility matured until it included business process reengineering.

One significant system that reflects this added responsibility was *material requirement planning* (MRP), now evolved into *enterprise requirements* (ERP). These systems reflected the need for cross-functional integration, as well as the need to have more and more end users involved.

Today, we call the department, the *IT department* (information technology department). With the new name, new challenges have been delegated to the department, specifically the responsibility both for the adoption of new technology as well as for leading the innovation process within the organization. The challenges brought with them new enigmas for the department that is reflected in an identity crisis: How many of us really know or understand the power of what the technology can bring? Why doesn't IT have a seat at the boardroom table? After all, the department is now responsible for all the technology implementation and innovation that embody the processes, procedures, policies, and goals of the business.

Progressing Beyond an IT Tower of Babel

Even though the pace of technology development and its adoption have accelerated considerably in the past 150 years, it still took 50 years to make the steam engine work efficiently, and even more time before this technology saw worldwide use. In great contrast, the microprocessor was developed in the early 1970s, yet by the early 1980s it was already the brain of easy-to-use personal computers. The small computer had become a commodity by the early 1990s, and today a laptop computer is more powerful than the largest research computers anywhere in the world thirty years ago. The introduction of microcomputers and their support introduced new challenges for the IT department. An IT department's responsibilities have become so extensive that version 4 of Control Objectives for Information and Related Technology (CobIT) lists thirty-eight different processes that an IT department should consider. CobIT is a document adopted by the IT Governance Institute (ITIG) to outline standard IT control activities to ensure best practices.

In addition, it is very likely that in another thirty years, today's state-of-the-art of computers will look like ancient devices. Since no two IT departments are the same, frequent migration of employees—in particular, IT employees from one company to another—has led to a very wide expectation spectrum of what services an IT department should provide. This situation is compounded by a very wide interpretation of the role an IT department has within the organization. This exacerbates the fluctuations in defining an IT department's responsibilities.

An Overview of the History of Science and Technology

In order to understand the power of what technology can bring, let's trace its development throughout the history of human kind. Perhaps the understanding of technology evolution will help us understand the identity and role the department should play within an organization.

One of the first expressions of human independent thinking was technology. Beginning in the Stone Age, and up to and including today, humans have been experimenting with ways to ease their daily chores and create working tools that would extend their capabilities. Science, the study of cause and effect, came much later, around 3,000 years B.C. with the emergence of the great ancient civilizations. Britannica (2003) defines technology as ". . . the systematic study of techniques for making and doing things. . . . [technology] is concerned with the fabrication and use of artifacts." Science, by contrast, is defined as "the systematic attempt to understand and interpret the world . . . [science] is devoted to the more conceptual enterprise of understanding the environment, and it depends upon the comparatively sophisticated skills of literacy and numeracy." (Britannica, 2003).

While science has been the subject of speculative philosophers, technology has been the practical concerns of craftsmen. It has only been from medieval times, with the growth of need for advanced tools, that technology started to capture men's interest. With an expansion of experimental science, humans realized that they could be in control of nature rather than nature being in control of them. In the seventeenth century, Francis Bacon made a first attempt to harmonize science with technology. Bacon led the scientific revolution with his new *observation and experimentation* theory. Over the next 200 years, while science was still in its infancy and progressing slowly through investigation and experimentation, craftsmen and mechanics continued developing iron bridges, textile machines, and steam engines. Finally, in the nineteenth century, there was a convergence of goals between science and technology, as theorists provided the scientific impulse leading to the development of practical objects.

As technology caused a positive influence in science by creating new tools and machines, it also created additional resources. A great example is the information technology of today, which has dramatically increased the efficiency with which material resources are used on a daily basis. There is no question that a significant portion of wealth generation of the modern economy comes from the production and consumption of information, which can be easily and efficiently duplicated and transported. According to Carlson (1994), thanks to technology, the entire U.S. economy has expanded by half since 1978, with virtually no increase in energy consumption.

Automobiles contain technologies to improve fuel economy, use less steel, and emit fewer pollutants than 25 years ago. A fax machine or e-mail is faster than a mail truck, cheaper to run, and environmentally friendly. Among all the technologies available to us, there is no doubt that the advent of information technology has had the biggest impact not only on science, but also on society and social change in general.

IT and the New Economy

This short history lesson teaches us that while science has always had goals, technology goals have evolved over time. As a result, the role of the IT department within an organization is continuously evolving.

Today, we find computers embedded in many activities and aspects of our lives. No one can argue that computers have changed all aspects of our daily living—the way we communicate, travel, work, shop, and even think. Negroponte (1995, p. 6) stated, "Computing is no longer about computers anymore. It is about living." We are just beginning to exploit the full power of modern communication technology, thanks to satellite, fiber optic, communication software, and other developments. More major transformations over the next decade will increasingly affect many aspects of life.

Negroponte (1995) argued that there has been a lot of discussion regarding the transition from the Industrial Age to a postindustrial or Information Age, but very little discussion about the current transition into a post-Information Age, characterized by a personalized delivery of information. In Negroponte's words:

> In the post-information age, we often have an audience the size of one. Everything is made to order, and information is extremely personalized. A widely held assumption is that individualization is the extrapolation of narrow casting—you go from a large to a small to a smaller group, ultimately to the individual. (p. 164)

The world is in the midst of an all-purpose technological revolution based on information technology (IT), defined here as computers, computer software, and telecommunications equipment. According to a study of the National Science Board, 2002, there are ten significant trends in information technology:

1. Information technology (IT) continues to develop and diffuse at a very rapid rate due to the substantial quality improvements and cost reductions in basic electronic components, microprocessors, storage, and networking. This cost reduction has enabled new applications and an expansion in the use of IT.
2. Businesses continue investing heavily in IT. Industry spending on IT equipment and software rose from less than $200 billion in 1993 to more than $600 billion in 2000.

3. E-commerce is having an increased significant impact in traditional businesses. E-commerce accounted for 12 percent of the total value of manufacturing shipments, or $485 billion.

4. Wireless communication and especially mobile phones are expected to be a major mean of accessing the Internet.

5. IT is commonly credited as being a key factor in the economy's structural shift from manufacturing to services. More evidence suggest that IT is contributing to the increase overall productivity in the economy.

6. There is a trend of more telecommuters working at home, enabled by IT and networking technologies.

7. Higher impact of IT for Science and Engineering as modeling and simulation are complementing theory and experimentation in many areas such as climate modeling, and engineering design.

8. The availability of large databases has become key resources in many areas of science and social science. For example: gene and protein databanks, collections of satellite sensing data, and social science databases.

9. IT also supports collaboration on large-scale research and development projects through shared databases, videoconferencing, and remote access to scientific instruments.

10. The number of Internet hosts and servers continues to growth both domestically and internationally. More than 100 million computers were connected to the Internet in January 2001 and more than 200 millions in 2004.

Based on these trends, one can conclude that information technology has created a *new economy*. The prosperity of manufacturing companies depends on timely delivery of products and speedy transactions. The key to successful competition is to save time for customers and suppliers. "Rapid comparison shopping on the Internet ensures that companies cannot hope to attract and retain customers on the assumption that information about competing alternatives is limited. Companies must provide immediacy of goods, services and information—they must be available when customers need them. Market makers are simplifying electronic commerce by focusing on convenience. The promise of large time-savings will be realized" (Wright 1999, p. 78). Using new systems for supply-side management, retailers cut costs and offer "everyday low prices." Companies retain profitability with higher sales volume and lower-priced goods.

Consequently, organizational changes, which have been tied to the infiltration of information technology, have yielded increased efficiency and improvements in the overall production process. These intra-firm changes have had pronounced affects on industries by displacing inefficient firms and promoting the spread of effective production procedures. In fact, studies by McKinsey Global Institute suggest that retail giant Wal-Mart had both a direct and an indirect impact on general merchandizing through "managerial innovation that increased competitive intensity and drove the diffusion of best practice" (McKinsey 2001). *Fortune* posed this question: "How did a peddler of cheap shirts and fishing rods become the mightiest corporation in America?" after Wal-Mart topped its Fortune 500 list in 2002, making it the first service-sector corporation to reach the top. From its small-town start in Arkansas, Wal-Mart has grown into an empire spanning the globe. In fact, Wal-Mart accounted for 6 percent of total U.S. retail sales in the fiscal year ending January 31, 2003.

Wal-Mart differed from other retailers in many of its strategies. Large retailers like Kmart and Sears, Roebuck, and Company targeted urban populations, believing that rural areas were not profitable. Wal-Mart, on the other hand, contended that a market existed in rural America as well. Though the advantage of building in urban areas came from proximity to distributors, Wal-Mart solved this problem by building capacity to install an internal distribution system. Essentially, Wal-Mart took on wholesaling in addition to the retail business (McKinsey 2001). As discussed earlier, retailers cut costs and saved time by establishing direct contact with manufacturers. Wal-Mart exploited this new practice by establishing direct contact with Procter & Gamble, and then warehoused merchandise in P&G's distribution centers. By centrally placing large orders, Wal-Mart was able to negotiate reduced prices on goods from manufacturers, helping it later to under-price competitors (McKinsey, 2001; Raff and Temin 1997.

IT as Change Agent

As mentioned earlier, the integration of computers into the firm's business processes led to the formation of the management information systems (MIS) department (Lane 2005). This has led to even greater organizational structure changes.

The introduction of microcomputers into the workplace during the 1980s ushered in a new era, which has had a profound effect on organizations. Advancement in the information technology utilization created the MIS department. More specifically, users are taking greater control for system development in their organization (Dearden 1987). After MIS followed creation of the centralized MIS department (CMIS) as a result of the high cost of the technology (Dearden 1987). CMIS centralized information processing, computing, and operations, making it exclusively run by IT specialists. It remained the major information system organization during the 1970s.

The introduction of inexpensive PCs in the 1980s significantly changed the preceding arrangement (Forcht, Kulonda and Moates 1987). Now, employees in non-MIS departments could use the less-complex software programs developed for the PC. The role of CMIS within the organization began to change as decentralization expanded. Its function became more of coordinating rather than controlling.

Nevertheless, the greater the dispersed environment becomes, the greater is the need for centralized planning and control. The CMIS department is still in demand to handle the information planning and control responsibilities for the organization as a whole—in particular, hardware and software standards formularies.

After 9/11, privacy issues and security concerns rose to the forefront. Although government in general is not on the leading edge of computer technology (Riley 1988), its size and function provides large dividends when adopting cost-efficient measures. Technology surveillance is considered an important role for CMIS in its new charter (Forcht, Kulonda, and Moates 1987). The background and experience of the professional CMIS staff is particularly well suited to perform the technology-tracking function within organizations (Halbrecht

1985). In addition, a major challenge for CMIS will be to facilitate the transfer of user-developed systems into an organizational resource (Henderson and Treacy 1986).

As was mentioned earlier, starting in the 1990s, the CMIS department assumed the responsibility to support and consult users and to form and educate users groups. As PCs become more numerous and powerful, computer networks become the preferred means of departmental communications. Nevertheless, common databases and connections between departmental networks still need to be planned, created, and maintained. It is unlikely that any department other than CMIS would choose to take on that responsibility. Although there will be a decrease in systems development work, the manpower required for systems maintenance is expected to increase (Swanson and Beath 1989).

The Macroeconomic Impact of IT

The world is in the middle of an all-purpose technological revolution based on information technology (IT). Stated differently, the Information Age is ongoing while the Industrial Age has not ended. The macroeconomic benefits of the IT revolution are already apparent in some economies, especially the United States. Historical experience has shown that such revolutions have often been accompanied by financial booms and busts, and the IT revolution has been no exception. However, while spending on IT goods is likely to remain weak in the immediate future, as past concerns over investment unwind, the longer-term benefits for the global economy are likely to continue, or even accelerate, in the years to come (Halal 1992).

At the core of the current IT revolution are advances in material science, which leads to increases in the power of semiconductors, which in turn results in rapidly declining semiconductor prices. Over the past four decades, the capacity of semiconductor chips has doubled roughly every eighteen to twenty-four months—a phenomenon known as *Moore's law*. Gordon Moore, the founder of Intel, made this prediction as early as 1965. At that time, he was a research director at Fairchild Semiconductor. Cheaper semiconductors have allowed rapid advances in the production of computers, computer software, and telecommunications equipment. The fall in relative prices of IT goods has also led to significant increases in consumer surplus in IT-using countries. "Over the near term, and despite the relatively rapid diffusion of technology around the globe, the IT revolution is likely to benefit advanced economies more than developing countries. In the long run, however, the distribution of the benefits will depend on specific country characteristics rather than relative incomes." (Halal 1992, p. 3).

"The result of the technological advances is to create a level field in providing goods and services worldwide" (Thomas Friedman: The World is Flat). We no longer know who is answering the request for assistance, making our complicated airline reservation, or preparing our legal document. This means that, for IT departments, a global perspective is an imperative.

IT and Labor Productivity Growth

The rapidly growing literature on IT and labor productivity growth (LPG) addresses two main issues: measurement problems and the contribution of IT to LPG. Alas, the IT sector in official statistics is often inadequate: In most countries, national accounts simply do not distinguish IT production, investment, or consumption:

> Information technology can contribute to labor productivity growth through both Capital Deepening and Total Factor Productivity (TFP) growth. [1] Capital deepening refers to the change in labor productivity attributable to higher levels of capital per worker. TFP growth refers to improvements in the efficiency with which capital and labor are combined to produce output. The existing literature has established that IT is contributing to labor productivity growth through both increases in the levels of IT capital per worker ("IT-related capital deepening") and TFP growth in IT production, though the precise magnitudes of these contributions remain a subject of debate. The main outstanding issue is whether IT has contributed to TFP growth more generally by increasing the efficiency of production, either through usage or knowledge spillovers from the production of IT goods (Fernald and Ramnath 2004).

Country-specific work broadly follows the pioneering studies of the United States, which generally agree that IT-related capital deepening and TEP growth in IT production made important contributions to the acceleration in labor productivity in the late 1990s.

[2] Labor productivity growth in the nonfarm business sector increased from about 1.5 percent in 1973 to 1995 to about 2.5 percent in 1996 to 2000. About a quarter to a half of a percentage point of the acceleration in labor productivity was attributed to capital deepening, more than accounted for by investment in IT, and another quarter percentage point to TFP growth in IT production.

[3] However, there is no consensus on the effect of IT on generalized TFP growth. More recent studies suggest that little of the acceleration in labor productivity is due to changes in factor utilization, factor accumulation, or returns to scale, and that virtually all of the acceleration is accounted for by IT-using and IT-producing industries. Together, these results—if they are borne out by further empirical work—suggest that we may soon see an impact of IT on generalized TFP growth.

Another way to measure the impact of information technology is to estimate the contributions of the IT-producing sector and of IT-intensive sectors to economic growth through capital deepening. Studies suggest that industries producing IT equipment or industries using IT equipment intensively contributed between 0.5 and 0.9 percentage points, or between 28 and 57 percent, to economic growth. For most G7 economies, the contribution of IT-using sectors is much stronger than the contribution of the IT-producing sector. The contribution of technological progress in IT production to labor productivity growth is also fairly uncontroversial. Substantial TFP growth in the IT sector, which is the counterpart of the rapid declines in quality-adjusted IT prices, made significant contributions to labor productivity growth in countries with relatively large IT-producing sectors (Fernald and Ramnath, 2004).

In summary, there is no convincing evidence of the impact of IT on the general efficiency of production, yet there are suggestions that IT is already making an important contribution to labor productivity growth through technological progress in IT production and IT-related capital deepening.

Although these developments don't necessarily impact an IT department, they have a huge impact on the way an IT department is perceived within an organization. Often, there is a deep resentment of IT as a displacement agent for human labor.

Long-Term Effects of IT on Macroeconomic Policies

In the long run, IT may affect fiscal, monetary, and financial policies in fundamental ways. First, IT has the potential to transform the way that governments do their work. Governments can use IT to improve the procurement of goods and services; the quality and delivery of the government services; especially information; and the efficiency with which applications are filed and taxes are paid. However, IT may undermine a government's ability to collect certain taxes, such as sales taxes in the United States, though the associated revenue loss is estimated to be small. In addition, IT may make it more difficult to define a *permanent establishment* for taxing the sale of digital products, like music, photographs, medical and financial advice, and educational services (Tanzi 2000).

Information technology also has the potential to reduce the demand for bank reserves held at the central bank, which would affect the central bank's ability to conduct monetary policy. At present, central banks have enormous leverage, even though the size of their balance sheet is small in relation to that of the private sector, because base money—especially bank reserves at the central bank—is the medium of final settlement. IT could allow final settlements to be carried out by the private sector without the need for clearing through the central bank. For example, private parties could settle a transaction by transferring wealth from one electronic account to another, with pre-agreed algorithms determining which financial assets were sold by the purchaser and bought by the seller (King 1999). The key to any such development is the ability of information and communication systems to allow instantaneous verification of credit worthiness, thereby enabling private sector real time gross settlement to occur with finality. While there would be a new need to ensure the integrity of the systems used for settlement purposes, base money would no longer have a unique role and central banks would lose their ability to implement monetary policy. However, the demand for bank reserves at the central bank is likely to remain strong for many years, given its current key role in final settlement (Cecchetti 2001).

Having said that, it is clear to see that the information technology is transforming financial services by changing the speed, scope, and nature of information, computation, and communication. To keep up with the financial institutions, banks have to offer new products and develop new processes to stay competent, and that, in turn, will bring greater risk in operations requiring expert guidance of IT personal. The impact of IT on the public sector helps create an aura of concern and dread that adds to the confusion of what an IT department mission should be within the organization, thereby blurring its supposedly distinctive features.

Why Doesn't IT Have a Seat at the Boardroom Table?

The investment in information technology has been steady since its inception and equally on the rise is the greater importance that organizations place on information resource management. Almost all organizations have developed formal policies governing the procurement of electronic data processing equipment. However, plans for distributed data processing, data sharing, and office automation are only available in about 50 percent of the organizations we have reviewed. Furthermore, progress in preparing privacy and security plans are minimal.

The future role for MIS is one in which more attention is focused on planning, consulting and monitoring the technology. These systems embody the processes, procedures, policies, and goals of the government and private sector business. Even with solid planning, IT departments have failed to make the case for the return that they bring. Intuitively organizations know that they can no longer compete or even remain in business without investing in Information Technology. However, unless the return on investment is presented with each investment, IT may never be given a seat at the table. This is a chicken and egg scenario. One would think that the "C" level personnel of an organization would be able to recognize the value and importance, but this has not occurred.

Technology departments have failed to make a public declaration of the mission, goals, principles, and policies of their organization. Often, technology departments will create an internal CobIT document but fail to make it public. The idea behind creating and maintaining a *technology manifesto* is to produce both an internal as well as an external marketing tool that explains the role and responsibilities of the technology department. The manifesto should encompass all the activities that the technology department is involved in. Suffice it to say here that the technology manifesto will introduce the CIO to the boardroom: It is the calling card. Other business disciplines such as accounting, finance, and marketing are relatively stable compared to the rapid evolution of technology and its leverage for an organization. For technology to be recognized, its contribution to the mission and vision of the organization must be elaborated and documented.

The technology manifesto should include a clear mission statement for the role that technology plays within the organization. It should detail the goals for the current and future periods derived from the mission. It should provide the guiding principles and processes within the organization that will accomplish the goals, and a clear statement of all the policies that govern the processes.

CIOs must, on a daily basis, take up the initiative to make their own individual organizations understand their value worth and importance. Only then can they be included a working member of the Board!

The Digital Divide—An IT Department's Social Responsibility

To date, the IT revolution has largely followed the pattern of past technological revolutions, including an initial phase characterized by a boom and bust in the stock prices of innovating firms, as well as in spending on goods embodying the new technology. The IT revolution is different from past technological revolutions in the globalization of production, which has strengthened real and financial linkages across countries. The rapid growth in the production of IT goods implies that changes in global demand conditions, driven mainly by IT-using advanced economies, have a significant impact on the exports of IT-producing countries. Although positive demand shocks helped to boost IT production in

1999 and 2000, in 2004 to 2005 the current slump in global IT spending is a heavy drag on these IT-producing countries.

Notwithstanding the adverse impact of the current IT slump on some countries, the economic benefits of the IT revolution are already significant and will likely continue. Thus far, the benefits arise mainly from the fall in the relative prices of semiconductors and computers, and accrue primarily to the users of these products. There is evidence that TFP growth in IT production and IT-related capital deepening have boosted labor productivity growth in some countries, and it is likely that—in the coming years—economic activities in a variety of countries will be increasingly reorganized to take advantage of IT, yielding further benefits. The fall in relative prices of IT goods has also led to significant increases in consumer surplus in IT-using countries.

The IT revolution has important policy implications. Structural policies should encourage the widespread adoption and effective use of IT, including promoting flexible labor markets and efficient service sectors. Uncertainty about the precise magnitude and likely duration of the acceleration in productivity imply that policy makers should place less weight on variables about which uncertainty has increased, such as the output gap, and more weight on observable variables, such as actual inflation and a wide array of indicators of future inflation.

Although the price of processing power is going down, what one can do with the processing power is not increasing at the same rate. Information technologies are basically self-enhancing technologies. They are causing rapid acceleration culturally as well as commercially, and people are now rewarded for being quick on uptake and are losing for being slow. These rapid accelerations are creating an event horizon over which it is difficult to see the future because of the pace of change. Nevertheless, we may be witnessing a self-limiting revolution; although it will never be choked off, it will never outpace our ability to understand. As we develop a city-quality information infrastructure in rural areas, education will become the largest issue on the new economy agenda. Information technologies are creating equal educational opportunity that will generate equality in the social fabric and bring dynamism and vibrancy to economic growth (Wright, 1999, p. 78).

> And as information becomes the primary resource in a knowledge-based economy, far greater attention must be devoted to its equitable distribution if the world hopes to avoid creating an underclass of information have-nots.
>
> What can we do? It is important that each product or service to be examined in terms of its contribution to the digital divide. Creating Web sites that very few people can productively access (David S. Platt: Why Software Sucks), is an example of what needs to be avoided. *Software should be written to serve users and not other programmers.*
>
> When people ask you where you work, and you can answer, "In IT," and not be concerned about the next question, IT has indeed established its identity.

The final message of the continuous evolution of IT is that the role of IT, the expectations and the measure of success within an organization must be *clearly defined at all times.*

References

(Britannica 2003, History of technology, Perceptions of technology, Science and technology section, paragraph 1).

(Britannica, 2003, History of technology, Perceptions of technology, Science and technology section, paragraph 1).

"The result of the technological advances is to create a level field in providing goods and services worldwide" (Thomas Friedman: The World is Flat)

AUTHOR BIOGRAPHIES

Stuart Appley

Stuart Appley is the Chief Information Officer for Shorenstein Properties, a national real estate investment firm headquartered in San Francisco. He brings more than 20 years' experience to his role as CIO, where he has responsibility for the long term strategy, planning, design and management of the firm's information systems, applications, and computing infrastructure.

Prior to Shorenstein, Stuart was the CIO at Walden International, a global venture capital firm, where he had world wide responsibility for the firm's technology needs. Additionally, Stuart acted as an advisor to Walden International's portfolio companies, while also participating in the due diligence of Walden's investments in IT related companies. Prior to Walden, Stuart held senior level technology and management positions at LGT Asset Management, First Nationwide Bank, and Lomas & Nettleton Information Systems. Stuart holds an MBA in finance from San Francisco State University and a bachelor's degree in finance and international business from San Diego State University.

Judy Armstrong

Judy Armstrong brings more than twenty years expertise to her role as a chief information officer (CIO). Most recently, she was CIO with Benchmark Capital. While there, Ms. Armstrong had worldwide responsibility for the design and implementation of information systems, applications, infrastructure, facilities, and human resource management for Benchmark, and acted as a strategic advisor to the Benchmark Portfolio Network.

Ms. Armstrong's expertise includes leading IT through both growth and contracting business cycles by evaluating, selecting, and implementing internal technologies, applications, and developing strategic plan. Before joining Benchmark, Ms. Armstrong, as VP of corporate services for C-Cube Microsystems, oversaw the replacement of the legacy ERP system (with Oracle) to help streamline the company's operating efficiency, the enhancement of employee communications through the development of a content-rich intranet, and assumed leadership for facilities and human resources organizations. In addition, she managed the transition and subsequent acquisition of DiviCom into Harmonic, and a year later the merger of C-Cube into LSI Logic.

Prior to C-Cube, Ms. Armstrong was engaged in business development and implementation of Oracle applications at KPMG Peat Marwick. Previously, she led the implementation of several applications and restructured IT to streamline workflow at Cadence Design Systems. She directed IT Operations at Quantum Corporation and held several IT positions at National Semiconductor.

Ms. Armstrong graduated from the University of Phoenix with a bachelor of science degree in business administration. She is past president of the Silicon Valley Chapter of the Society of Information Management (SIM), a member of the Governance Committee of the CIO Collective, a mentor for Women Unlimited, the past president of the Child Abuse Prevention Center, and has co-authored a book, *CIO Wisdom*.

Sunny Azadeh

Sunny Azadeh serves as Senior Vice President of Information Technology at Agile Software, where she has worldwide responsibility for the strategy, design and implementation of information systems. Prior to her role as SVP of IT at Agile, she held the position of CIO at ZiLOG Inc. Ms. Azadeh has 22 years of experience in Information Technology, and in leveraging upcoming technologies to solve business problems.

Ms. Azadeh has been an active member of the Consortium of Information Systems Executives since 2003, and is a member of Open IT Works focused on open source and collaboration in Information Technology. She is currently on advisory boards for several companies in the Bay Area including Groundwork, Fastscale, Jaspersoft, TriChiper, Agistics and Open IT Works. She is also a mentor and alumni at Women's Unlimited.

Ms. Azadeh holds BSCSE degree from San Jose State University.

Cliff Bell

Cliff Bell is the Chief Information Officer of Infogain. He bring 25 years+ years of IT experience to his role. In addition to his role as CIO, Mr. Bell is has a business development role. Mr. Bell also serves in an advisory capacity to several startups providing guidance to companies with emerging technologies.

Mr. Bell is on the board of two non-profit organizations. *The providence Foundation of San Francisco* provides health and welfare services to families of the inner city of San Francisco. The fifty thousand member *Professional Businesswomen of California* allows leaders to mentor and role model professional women, foster upward career mobility and gain instant access to a large network of other professionals.

Prior to Infogain, he was CIO of Phoenix Technologies from 2002 to 2006. He was also Vice President and Chief Information Officer at two Internet startup companies from 1999 to 2002. From 1997 to 1999, Mr. Bell served as Regional IT Director at Iomega Corporation based in Singapore and has held IT management positions at Bay Networks and Apple Computer.

Mr. Bell earned an undergraduate degree in mathematics from Wabash College and an M.B.A. in finance from Purdue University's Krannert School of Business

Sam Chughtai

Sam Chughtai has held a number of major leadership positions during his career. He served as an executive management consultant for Price Waterhouse Coopers, KPMG, Equifax, and Lawrence Berkeley Lab and Govt. of Malaysia / Melaka State. Currently, Mr. Chughtai is leading the Future State Architecture and Business Capability Model team for Microsoft Corporation.

Mr. Chughtai has a track record of over eighteen years in business development, information technology management, information risk management, marketing campaign management, public policies development, executive relationship management, and FSA (future state architecture) advisory to C-level management.

With his in-depth knowledge, industry relationship, and years of experience in marketing and business development, he has managed and delivered multimillion-dollar projects for various multinational Fortune 100 companies and the public sector.

Jennifer Diamond

Jennifer Diamond, MAOM, PMP, has more than twenty years of operational and professional services experience, emphasizing technology implementation and operational improvement. Ms. Diamond is president of Management Agility, Inc., a professional services firm currently emphasizing organizational guidance and support for IT organizations navigating Sarbanes-Oxley compliance.

Prior to founding the now Management Agility consulting network in 2000, Ms. Diamond worked with both Ernst & Young LLP and Deloitte & Touche LLP in Silicon Valley and Southern California, most recently as a senior manager with Deloitte emphasizing CFO-optimization services. Prior to consulting, Ms. Diamond worked for Applied Materials, Inc. in finance and systems implementation roles for the global semiconductor equipment maker during its highest growth years.

Ms. Diamond holds a bachelor of arts in business/economics from the University of California at Santa Barbara and a master of arts in organizational management from the University of Phoenix. She has been certified as a project management professional by the Project Management Institute.

Richard Diamond

Richard Diamond is chief information officer at FormFactor Inc. and a veteran of over thirty-five years in the information systems field, including more than twenty years as chief information officer of global companies that include Applied Materials, AST Computers, Madge Networks, and Verbatim.

He is a frequent speaker on the subject of information system strategy and governance at business graduate schools including San Francisco State University, University of Southern California, and University of California, at Irvine.

In addition to management consulting, he is a recognized consultant in litigation involving major IT projects.

Mr. Diamond holds a bachelor of science degree in industrial engineering from New York University and an MBA from The University of Louisville. He is a graduate of the 1986 Stanford Executive Program.

Mark Egan

Mark Egan is a partner with the StrataFusion Group, Inc. and has over thirty years of experience in information technology from a variety of industries. His expertise includes information technology strategy, information security, and mergers and acquisitions. He was previously CIO at Symantec for six years and led the IT organization through rapid growth while the company transformed from a software publisher to the third-largest software company. Mr. Egan led the information technology integration for over 30 acquisitions, including the $13B acquisition of Veritas Software.

Mr. Egan has held several senior-level positions with companies including Sun Microsystems, Price Waterhouse, Atlantic Richfield Corp., Martin Marietta Data Systems, Walden International Investment Group, and Wells Fargo Bank.

He serves on the board for Sigue Corporation and CIO Scholarship Fund, and on the technical advisory boards for Golden Gate University and San Francisco State University. Mr. Egan is a member of the American Management Association's Information Systems and Technology Council and is co-chair of TechNet's Cyber Security Practices Adoption Campaign.

Mr. Egan is author of *Executive Guide to Information Security: Threats, Challenges, and Solutions* from Addison Wesley and was a contributing author to *CIO Wisdom*. He writes a monthly column for CIO Update.com on best practices for information security.

He holds a master's degree in finance and international business from the University of San Diego and a bachelor's degree in computer sciences from the University of Clarion.

Sam Gill

Sam Gill is a professor in the information systems (IS) department at the College of Business at San Francisco State University (SFSU). He is also the director of a research and service organization for IS/IT internships—CampusSolutions.

Dr. Gill's career spans five decades of computing, from the infant days of MAMRAM, the Israeli Ministry of Defense Computing Center, through his latest professional engagements as a consultant to Fortune 1,000 companies and state and federal agencies. During this span, Dr. Gill has been involved in several IT start-ups. He has also managed several computing centers. Dr. Gill's latest venture was DataWiz Centers, one of the first Microsoft Solution Provider partners and the first Microsoft certified training partner.

Dr. Gill publishes (articles, books, and courseware) and teaches in many areas of information systems focusing on strategy, management, and technology. Recently, he collaborated with Jim Cates and Natalie Zeituny on the book *Climbing up the Business Intelligence Ladder*.

Dr. Gill's current research interests include the strategic, tactical, and operational management of information systems, business intelligence, software testing and quality assurance (SQA), information technology (IT) budgeting, offshore and outsourcing of IT, development methodologies and frameworks, and development architectures, platforms, and languages, including .NET, PHP/MySQL, Ruby on Rails, WebSphere, Visual Basic, C#, AJAX, and Java.

Dr. Gill holds a Ph.D. from the University of California, Berkeley.

Roger J. Gray

Roger Gray has almost twenty-five years of experience in the electric utility and telecommunications industries. He currently runs a consulting business (Great Northern Exchange, LLC) and consults in the utility and telecommunication sectors. He has recently served both on boards and executive management at a couple of different start-up companies. He retired from PG&E in 2004, where his last position was chief information officer. Earlier in his career he worked in a variety of positions, ranging from electric operations to power planning and trading at PG&E, as well as positions at Duke/Louis Dreyfus, Southern California Edison, and the Los Angeles Department of Water and Power.

Mr. Gray was born in Panama. He has degrees in electrical engineering–power systems and computer science from UC Berkeley, and has completed course work in public policy.

Frank Hannig

Frank L. Hannig, with a career that spans close to 30 years in the Information Technology industry, is currently working as an Executive and Technology Consultant. His focus areas include assisting new companies in the formation and early development stages and advising established companies on how to improve their IT departments. Frank was most recently the Vice President and Chief Information Officer for Altera Corporation for over 8 years. In addition to his other high tech experience, he has experience in VC funded startups as well as consulting experience with Price Waterhouse. Frank holds a BS degree from California Polytechnic State University in San Luis Obispo and an MBA degree from the University of Santa Clara. He also holds a CPIM certification. Frank is currently on the Board of Trustees for Notre Dame de Namur University and is the Chairman of the Sequoia Hospital Foundation.

Tim Hanrahan

Tim Hanrahan is currently General Manager for the Iheira Group, a systems and management consulting firm. Mr. Hanrahan most recently held the position of vice president of information services and chief information officer at Adaptec for 5 years where was responsible for all of the company's worldwide computer operations, networks, and application systems.

Previously, Mr. Hanrahan spent twenty-two years with Sun Diamond Growers of California in various positions, culminating as vice president of information systems and services. Earlier career stops included system-related positions with United Airlines and the U.S. Air Force.

Mr. Hanrahan holds a bachelor of science degree in engineering from Arizona State University.

Doug Harr

Mr. Harr's career has been focused on building information technology and professional service organizations that design, deliver, and support business solutions involving multiple technologies, applications, and industries. Mr. Harr is currently CIO at Ingres Corporation in Redwood City, California, building and delivering IT solutions for the company. Before joining Ingres, he worked in the same capacity for Portal Software in Cupertino, California. Earlier in his career, Mr. Harr worked at various companies as programmer, IT manager, director, and vice president, with increasing responsibilities for managing internal IT. For half of his career, Mr. Harr was vice president in charge of professional services for Core Technology Group, providing services to deploy packaged and custom business applications for a wide variety of clients.

Mr. Harr holds a bachelor of science degree in business administration w/computer science (MIS) minor from California Polytechnic State University, San Luis Obispo. He is a member of the Consortium for Information System Executives (CISE), and a guest lecturer at the San Francisco State University system MBA program.

Gordon Jones

Gordon is a Partner of the StrataFusion Group, Inc. Mr. Jones has over 30 years of global technology experience within multi-billion dollar organizations, as well as small companies. His extensive industry experience spans financial services, e-Commerce, high technology, and large distribution and manufacturing companies.

Recently, he oversaw IT and Engineering at Billpoint, then a subsidiary of eBay and Wells Fargo. Mr. Jones has also served as CIO for the Franklin Templeton Group, the fifth largest mutual fund company and as CIO of Novell for 5 years during the company's explosive growth period in the early 90's, as well as several start-ups.

Mr. Jones has extensive experience include managing large volume, mission critical transaction systems and galvanizing teams to improve processes that deliver better business returns/improve shareholder value for technology investments. He received CIO Magazine award—CIO 100 for Performance Excellence. He has served as an executive board member of the SIIA (Software and Information Industry Association. Mr. Jones holds a Management Studies degree from Buckinghamshire University in the United Kingdom.

Gary Kelly

Gary Kelly has over twenty years experience in systems management, focused on financials, manufacturing, and computer forensics. Success in positions at Boeing, Symantec, St. Paul Travelers Ins., and Xilinx along with an MBA from UCLA have prepared Gary for his current position as Global IT Applications Compliance Manager for Seagate Technology; the world's largest hard-disk drive manufacturer and *Fortune* magazine's 2006 Company of the Year. His active certifications include CISA, CISSP, CPA, PMP, CCE, CPIM, and CIRM. Gary lives with his wife, Patricia, in Scotts Valley, California while his son, Jeffrey, pursues a Business Law degree at Indiana University in Bloomington.

Dean Lane

Dean Lane has over twenty-five years of experience in IT management. Mr. Lane currently serves as CEO of VariTRAK. Prior to joining VariTRAK, he was responsible for all global business systems, applications, and Web architecture at Symantec.

Mr. Lane has been a CIO four times and a corporate director of manufacturing. Mr. Lane has served as the EVP and CIO for Masters Institute of Technology, as VP and CIO for Plantronics, the telephone headset company, as the corporate office CIO and strategic planner for the Thiokol Corporation, and as Allied Signal's corporate materials manager and CIO.

Additionally, Mr. Lane has been a consultant for Ernst & Young, AT&T, and the Gartner Group. He serves on the advisory boards for Search CIO, ITP Systems, Cranium, Inc., HBS Consulting, and San Francisco State University's Center for Electronic Business. He is an active member of Executive World, Secretary for the CIO Scholarship Fund, member of the Project Management Institute, APICS, the CIO Collective, the Consortium of Information Systems Executives, Silicon Valley's Community of Practice and was president of SIM's Silicon Valley Chapter from 2005 to 2006. His book *CIO Wisdom* was published last year. Mr. Lane speaks internationally, delivering keynote addresses to the Adam Smith Society, the Russian IT Summit in Moscow and a CIO Conference of 200 CIOs from all over Russia. He was a representative on the Hi-Tech Economic Mission to Israel. He is a contributing editor to CIO *Insight* magazine and is a highly decorated U.S. Navy officer.

Mr. Lane obtained his undergraduate degree from the University of California (UCLA) and his MBA from National University.

George Lin

George Lin is Vice President and Chief Information Officer of Dolby Laboratories. He is responsible for Dolby's worldwide IT organization and leads global business process optimization, integration, and automation efforts for the company. Before joining Dolby, Mr. Lin was CIO of Advent Software, a financial services company. Prior to Advent, he managed the consolidated IT organization of EMC Software, a division of EMC Corporation, the world's leading developer and provider of information infrastructure technology and solutions.
Before it was acquired by EMC, Mr. Lin was CIO of Documentum, a provider of enterprise content management solutions.

Named a Premier 100 IT Leader by Computerworld magazine in 2003, Mr. Lin won CIO Decisions magazine's prestigious Mid-Market Leadership Award in 2006. He is a contributing author of the Prentice Hall PTR book CIO Wisdom: Best Practices from Silicon Valley's Leading IT Experts. He serves on the advisory boards of the Fisher IT Center at the University of California, Berkeley Haas School of Business and Tablus, a leading content security solutions provider. Mr. Lin graduated with a Bachelor of Arts degree from the University of California, Berkeley.

John Mass

Mr. Mass is the Western Region Managing Director for Exeter Group Inc. He has an extensive background in information technology consulting, with a strong interest in project and operational risk and using process control models to measure and mitigate operational risks. While working for Exeter he has overseen projects that include IT strategy, Outsourcing, Systems Implementation, Application Development and Operational Risk Analysis. Mr. Mass has served Exeter Group in this capacity since 1996. Exeter Group is a Cambridge MA. consulting organization.

Mr. Mass obtained a Masters of Science from the Massachusetts Institute of Technology, and holds an undergraduate degree in Electrical Engineering from Marquette University.

Marti Menacho

Marti Menacho has had an impressive twenty-year career working for some of the Who's Who of manufacturing and high-tech companies in Silicon Valley. She has successfully blended her knowledge of business operations and technology to develop strategies and create solutions that have enabled companies to achieve substantial growth.

Ms. Menacho has held CIO positions at Brocade Communications, TIBCO Software, Nortel Networks, and Clarify Corporation. She has held IT management positions at 3Com, SGI, ASK Computer Systems, and Syntex. Additionally, she was Sales and Marketing EVP at Saama Technologies and VP Operations at Clarify Corporation. Currently Ms. Menacho is providing strategic consulting services to businesses in the San Francisco Bay Area.

As an Internet pioneer, Ms. Menacho was a member of Vice President Gore's eGovernment committee during the Clinton administration and was involved in developing the first federal government Web site.

Al Pappas

Al is a Partner of the StrataFusion Group, Inc. and is a well-known technology veteran with over 40 years experience in the fields of information technology (IT), development engineering, marketing and business management. Al's expertise spans internet technology, enterprise applications, CRM applications, PostScript development, communications systems, global manufacturing, professional services and automated test systems.

Most recently as the CIO for VMware, Al led the IT organization during the period of hyper-growth. Al was also the CIO for Hotwire responsible for all development and information technology operations of this internet based travel provider. Prior to Hotwire, Al was the CIO for Portal Software, VeriFone/HP and Adobe Systems were he was responsible for leading all IT activities.

Prior to his CIO positions, Al was a VP of Engineering at Adobe Systems, a Test Engineering manager at Apple Computer, a Business Unit Director & VP of Engineering (VPE) for Schlumberger Technologies, a Director of Software at MSI Data and held various technology and marketing positions with the Xerox Corporation. Al is an active member of several CIO & VPE communities of practice and service organizations.

Al holds a Certificate of Technical Business Management from UCLA and BA in Mathematics from Brooklyn College of the University of the City of New York.

Steve Paszkiewicz

Steve Paszkiewicz has been involved in technology and operations management for the past twenty-three years. He has served in the capacity of chief operating officer and president at Media Arts Group Inc. (MDA), chief operating officer at Saama Technologies, chief information officer at Sanmina Corporation (SANM), director of information resources at Sun Microsystems (SUNW) responsible for American, European and Asian Pacific Operations, and director of WW Information Technology at Silicon Graphics (SGI).

While at Sun Microsystems, he received the prestigious Manager of the Year award. Mr. Paszkiewicz currently works at Risk Management Solutions Inc., where he is responsible for architecture and applications. Stephen has delivered keynote speeches at customer conferences and participated in several panel discussions on the application of technology management in the Silicon Valley. Stephen's undergraduate work was in business administration at Rivier College in New Hampshire, and he received his technical training while serving in the U.S. Marines.

Christine Rose

Fulfilling the role of CIO for Finisar since 2002, Christine Rose is responsible for the management of all aspects of information technology. She directs the efforts of more than forty employees in the department of information technology worldwide. She provides leadership and develops and implements strategies to enhance security and business continuity for Finisar. She is also responsible for technology planning and budgets, and for ensuring that Finisar is in compliance with Sarbanes-Oxley, ISO 9001, and ISO 14001 and other entity-level security policies and procedures.

Ms. Rose reports directly to the chief financial officer. She leads IT strategic and operational planning to achieve business goals by fostering innovation, prioritizing IT initiatives, and coordinating the evaluation, deployment, and management of current and future IT systems across the organization. She serves as the chair of the Information Technology Steering Committee.

Ms. Rose has worked in the information technology field for over eleven years, serving private-sector companies in finance, Internet, and manufacturing, and the public sector in heath care. She believes in promoting information technology as a career, and has implemented a summer internship for high school seniors interested in the field.

Ms. Rose has managed multimillion-dollar projects among a diverse portfolio of needs in project management, disaster recovery, full lifecycle system development, IT visioning and strategic planning, and business process redesign.

Ms. Rose holds an MBA from the University of Phoenix and a bachelor in communications degree from San Francisco State University. She is a member of Information Systems Audit and Control Association, and she holds certifications as a Project Management Professional (PMP) and in Foundations Information Technology Infrastructure Library (ITIL).

Ron Sha

As Vice President and CIO for Glu.com, Ron Sha is responsible for global IT strategy, application and infrastructure development and support. Prior to joining Glu, Mr. Sha was Vice President and CIO at Borland Software.

Mr. Sha was senior vice president of Internet operations at WebMD. While at WebMD, he established and implemented various processes related to system performance, reliability and capacity, change control, and product releases. He also redesigned and expanded the companywide network and system infrastructure to a high-performance and scalable environment. Prior to WebMD, Mr. Sha was CIO at Responsys and Visto Corporation. He also held various senior-level IT positions at Sun Microsystems.

Mr. Sha has broad experience in managing operations, information technology and application development initiatives in high growth companies. He has extensive experience in leading data center operations, customer service, application software development, and information systems management. Mr. Sha also holds multiple US patents. Mr. Sha holds a M.S. in Engineering Management from Santa Clara University, and a B.S. degree in Computer Science from San Jose State University, California.

Dani Shomron

Dani Shomron is a veteran of the software industry, with twenty-three years of experience in development, managerial, and executive roles. He spent the first half of his career in software start-ups and co-founded QXI, specializing in the Japanese software market, where he served as the executive vice president of research and development and a QXI board member.

Mr. Shomron's experience spans multiple industries and geographies. Some of the firms that have benefited from his involvement include the Bank of New York, AMDOCS, and Mercury Interactive. His expertise covers software-as-a-service, performance testing and monitoring, network management, and localization.

Mr. Shomron holds a Bachelor of Science in computer science from the Hebrew University and a Master of Science degree in artificial intelligence from the University of Edinburgh. Currently, he is the VP of Operations and Services at Contactual, a vendor offering contact centers in the software-as-a-service model to the SMB market.

Pamela Vaughan

Pamela Vaughan is the Vice President of Information Technology for Ariat International, the leader in performance footwear and apparel for equestrian athletes. She has global responsibility for strategy, design and implementation of information systems, applications, and infrastructure. Prior to Ariat, she was the Vice President of Information Technology at THE SAK, a leading handbag and fashion accessory company. Pamela has also held IT Executive positions at Acumation, a subsidiary of American Century Investments, that set the company's overall strategic direction in the online financial advice market; The Dialog Corporation, the world's first online information retrieval system; and Hub Group Distribution Services, a third party logistics provider and four time Inc. 500 company during her tenure.

Pamela holds both an undergraduate degree and a postgraduate degree, in Applied Statistics and Computing, from the University of Wales. She is the Chairperson for the Northern California Cognos User Group, and a member of both the Consortium of Information Systems Executives and San Francisco Bay Area Society of Information Management.

Jeffrey J. Ward

Jeffrey J. Ward is a management consultant who specializes in helping CIOs transform IT organizations. He combines academic training in cultural anthropology with more than twenty years of experience in high technology. His technical career has been diverse. He has worked in software technical support, technical writing, and software quality assurance, has managed projects and programs in software development, IT, and construction, and has held several executive positions in software product development and IT.

Mr. Ward was an early employee at both Informix and Sybase (where he wrote the first stored procedures, triggers, and constraints used in a production application). His most recent non-consulting position was as director of Global IT Services at Documentum. He has worked in the United States and Europe.

Mr. Ward lives and works in San Francisco.

Martin Wegenstein

Martin Wegenstein is a senior executive with extensive experience in operations and information technology leadership at companies ranging from small start-ups to Fortune 500 corporations. He is focusing his experiences and skills on bringing new technologies to market.

Wegenstein serves on the Board of Advisors for Coghead, and Voxify. He also serves on the Board of Advisors of the Center for Electronic Business, San Francisco State University.

Wegenstein retired from Autodesk as VP and CIO in where he was responsible for the world wide information technology infrastructure and IT based systems solutions. At Autodesk he completely overhauled the global Information Technology organization and system infrastructure to enable new business initiatives and drive margin improvements for this leading design software and digital content company. In 2004 he was recognized as a Computerworld Premier 100 IT Leader.

Prior to Autodesk Martin was VP of Operations at Slam Dunk Networks, a managed network services provider for secure, guaranteed delivery of applications to applications transaction messages. At Slam Dunk he established complete operational and customer support capabilities for a global 7×24 network service and achieved consistent performance with 100% network uptime for over 15 month running.

Before Slam Dunk Wegenstein was Senior VP of Operations and Customer Service at Pilot Network Services, a provider of highly secure Internet access and web hosting services, where he established a scalable infrastructure and customer focused operations and client support capabilities.

Prior to Pilot, Wegenstein served as CIO at Applied Materials and Raychem, following a long career at Emerson Electric Co. He was recognized with the CIO-100 Award for Best Practices in Human Resources for his work at Raychem.

Wegenstein brings broad knowledge and considerable experience in IT, the software, as well as the managed services industry. He has a degree in Mathematics from the Swiss Federal Institute of Technology and a M.S. degree in Computer Science from Union College.

Shawn Wilde

Shawn Wilde joined Trimble in 2001 as director of worldwide IT operations. In 2005, he was promoted to the position of chief information officer. Mr. Wilde's background includes over twenty-five years of industry experience in both information technology and software engineering. Since joining Trimble, Mr. Wilde has overseen the integration of multiple IT organizations into regional centers of excellence, systems consolidation into a corporate data center, the design and deployment of a global data network, and the integration of VoIP in the USA and Europe.

Most recently, Mr. Wilde was a senior engineering manager at an Internet start-up, and prior to that he spent fifteen years with Bell Northern Research/Nortel as a senior engineering manager in software development, quality systems and R&D information systems.

Mr. Wilde began his career at DeHavilland Aircraft in Toronto, Ontario. He attended the University of Guelph, where he received his bachelor's degree in computer and information science in 1979.

Tony Young

Tony Young serves as vice president and chief information officer of Informatica, with responsibility for the strategic direction of Informatica's global information systems and technology infrastructure. During his tenure at Informatica, Mr. Young and the information technology department have won two prestigious industry awards, including the 2006 CIO Decision Midmarket Leadership Award and the 2006 Ventana Research IT Performance Management Leadership Award.

Prior to joining Informatica in 2002, Mr. Young served at Mindcrossing and Converge, where he was responsible for overseeing product development and product management. Mr. Young began his career at Hewlett-Packard, where he served for eleven years in a number of information technology and marketing roles. A major milestone at H-P included building the first partner portal, as well as building the enterprise portal and e-commerce. Mr. Young earned a bachelor's degree in information systems and a master's degree in business administration from Santa Clara University.

INDEX